WITHDRAWN
UTSA LIBRARIES

Locked in the Poorhouse

Locked in the Poorhouse

*Cities, Race, and Poverty
in the United States*

edited by
Fred R. Harris
and
Lynn A. Curtis

A Milton S. Eisenhower Foundation Update
of the Kerner Commission Report

ROWMAN & LITTLEFIELD PUBLISHERS, INC.
Lanham • Boulder • New York • Oxford

ROWMAN & LITTLEFIELD PUBLISHERS, INC.

Published in the United States of America
by Rowman & Littlefield Publishers, Inc.
4720 Boston Way, Lanham, Maryland 20706

12 Hid's Copse Road
Cumnor Hill, Oxford OX2 9JJ, England

Copyright © 1998 by the Milton S. Eisenhower Foundation

British Library Cataloguing in Publication Information Available

Library of Congress Cataloging-in-Publication Data
Locked in the poorhouse : cities, race, and poverty in the United
   States / edited by Fred R. Harris and Lynn A. Curtis.
      p.   cm.
   "A Milton S. Eisenhower Foundation update of the Kerner Commission
report.
   Includes bibliographical references and index.
   ISBN 0-8476-9135-7 (cloth : alk.)
   1. Riots—United States.   2. Urban poor—United States.   3. Afro-
Americans.   4. United States—Race relations.   I. Harris, Fred R.,
1930.   II. Curtis, Lynn A.   III. Milton S. Eisenhower Foundation.
HV6477.L63   1998
305.569'089'00973—dc21   98-29542
                                                         CIP

Printed in the United States of America

∞ ™ The paper used in this publication meets the minimum requirements
of American National Standard for Information Sciences—Permanence of Paper
for Printed Library Materials, ANSI Z39.48–1984.

To Ying, Julie, and Miranda
—Lynn A. Curtis

To Margaret S. Elliston
—Fred R. Harris

Contents

Introduction   1

1   The Kerner Report Thirty Years Later   7
    Fred R. Harris

2   Urban Poverty, Welfare Reform, and Child Development   21
    Greg J. Duncan and Jeanne Brooks-Gunn

3   Poverty as a Public Health Issue: Since the Kerner Report
    of 1968   33
    Gary Sandefur, Molly Martin, and Thomas Wells

4   The New Urban Poverty: Consequences of the Economic
    and Social Decline of Inner-City Neighborhoods   57
    William Julius Wilson, James M. Quane,
    and Bruce H. Rankin

5   Urban Poverty, Race, and the Inner City: The Bitter Fruit
    of Thirty Years of Neglect   79
    Paul A. Jargowsky

6   Race, Violence, and Justice since Kerner   95
    Elliott Currie

7   Racism and the Poor: Integration and Affirmative Action
    as Mobility Strategies   117
    William L. Taylor

8   Policy for the New Millennium   129
    Lynn A. Curtis

Conclusion   151
Notes and Sources   155
Index   .   179
About the Contributors   187

Introduction

"Our nation is moving toward two societies, one black, one white—separate and unequal." These were the stark and distressing words of the Kerner Commission—the National Advisory Commission on Civil Disorders—in its landmark report issued on March 1, 1968.

President Lyndon B. Johnson had appointed the blue-ribbon citizens' commission following the terrible riots that broke out in the black sections of many American cities during the summer of 1967. The Kerner Report recommended "compassionate, massive, and sustained" federal efforts to combat the nation's intertwined problems of racism and poverty that, the commission found, had most harshly impacted the nation's inner cities and that were the root causes of the urban disorders.

After the 1968 assassinations of Dr. Martin Luther King Jr. and Senator Robert F. Kennedy, President Johnson appointed another citizens' body, the National Commission on the Causes and Prevention of Violence, headed by Milton S. Eisenhower. Its December 1969 report declared: "The greatness and durability of most civilizations has been finally determined by how they responded to challenges from within. Ours will be no exception."

Since the reports of these two national commissions, the divide between rich and poor in the United States has become greater and the challenges from within more formidable.

The Milton S. Eisenhower Foundation is the private sector continuation of the Kerner and the Eisenhower commissions. It is a nonendowed and nonprofit foundation and a national intermediary organization. The foundation replicates and evaluates multiple-solution successes for children, youth, and families and for the inner city. And it communicates what works to citizens, the media, and decision makers.

1

To mark the thirtieth anniversary of the Kerner Report, the Eisenhower Foundation has sponsored two complementary volumes. *The Millennium Breach* was released on March 1, 1998—thirty years to the day after the original Kerner Report. Written by the editors of the present volume and other Eisenhower Foundation Trustees and published by the Foundation, *The Millennium Breach* presents the Foundation's position on practical policy and on how to replicate the grassroots non-profit inner-city programs that are responsible for much of what works. It is targeted to private and public policy makers and to community practitioners on the front lines in inner cities.

Locked in the Poorhouse is a compilation of essays by a distinguished panel of experts who give their assessments of where America is now in regard to the problems with which the original Kerner Report dealt. It concludes with a summary of *The Millennium Breach,* which, in turn, drew on some of the analyses in *Locked in the Poorhouse.*

In chapter 1 of *Locked in the Poorhouse: Cities, Race, and Poverty in the United States,* "The Kerner Report Thirty Years Later," Fred Harris, who was a member of the Kerner Commission, briefly relates the details of the urban riots that gave rise to the creation of the Kerner Commission, outlines the contents of its 1968 report, and assesses the present situation in America. He shows how economic shocks and trends, as well as government action and inaction, caused the nation's progress on the problems of race, poverty, and the inner cities to stop toward the end of the 1970s and even, in some ways, to be undone. Today, thirty years after the Kerner Report, there is more poverty in America, it is deeper, blacker, and browner than before, and it is more concentrated in the cities, which have become America's poorhouses.

In chapter 2, "Urban Poverty, Welfare Reform, and Child Development," Greg Duncan and Jeanne Brooks-Gunn call attention to the fact that one in five of American inner-city residents are poor, half again more than thirty years ago, and that child poverty is twice the rate for adults. Childhood poverty, especially in the earliest years, can have an alarmingly depressing impact on children's school achievement and cognitive and verbal ability. The authors point to important national policy initiatives to which these findings should lead us.

Chapter 3, "Poverty as a Public Health Issue," by Gary Sandefur, Molly Martin, and Thomas Wells, emphasizes that poverty in America is at least as prevalent as it was thirty years ago and is not just a city, nor a black, issue. However, what is now distinctive about inner-city poverty is the geographical concentration of large numbers of black and

Hispanic poor people. Poverty, wherever it occurs and whatever group it affects, should be viewed by the nation as a public health problem, as a failure of national will and political courage, rather than as a moral failure on the part of poor people.

In chapter 4, "The New Urban Poverty: Consequences of the Economic and Social Decline of Inner-City Neighborhoods," William Julius Wilson, James M. Quane, and Bruce H. Rankin demonstrate how continued high levels of poverty, together with the disappearance of well-paying blue-collar jobs and an outmigration of working- and middle-class African Americans (paralleling a similar, and greater, white outmigration), have concentrated poverty and chronic joblessness in the inner cities and have increased the number of urban ghettos. The concentration effects are increased social disorganization, crime, and isolation from the outside world. The authors conclude that "the ominous predictions of the Kerner Report have become our urban reality."

Chapter 5, "Urban Poverty, Race, and the Inner City: The Bitter Fruit of Thirty Years of Neglect," by Paul A. Jargowsky, demonstrates that, as a result of inaction and neglect, the conditions that spawned the 1967 riots have grown worse. Today's urban crisis can be summed up as "increasing economic segregation interacting with rising inequality in the context of the aftermath of three hundred years of poverty and racism," which "poses the greatest threat to the United States' long-term economic and political stability."

In chapter 6, "Race, Violence, and Justice since Kerner," Elliott Currie shows that, despite a falling national crime rate, crime and violence in minority communities remain "a public health disaster of staggering proportions." An explosion in minority incarceration and a massive expansion in the prison system—which is what America has *instead of* effective antipoverty, public housing, drug treatment, and mental health programs—are crippling the chances for a stable and successful future for millions of minority people.

Chapter 7, "Racism and the Poor: Integration and Affirmative Action as Mobility Strategies," by William L. Taylor, describes how affirmative action and desegregation laws have helped lift many minority people out of poverty, but the nation's "drive for equality has been running on empty for a quarter of a century." Taylor argues that it is in America's national interest to renew and build on these past efforts.

In chapter 8, "Policy for the New Millennium," Lynn A. Curtis, President of the Milton S. Eisenhower Foundation, argues that, if we reduce by only a fraction the $100 billion-plus that taxpayers pay for affirmative action for the rich and for corporate welfare, we could finance both a full employment program for the truly disadvantaged in our inner cities and the reform of our urban public education system. Such reform should be based on replicating scientifically proven models of success and programs that work. Curtis shows how the 1980s policy of tax breaks for the rich and prison building for the poor has failed. He says that leadership and the political will to act must be forged through a new alliance among the working class, the truly disadvantaged, and the anxious middle class, all of whom have lost ground because of present policies. Curtis concludes with public opinion information that suggests the political feasibility of such an alliance and of a "what works" policy.

The Conclusion summarizes the findings and recommendations of the earlier chapters and makes a final analysis:

> America made progress for nearly a decade on the problems with which the Kerner Report dealt. Then, because of certain economic shocks and trends and government action and inaction, that progress stopped and, in some ways, went into reverse.
>
> A growing number of working-class families fell into poverty and a lot of already-poor Americans became deeply poor.
>
> There are more poor people in America, now, than there were thirty years ago—36.5 million, 13.7 percent of our population, compared to 25.4 million, 12.8 percent. Child poverty is greater. The income gap between rich and poor is wider. Those who're poor are poorer: 14.4 million Americans have incomes that are 50 percent or less of the poverty line.
>
> Poverty is more concentrated now. Three-fourths of the poor live in metropolitan areas, compared to about half in 1968, and forty-two percent of today's poor live in the very central cities.
>
> Many working- and middle-class whites and African Americans have moved out, and inner-city poverty has become more densely packed. Housing and schools are resegregating. Poverty concentration has produced social disorganization and crime and social isolation for inner-city residents—largely African American and Hispanic, with some American Indian and Asian-American, as well. Children are often damaged by growing up in poverty, especially in high-poverty neighborhoods, severely curtailing their life-success chances.
>
> America's inner cities have become the nation's poorhouses from which many, now, have little hope of escape.
>
> It's not true that government can do nothing right. What we tried after the Kerner Report largely worked. We just stopped trying it or we didn't try it hard enough.
>
> We know what works—Headstart and early childhood development,

sensible and working follow-on programs for older children and youth at risk, jobs, public school reform, job training and job retention, affirmative action and proven desegregation efforts, investments in housing and community development organizations that are more directly targeted at generating jobs for the poor, and a livable minimum wage.

We know what doesn't work. Tax breaks and other incentives for the rich don't work, not for most Americans. Neither do disinvestment from the inner city or massive prison building and the explosion in incarceration.

We have the money. We must reorder the federal budget and its priorities—moving back from programs and policies that don't work and cutting down on unneeded military expenditures and corporate welfare. We must return to human investment—in programs that do work.

To accomplish this, we must, first, help Americans see that things are getting worse again for millions. Many don't know this. We must communicate what works. We must reduce the alarmingly growing power of money in American politics. We must form political coalitions across racial, ethnic, and class lines.

We must begin to think of our inner cities, and wherever else great American poverty exists, as internal wasteful, underdeveloped areas and commit to the required human and infrastructure investments. This makes economic, fiscal, and moral sense. And it will ensure a more stable and secure America for us all.

1

The Kerner Report
Thirty Years Later

Fred R. Harris

The thirtieth anniversary of the historic 1968 report of the National Advisory Commission on Civil Disorders (called the Kerner Commission, after its chairman) offers an opportunity for America to take stock of where we are now in regard to the intertwined problems of race, poverty, and the inner cities. Should this thirtieth anniversary be the occasion for celebration? The answer is, unfortunately, no. And in fact these problems have in some ways worsened.

But first, a brief review of the Kerner Commission and the reasons for its appointment.[1] For the two decades following World War II—roughly 1945–65—African Americans began to flood into the nation's cities. These were refugees from the wretched poverty and brutal degradation of the rural and small-town South. They came to places like Detroit and Newark for jobs, which by the later years of the migration often proved nonexistent. Furthermore, they found that racial segregation was as rigid in the North as in the South. Three or four families might crowd into the rented rooms of one old single-family house, situated in what would soon become an all-black section of the inner city. City housing projects were packed, too. Yet African Americans continued to come, looking for work, even though many of the better manufacturing jobs were beginning to disappear altogether or were being moved to the white suburbs.

Black frustration rose. But so did black expectations, especially as a result of civil rights activism and laws and the antipoverty and other new social programs of the 1960s. Clearly, the combination was explosive.

As Alexis de Tocqueville wrote in the 1800s, "Evils which are patiently endured when they seem inevitable become intolerable when once the idea of escape from them is suggested."

Consider Newark in 1967, whose population had dramatically changed to 62 percent black from 65 percent white in 1960. In spite of their numbers, only two black members served on Newark's seven-member city council, and Newark's white mayor, over black objections, appointed a white school board secretary. Inner-city housing was run-down and deteriorating, neighborhoods were dismal, the unemployment rate for blacks was 12 percent, and 40 percent of black children lived in single-parent homes. Newark's schools, whose student enrollment had grown by a third since the late 1950s and which spent much less per child than white suburban schools, had a dropout rate of 33 percent; about half of all blacks between the ages of sixteen and nineteen years were not in school. The city also had the highest crime rate in the country.

The 1967 situation in Detroit was no better. Its African American population had grown by 40 percent in the preceding six years. Detroit schools, up 60,000 in enrollments during the same period, were 57 percent black and would have required 1,700 more teachers and 1,000 more classrooms just to meet state standards. The dropout rate in Detroit schools was 50 percent. Surrounding suburban schools spent $500 a year more per student. In Detroit's black Twelfth Street area, where 21,000 people were crowded into each square mile (twice Detroit's average), more than a fourth of the apartment buildings were so run-down as to require demolition, and another 20 percent were below livable standards.

During the summer of 1966, a year after riots had seared the Watts section of Los Angeles, urban disorders occurred in twenty inner-city communities, the largest being in Chicago, San Francisco, and Cleveland. But these disorders were small compared to the terrible explosions of the long hot summer of 1967, the worst of these being in Newark and Detroit.

The Summer of 1967

Random sparks ignited black frustration in Newark, whose all-white police force had become the flashpoint for black hostility toward what blacks saw as an unresponsive and neglectful city system. In fact, the police were almost the only part of that system that many Detroit African Americans had any contact with.

On a hot July night, a Newark police car stopped a taxi driven by a black man whose license had been revoked. The man, one John Smith, was taken to the Fourth Street Precinct station, where a number of local African Americans watched as Smith was dragged and carried, unable or unwilling to walk, from the police car and into the precinct house. Reports and rumors spread. A hostile crowd gathered. Police reinforcements arrived. Tensions increased. Two black mediators tried unsuccessfully to calm and disperse the crowd. Suddenly, a Molotov cocktail crashed against the station wall. The police scattered the crowd, and quiet returned for a time. But not for long.

The following day, the mayor agreed to an investigation of Smith's arrest and treatment, even though he called it "an isolated incident." A black "police brutality rally" in front of the precinct station grew into a riot when the rumor spread that Smith had died. Young African Americans began roaming the streets, breaking windows. Disorder grew rapidly. Looting, burning, and damage to property mounted. There were reports of gunshots.

Local law enforcement officials were soon joined by state police and the New Jersey National Guard. Untrained and unprepared, the often-frightened young National Guardsmen frequently fired their weapons indiscriminately. Before the riot was over, twenty-five people were dead, twenty-one of them innocent civilians (including an eleven-year-old African American youngster who was carrying out the garbage and a black woman killed by National Guard fire as she watched the riot from her window). Six of the civilian dead were women. Several were children. Damage to property was estimated at $10.2 million, primarily in lost merchandise. Damage to buildings and fixtures was estimated at $2 million.

A little over a week later, Detroit's time was up. The police raided a "blind pig" (an illegal after-hours drinking joint) at the corner of Twelfth Street and Clairmont, expecting to find ten to twenty people. Instead, they arrested eighty-two people, whom they herded down to the street to wait for more patrol wagons. A crowd of about two hundred neighborhood African Americans rapidly gathered. Their initial good humor quickly changed to surliness. A bottle was thrown against a police car window, and the riot began. False rumors spread about the arresting methods used by the police officers. By the following morning, the angry crowd numbered in the thousands. Looting, window breaking, and burning were widespread. The state police were called in, then the National Guard, and finally, on President Lyndon B. Johnson's orders, federal troops.

Thirty-three blacks and ten whites were killed in the Detroit riot; seventeen of these were looters (including two white men). Two of the deaths resulted from a fallen power line. Seventeen of the dead were killed by accidental gunshots, or were murdered. Two persons were burned to death. One police officer was accidentally killed by another officer while he was scuffling with a looter. One white man was killed by a looter. The injured numbered 279, including 85 police officers. Damage estimates ranged up to $45 million. Nearly 700 buildings were burned, and 412 of them were totally destroyed. More than seven thousand people were arrested.

Sadly, there was more. Riots also occurred that summer in Atlanta, Buffalo, Cambridge (Maryland), Cincinnati, Grand Rapids, Milwaukee, Minneapolis, Tampa, and Plainfield (New Jersey). Twenty-eight other cities had serious disorders, lasting one to two days, and ninety-two cities had smaller outbreaks. In all, this violence brought death to eighty-four people, injuries to several hundred more, and property damage between $75 and $100 million.

In the aftermath of the widespread violence, while cities were still smoldering, President Johnson urgently assembled a blue-ribbon citizens' commission, charging it to find the causes of the violence and to recommend steps to prevent it. He made me a member of this commission, the National Advisory Commission on Civil Disorders.

The Report of the Kerner Commission

"Let your search be free," President Johnson told commission members. "As best you can," he said, "find the truth, the whole truth, and express it in your report." By the "whole truth," the president meant answers to three basic questions that he posed to the new commission: What happened? Why did it happen? What can be done to prevent it from happening again and again?

What Happened?

President Johnson, as did many other people at the time, believed that a conspiracy, some organization, was behind the riots. Kerner Commission members soon knew that this was not true. "The urban disorders of the summer of 1967 were not caused by, nor were they the consequence of, any organized plan or 'conspiracy,' " the report stated. Instead, the commission found, hostility levels were so high in all of America's cities that almost anything could have set them off.[2]

Why Did It Happen?

At first, commission members thought that the commission should make two reports: a quick one, before the next summer's "riot season" began, that would deal only with short-range solutions for preventing and quelling riots; and a later, deeper, final report that would deal with long-range solutions to the underlying racial and economic problems. But we soon realized that there were no short-range solutions; the causes of the riots were too profound and serious. The causes were racism and economic deprivation: "Segregation and poverty have created in the racial ghettos a destructive environment totally unknown to most white Americans." "Our nation," the commission stated, "is moving toward two societies, one black, one white—separate and unequal."

What Can Be Done to Prevent It from Happening Again?

By the time the commission turned its attention to the last of the three questions put by President Johnson, the straightforward answers to the first two questions locked it into an inevitable answer to the third: an urgent and massive national commitment against racism, unemployment, and poverty: "It is time to make good the promises of American democracy to all its citizens—urban and rural, white and black, Spanish-surname, American Indian and every minority group."

The Kerner Report then called for specific, great, and sustained federal efforts for new jobs, improved education and training, adequate housing, livable income support, and vigorous civil rights enforcement.

Progress and Reversals

During most of the decade that followed the Kerner Report, America made progress on the principal fronts that the report dealt with: race, poverty, and the inner cities. Then progress stopped and, in some ways, went into reverse. What caused this halt and retreat? First, a series of

economic shocks and trends had a depressing impact, especially on minorities. And second, the government's action and inaction bore a good
deal of the blame.

Economic Shocks and Trends

The nation suffered a series of economic recessions, most often pre-
cipitated or accentuated by tight money policy and high interest rates.[3]
One of these recessions, during the first part of President Ronald
Reagan's administration, was the nation's worst economic crisis since
the Great Depression. Another recession, during the last of the George
Bush presidency, was especially persistent and had a lasting effect. Over
time, too, economic growth rates, which had been high during the
1950s and 1960s, leveled off.

One serious effect of the recurring recessions and slowed economic
growth, compared to the two postwar decades, was a kind of Jekyll and
Hyde economy, as Jerry Jones, writing for the Center for Community
Change, puts it.[4] Economic recoveries, including the particularly long
and robust one after 1991, were markedly uneven in their effect: wages
stagnated, and after each recession, middle- and lower-income families
never fully regained the ground they had lost.

Better-paying blue-collar manufacturing jobs for low-skilled workers
dwindled or vanished. Some of these jobs moved from the inner cities
to the suburbs or, as a result of enormously heightened global competition, to other countries. Other jobs disappeared altogether as a result of
technological developments and greater use of computers. New domestic jobs were largely low-paying service jobs or jobs, often in the hard-
to-get-to suburbs, that required a dauntingly high level of skills and
education. The gap between the average wages of high school graduates
and those of college graduates widened. Unions were weakened.
Unionization declined, as membership fell from 20.7 percent of the
workforce in 1975 to 14.5 percent by 1996.[5] Wages were kept low.

As a result of these economic shocks and deleterious trends, a growing
number of American working families fell into poverty, and many already poor Americans became deeply poor.

Government Action and Inaction

Particularly with the advent of the Reagan administration in 1981,
public policy took on a decidedly antigovernment and anti–public sector

cast. Social programs and social investment suffered. The safety net was rent. Poverty expert Gary Burtless writes:

> The trend toward increased public generosity to the poor came to an abrupt halt at the end of the 1970s. Although total outlays continued to mount, almost all of the increase was due to rising poverty. None was due to more generous government provision for the low-income population. Many programs, including the main cash assistance program for indigent children, were severely curtailed. Despite increased outlays, spending per poor person did not rise.[6]

For the typical family of three with no other income, welfare benefits, when adjusted for inflation, fell an average of 40 percent between 1975 and 1996 (even before the full implementation of new federal welfare reform laws).[7] Job and training programs suffered, too. In 1980, the federal government spent $9.3 billion (in constant 1986 dollars) for such programs; by 1986, that figure had fallen to $3.7 billion.[8] Over a twenty-year period prior to 1997, public investment in education and training, infrastructure, and research and development fell by half.[9]

By the late 1980s and early 1990s, some of these governmental trends began to change. But they were not halted, not even by President Bill Clinton. As Robert Reich says concerning the first part of the Clinton administration, in which he served as secretary of labor:

> Over five years, the national debate shifted, and it shriveled. At first the central question was: Shall we invest in our future—including providing universal health care—by raising taxes or by borrowing (or by what combination)? The question quickly became: Shall we invest in our future or shall we balance the budget (or what combination)? And then: Shall we balance the budget in ten years *or* by 2002? Then: Shall we balance the budget by 2002 and *also* cut taxes? Then: Shall we cut taxes equitably *or* will most of the tax cuts go to the wealthy? At each step, the frame got smaller, the options less relevant, and the broad public less interested in the outcome.[10]

Similarly, as Jeff Faux points out, as a share of gross domestic product, present public investment in education and training (including the effect of the 1997 tax cuts for education) amounts to 40 percent less than what it was during the 1970s. Furthermore, "as a result of the 1997 budget agreement, the human investment share will drop another 20 percent by 2007. Investment in infrastructure—roads, schools, water systems—is 36 percent of its 1970s level and on our current budget trajectory will drop another 37 percent."[11] Nor has the minimum wage, set by the federal government, kept pace with inflation. It is now $5.15 an hour. Adjusted for inflation, that is 18 percent below its average value during the late 1970s.[12]

Worsening Poverty

There is more poverty in America today than there was thirty years ago, both in actual numbers and as a percentage of total population. In 1968, about one in eight Americans was living in poverty; that is 25.4 million people, or 12.8 percent of the population. In 1997, about one in seven was poor. This means that 36.5 million Americans, or 13.7 percent of our people, are living in poverty.[13] This is true despite an unemployment rate below 5 percent and an economy that has continued to grow since 1991.

Median family income grew in 1996 by about 1 percent over the preceding year (to $35,500 a year). But the typical family's living standard was still below what it was in 1989, just before the last recession. And the small increase in 1996 median family income was actually the result of women earning more, offsetting an actual drop in median earnings for full-time male workers. Child poverty in America is greater now than it was thirty years ago. The rate of child poverty grew by more than 20 percent in the decade of the 1980s. Even with some improvement in the most recent years, one in every five children in America—20.5 percent—is still living in poverty. That is four times the average child poverty rate of Western European countries.

Income inequality in America is stark. Although during most of the 1970s the income of the poorest fifth of Americans grew faster than the richest fifth, that income relationship changed dramatically after 1980. From that year until 1995, the inflation-adjusted earnings of the wealthiest one-fifth rose 10.7 percent, while median-income worker's wages fell 3.6 percent, and wages of workers in the lowest brackets declined by 9.6 percent.[14] In 1995, the wealthiest 1 percent of Americans (2.5 million people) enjoyed nearly as much after-tax income as the entire lowest 40 percent (about 100 million people), and the top 20 percent as much as the bottom 80 percent.[15] These income trends continued through 1996. The upper one-fifth of Americans saw their aggregate income share steadily increase between 1967 and 1996, while the aggregate income shares of the fourth, third, second, and lowest fifths fell.[16]

Poor people are poorer than they were thirty years ago. In 1994, half of the poor children in America under the age of six lived in families whose incomes amounted to only one-half or less of poverty-line income, an indicator of deep poverty that had doubled in the preceding twenty years.[17] This deepening poverty trend continued, and by the end of 1996, 14.4 million Americans had incomes less than half their poverty threshold, an increase from 13.9 million in the preceding year.[18]

Growing up in poverty has grave consequences for America's children and for America. In chapter 2, sociologists Greg Duncan and Jeanne Brooks-Gunn show that childhood development is often seriously impaired in poor children. Poverty in the early years is closely associated with the diminution of a child's achievement and cognitive and verbal skills and substantially reduces the chances the child will finish high school. These deleterious effects are especially pronounced for the poorest children and for those who grow up in neighborhoods of concentrated poverty. Today, poverty is more concentrated than ever before in the inner cities, where so many African Americans and Hispanic Americans live.

Race, Poverty, and the Inner Cities

In 1968, only about a half of all America's poor people lived in a metropolitan area. Today, according to the Census Bureau, more than 77 percent do. Then, 30 percent of all poor people lived in the inner city; now, 42 percent do.[19]

Many of America's inner cities have been losing population, as new jobs have moved to, or have been created in, the suburbs and as middle-class residents (including a good many African Americans) have moved out of the cities. The U.S. Department of Housing and Urban Development reports that in seventy-seven large metropolitan areas during the first three years of the 1990s, 97 percent of the new businesses created and 87 percent of new entry-level jobs were located in the suburbs.[20]

Consider Detroit, one of the two hardest-hit riot cities of the summer of 1967. Thirty years later, it is smaller, blacker, and poorer. In 1967, 1.6 million people—only a third of them black—lived in Detroit. By 1990, Detroit was down to 992,000 people, and 76 percent of them were black. The median family income in Detroit is three-fifths that of the national median, and one in three residents lives in poverty, compared to one in thirteen in the city's suburbs. According to Representative John Conyers (D. Mich.), who has served in Congress from Detroit since 1965, "We still have a huge inner-city problem in Detroit—of housing, homelessness, joblessness, an incredibly decrepit education system, high crime rates, drug abuse, welfare dependency, teen-age pregnancy. All the statistics may have gotten worse in the last 30 years."[21]

Thirty years ago, at the time of the Kerner Report, federal desegregation and affirmative action efforts were already well under way. And in the ensuing years, these efforts had enormous and beneficial effect (see chap. 7). Studies show that educational outcomes were much better for children attending socioeconomically integrated schools. African Americans (and Hispanics, other minorities, and women, too) entered professional schools or went into business, and many joined the middle class. The number of black parents with college degrees quadrupled. And contrary to the claims of some critics, affirmative action did not help only the middle class; occupations and trades—such as law enforcement, fire fighting, long-distance trucking, and skilled construction work—opened up, too.

Then in 1981, with the advent of the twelve Reagan-Bush years, progress on racial discrimination slowed. An assault was launched on affirmative action, both in the executive branch and in the Supreme Court (to which Reagan appointed conservative William Rehnquist as Chief Justice and Bush appointed conservative Clarence Thomas to replace the late Thurgood Marshall).[22] By the 1990s opposition to affirmative action had spread to many members of the U.S. Congress and to a number of state governments, as well.

This official hostility to affirmative action and civil rights laws was to have dire consequences. In California, for example, where affirmative action was abandoned, University of California law schools saw a one-year (1996–97) drop of 63 percent in new African American students (from forty-three to sixteen), a 60 percent drop in new American Indian students (from ten to four), and a 34 percent drop in new Hispanic students (from eighty-nine to fifty-nine). The university's five business schools saw similar decreases in new minority students: a 26 percent drop in African American students (from twenty-seven to twenty) and a 54 percent drop in Hispanic students (from fifty-four to twenty-five), with American Indian new enrollments remaining the same (at three).[23]

With attacks on affirmative action, wage discrimination against African Americans increased.[24] And studies demonstrate that many employers still base hiring decisions on racial stereotypes, preferring white over African American or Hispanic applicants, Hispanics over African Americans, African American women over African American men, and young African American men least of all.[25]

While overall February 1998 unemployment was 4.7 percent of America's workforce, the figure for African Americans was more than twice that, at 9.9 percent. For white teens, unemployment stood at 11.2 percent, while for black teens it was more than three times higher.[26] Despite some recent improvement, median African American family income is still only 56.2 percent, and for Hispanic families only 55.6 percent, of median family income for non-Hispanic whites.[27] About 30 percent of Hispanic families and 28.4 percent of African American families live below the poverty line, rates that are nearly three times those for non-Hispanic whites.[28] Even with some narrowing of the gap, the median net worth of non-Hispanic white families is still 4.5 times that for African American and Hispanic families.[29]

And America is resegregating. Income levels of residents explain only a small fraction of America's segregation in housing. Instead, as Gary Orfield demonstrates, despite open housing laws, massive discrimination against African Americans and Hispanics still exists in housing and home finance markets, subsidized housing has been openly segregated and excluded from middle-class suburban areas, and housing subsidies have often helped resegregate integrated neighborhoods.[30]

America's schools are resegregating. Orfield told the President's Initiative on Race that two-thirds of African American students and three-fourths of Hispanic students now attend predominantly minority schools and that one-third of each group attend intensely segregated schools.[31] Government has abandoned the policy goal of school desegregation—to the degree that Gary Orfield has termed this development a "quiet reversal of *Brown v. Board of Education.*" Polls in recent years show that a majority of Americans think that African Americans are as well off or better off than whites, insofar as education is concerned.[32] That is not true. After noting that intensely segregated minority schools are sixteen times as likely as nonsegregated schools to serve areas of concentrated poverty (more than 50 percent poor), Orfield points out that, to a considerable extent, "concentrated school poverty is a problem affecting minority students only," adding that

schools with large numbers of impoverished students tend to have much lower test scores, higher dropout rates, fewer students in demanding classes, less well-prepared teachers, and a low percentage of students who will eventually finish college. . . . Segregated schools are unequal not because of anything inherent in race but because they reflect the long-term corrosive impact on neighborhoods and families from a long history of racial discrimination in many aspects of life. If those inequalities and the stereotypes associated with them did not exist, desegregation would have little consequence.

Poverty researchers Gary Sandefur, Molly Martin, and Thomas Wells find that, while there is still much poverty outside America's metropolitan areas and inner cities, what is most distinctive about today's inner-city poverty is the geographical concentration of large numbers of African American and Hispanic poor people (see chap. 3). Sociologist William Julius Wilson has documented how work has disappeared in the inner city, ghettos have proliferated, and poverty has become more densely massed.[3] Another sociologist, Paul A. Jargowsky, reports that the problems of the ghetto have become dramatically worse. He states:

> High-poverty areas in central cities have expanded rapidly; more of the overall black population resides in such neighborhoods; and the black poor are increasingly concentrated within them and isolated from the social and economic mainstream. . . . For blacks, therefore, neighborhood poverty goes hand in hand with segregation. . . . The combination of population growth, increasing metropolitanization, and increasing neighborhood poverty resulted in a 70 percent increase in the number of blacks residing in impoverished ghetto neighborhoods—rising from about 2.5 million in 1970 to more than four million persons in 1990.[34]

Locked in the Poorhouse

Inner cities, then, have become America's poorhouses, Jargowsky concludes. Millions of African Americans and Hispanics, as well as a good number of American Indians and Asian Americans, are almost locked in them, with little hope of escape. Living in concentrated poverty can have devastating effects. Sociologists William Julius Wilson, James Quane, and Bruce Rankin point out that

> ghetto neighborhoods have less effective institutions, weaker informal networks, and social milieus that discourage collective supervision and responsibility. Lacking these important social resources, high poverty neighbor-

hoods are more likely to experience a breakdown of public order, whereby crime, delinquency, and other forms of social disorder flourish. Thus poor ghetto residents are doubly disadvantaged—first, by being poor and, secondly, by residing in neighborhoods characterized by low levels of social organization.[35]

They write that the impact of inner-city poverty on a person is made worse by the social isolation that goes with it "by residing in neighborhoods that offer few opportunities to interact with individuals and institutions representing mainstream society. Ghetto residents lack contact with regularly employed persons who can provide social support."[36]

So this thirty-year anniversary of the Kerner Report is no occasion for celebration. It is not right that in a land of plenty so many Americans, especially so many American children, should be left out and left behind.

We know what to do. Martin Carnoy makes that clear:

When government has focused its power on racial and ethnic income differences and discrimination in the past, it has had a major impact on the economic conditions of blacks and other disadvantaged minorities. It can have a similar impact if policies combine investment in the education of disadvantaged children and minority college education with expansionary economics. It can have an impact if it combines pro-labor wage and training legislation with the implementation of existing anti-discrimination laws. Government can do all this.[37]

And more. It does not make economic sense for America to continue on its present path in regard to race, poverty, and the inner cities. It does not make economic sense for America to continue to have such underdeveloped areas or to leave so many of our fellow citizens underskilled, undereducated, and underemployed and underutilized. It does not make fiscal sense to continue to spend so much more on crime and prisons than it would cost us to invest appropriately in education, jobs, and skills in the first place. Human development investment would pay untold dividends.

Further, it does not make moral sense to consign so many Americans to wasted lives. It's not good public health policy, what we're doing. Nor does our present course adequately provide internally for the kind of national security and public safety that Americans have a right to expect from their government.

2

Urban Poverty, Welfare Reform, and Child Development

Greg J. Duncan and Jeanne Brooks-Gunn

In 1968, when the Kerner Report was published, one in eight (12.8 percent) residents of our nation's inner cities was poor (see figure 2.1).[1] This poverty count is based on a Census Bureau comparison of total family income with a poverty threshold that varies by family size. Expressed in 1996 dollars, the poverty thresholds for families with three and four persons in the late 1960s were roughly $12,500 and $16,000, respectively. Individuals living in families with incomes below these thresholds were counted as poor. Since poverty thresholds are adjusted only for inflation, these same dollar thresholds hold today.

The fraction of inner-city residents who are impoverished has generally increased over the past thirty years and has always been much higher than poverty rates for metropolitan residents who live outside of inner cities. By 1997, one in five (19%) inner-city residents was poor, half again more than thirty years earlier. Worse yet, the extent of poverty is twice as high for urban children as urban adults. In 1996, some 31 percent of children living in the inner cities of our nation's metropolitan areas were poor, as compared with 16 percent of adults living in inner cities.[2]

What have we learned in the past thirty years about the likely consequences of these high rates of urban poverty on the development of children and on the life chances of children when they become adults? A fortunate legacy of the War on Poverty was the initiation of what has become a series of large-scale national survey studies of child development.[3] These studies provide information on both family poverty status,

FIGURE 2.1
Poverty Rates in Inner Cities and Other Metropolitan Areas, 1967–1996

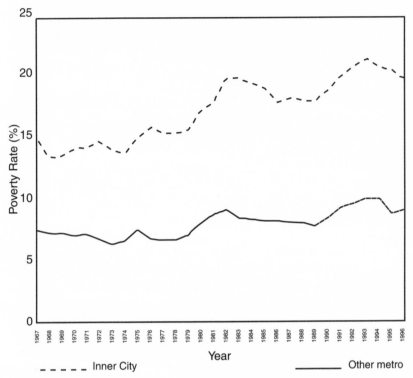

Source: U.S. Bureau of the Census, *Historical Poverty Tables, 1997* (Washington, D.C.: Government Printing Office, 1997), http://www.census.gov/hhes/poverty/histpov/hstpov8.html.

measured during childhood, and outcomes for the children, measured during childhood as well as adulthood. Thus, they provide a basis for evaluating the likely developmental impacts of the high rates of child poverty both within and outside of our nation's urban areas.

The future extent and effects of urban poverty among children will depend critically on the effects of the Personal Responsibility and Work Opportunity Reconciliation Act, which was signed by President Bill Clinton on August 22, 1996. Ending six decades of guaranteed government aid for economically deprived children, this law eliminated the open-ended federal entitlement program of Aid to Families with Dependent Children (AFDC) in favor of providing block grants to states to be used for time-limited cash assistance replacement programs (TANF, or

Temporary Assistance for Needy Families). This legislation is likely to spur welfare-to-work transitions among a substantial number of recipients. But just as certain is an increase in the depth of the poverty among families in which mothers are unable to make successful transitions to full-time work. Given the importance of welfare reform for the well-being of future generations of children, we evaluate below its likely effect on poor children.

Consequences of Child Poverty

A plethora of studies, books, and reports demonstrate correlations between child poverty and various measures of child achievement, health, and behavior.[4] The strength and consistency of these associations is striking. For example, in terms of physical health, the risk to poor children relative to nonpoor children is 1.7 times for a low-birthweight birth, 3.5 times for lead poisoning, 1.7 times for child mortality, and 2.0 times for a short-stay hospital episode.[5] In terms of achievement, the risk to poor children relative to nonpoor children is 2.0 times higher for grade repetition and high school dropout and 1.4 times for learning disability. For other conditions and outcomes, these risk ratios are 1.3 times for parent-reported emotional or behavioral problems, 3.1 times for a teenage out-of-wedlock birth, 6.8 times for reported cases of child abuse and neglect, and 2.2 times for experiencing violent crime.

Although there is a substantial body of literature on the effects of poverty on children, it has major shortcomings: family income and child outcomes are often not well measured, and information on some topics is old or taken from studies narrowly focused on local communities. Most important, family income is not reported in many data sources (such as vital statistics) that contain crucial information about child outcomes. As a result, studies using these kinds of data have often used variables such as occupation, single parenthood, or low maternal education to infer family income levels. But income and social class are far from synonymous. Since family incomes are surprisingly volatile, there are only modest correlations between economic deprivation and typical measures of socioeconomic background.

Several national, longitudinal data sources do collect the requisite information, however, making it possible to distinguish between the effects on child development of income poverty and those of its correlated events and conditions. The distinction is crucial, both conceptually and because policy changes such as welfare reform will have a much bigger impact on family income than on such correlates of poverty as low levels of schooling or lone-parent family structure.

Research that isolates the impact of poverty per se suggests that family income has at times large but rather selective effects on children's attainments.[6] Most noteworthy is the importance of the type of outcome being considered. To the extent that family income affects children's development, it appears to affect verbal ability and achievement rather than problem behavior, mental health, or physical health.

Also important is the childhood stage at which income is measured. Family economic conditions in early childhood appear to be far more important for shaping ability and achievement than economic conditions later in childhood. A study of completed schooling illustrates the importance of avoiding poverty early in childhood.[7] Controlling for income later in childhood as well as for demographic characteristics of households, the authors estimate that a $10,000 increment to income averaged over the first five years of life for children in low-income families is associated with a 2.8-fold increase in the odds of finishing high school. This estimated effect was much larger than the corresponding estimated effects of income measured later in childhood.

Other studies have found associations between income and school-related outcomes before high school—including children's achievement and cognitive and verbal ability test scores—when other family conditions such as maternal education, maternal age at child's birth, single parenthood, and employment are controlled.[8] Children in households with incomes below the poverty threshold have substantially lower test scores than children in households with incomes above the poverty threshold. Effects are seen for children from age two through age eight and are most pronounced for children who are persistently poor (with multiple years of low income), although there are also some effects of transient poverty. Children who are just above the poverty threshold (family income at the threshold to twice the threshold) have significantly higher scores than those below the threshold. And the lowest scores are seen in children who are extremely poor (family incomes below 50 percent of the poverty threshold).

Completed years of schooling are strongly predicted by early cognitive, verbal, and achievement test scores. Indeed, the few studies that include measures of early test scores, high school completion, and measures of poverty (or proxies, such as welfare receipt) find that about one-half of the variance in high school completion rates is accounted for by early test scores.[9] In these analyses, poverty exerted much of its influence upon high school completion through its effect on early test scores.

How is it that low income affects children? We need to learn more about possible pathways in order to understand more completely the effects of poverty on children and identify leverage points amenable to policy intervention. Research here is often far from definitive, but it is useful to identify what might ultimately prove important.

A first important pathway is the quality of a child's home environment. Warmth of mother–child interactions, the physical condition of the home, and especially opportunities for learning account for a substantial portion of the effects of family income on cognitive outcomes in young children. Several studies have found that differences in the home learning environments of higher- and lower-income children account for up to half of the effect of income on the cognitive development of preschool children and between one-quarter and one-third of the effect of income on the achievement scores of elementary schoolchildren.[10] The home environment is assessed during a home visit to see what learning experiences parents provide their children, both inside and outside the home. These include access to a library card, reading to the children, provision of learning-oriented toys and experiences, and use of developmentally appropriate activities.[11]

School readiness also depends on the quality of the care that children receive outside the home. High-quality, developmentally appropriate, early childhood education in the toddler and preschool years is associated with enhanced school readiness for poor and middle-income children alike.[12] In addition, randomized trials have demonstrated that early childhood education programs for poor children increase verbal ability and reasoning skills through the early elementary years.[13] Such programs may also decrease behavioral problems and increase persistence and enthusiasm for learning, although few early childhood programs have assessed these outcomes.[14] Early childhood programs also influence maternal outcomes, including mental health, coping skills, knowledge about child rearing, and mother–child interactions.[15]

For adolescents, a second pathway is through family economic pressure that leads to conflict with parents and results in lower school grades, reduced emotional health, and impaired social relationships.[16] Other work suggests that income loss or economic uncertainty due to unemployment, underemployment, and unstable work conditions, rather than poverty or low income per se, is a source of conflict between parents and teens, leading to emotional and school problems.[17]

A third possible pathway is parental health. Parents who are poor are likely to be less healthy, both emotionally and physically, than those who are not poor.[18] And parental irritability and depressive symptoms are associated with more conflictual interactions with adolescents, leading to less satisfactory emotional, social, and cognitive development. Some studies have established that parental mental health accounts for some of the effect of economic circumstances on child health and behavior. Additionally, poor parental mental health is associated with impaired parent–child interactions and fewer learning experiences in the home.[19]

A fourth possible pathway through which family income operates is with neighborhoods.[20] The possibility that neighborhood poverty affects child development independently of family poverty is particularly acute in large urban areas, where concentrated neighborhood poverty is most severe. Poor parents are constrained in their choice of neighborhoods and schools. Low income may lead to residence in extremely poor neighborhoods, characterized by social disorganization (crime, many unemployed adults, neighbors who do not monitor the behavior of adolescents) and few resources for child development (playgrounds, child care, health care facilities, parks, after-school programs).

Research on the impact of neighborhood conditions on child development has tended to rely on neighborhood measures that can be gleaned from data collected in the decennial census. Some of it has found that the presence or absence of affluent neighbors is associated with both child (preschool intelligence test scores) and adolescent (high school graduation rates and total years of completed schooling) outcomes, independent of the individual family's economic situation.[21] By implication, the trend toward increasing concentrations of poverty in urban neighborhoods over the thirty years since the publication of the Kerner Report is especially worrisome.

The most recent research on neighborhood effects has developed innovative measures of neighborhood conditions. As part of a survey of a Chicago neighborhood in the 1990s, the collective efficacy of neighborhoods was measured.[22] Collective efficacy combines social cohesion (the extent to which neighbors trust each other and share common values) with informal social control (the extent to which neighbors can count on each other to monitor and supervise youth and protect public order). Collective efficacy is thus a capacity for collective action. The study found that, in Chicago, collective efficacy relates strongly to neighborhood levels of violence, personal victimization, and homicide (controlling for social composition, as indicated by census variables, and for prior crime). Key, then, is not so much the criminogenic character of neighborhoods but rather the capacity of adults informally to regulate social behavior, particularly that of young people.

Welfare Reform and Urban Poverty

Research on the impact of poverty on children suggests that avoiding the adverse consequences of deep poverty in early childhood is key to the cognitive development of children. Looking to the past, the increasing degree of poverty in America's inner cities has almost certainly harmed the development and life chances of urban children. For the future, the crucial question is to what extent welfare reform, other child- and family-based programs, and macroeconomic conditions will affect the development of children.

In addition to eliminating the AFDC program, the 1996 welfare legislation makes other sweeping changes affecting child care, the food stamp program, Supplemental Security Income for children, benefits for legal immigrants, and the Child Support Enforcement program, and it offers states numerous options, such as capping benefits so payments do not increase if recipients have additional children and denying assistance to unmarried teen parents and their children.

The 1996 legislation introduced two provisions linked to the length of welfare receipt. First, after twenty-four months of receipt, recipients are required to participate in "allowable work activities" or else face sanctions or penalties. Second, recipients are limited to sixty months of total receipt (whether or not consecutive), regardless of work effort. This limit applies to the entire household and to all forms of assistance under the grant. States are allowed to impose shorter time limits on total receipt than the sixty-month period specified in the legislation; nearly half of the states have already opted to do so. For families currently receiving assistance, the five-year clock starts on the date that the state of residence begins implementation of the block grant. States are permitted to exempt up to 20 percent of their caseloads from the lifetime limits by reason of hardship.

Early returns on the new state-designed welfare reforms appear to be stunningly positive. Caseloads have fallen by roughly 25 percent since 1994, and by as much as 80 percent in some counties in Wisconsin. News accounts often feature former welfare-recipient mothers who are thankful for having been spurred into action by the reforms. But although some optimism is warranted, research suggests that much of the euphoria over welfare reform is unfounded and that states should prepare for almost half of their welfare families to hit the five-year benefit cutoff within eight years.[23] This research suggests that more than twice the number of families and children as can be exempted from the benefit cutoffs will accumulate five years of welfare receipt. And while some of the families facing benefit cutoffs will respond with successful transitions into the labor force, many will not.

It is wrong to view falling caseloads as evidence that welfare reform will be easy. Caseloads started to fall well before welfare reform legislation was signed in 1996. In fact, a thirty-year look at the size of national welfare caseloads in the United States shows little change, except for an increase in the early 1970s and early 1990s and the sharp fall in recent years. The drop in caseloads in the years 1994 to 1997 followed a period in the early 1990s when caseloads soared and actually represents a return to more typical levels. Caseloads in states like Wisconsin, whose economy began booming before that of most other states, have indeed fallen dramatically, but the more typical reductions are modest. Since the labor market is almost certain to sour again before time limits hit, and since welfare reform has already pushed many work-ready recipients into work, it cannot be presumed that the decline in the number of welfare recipients will continue.

Photographs of former welfare mothers now hard at work make wonderful news copy, but the truth is, every year hundreds of thousands of women, some but not most of them living in our inner cities, have made successful exits from the welfare rolls. Numerous studies have shown that spells of AFDC (i.e., continuous periods of receipt) typically last less than two years.[24] For many recipients, welfare provides a kind of short-term insurance against the economic consequences of a divorce, a nonmarital birth, or a job loss. And the booming economy of the mid-1990s made the transition to work even easier and faster.

But the story that is eclipsed in the widespread optimism about welfare reform concerns the people the politicians and pundits have been arguing about for years: long-term welfare recipients. Families least likely to be able to support themselves and most likely to reach the welfare time limits have always been an important part of the caseload. The characteristics of recipients most likely to hit the five-year time limit are very similar to the characteristics of previous long-term recipients: two-thirds lack high school diplomas, a majority lack work experience, two-thirds were age twenty-one or younger when they started receiving benefits, and most have a low level of cognitive skills.[25]

Many provisions of the welfare reform legislation will affect the amount of income available to low-income children. For example, most states have adopted family caps, which prevent an increase in benefits paid to women who have additional children while receiving public assistance. This will lower the per capita incomes of recipient families but not dramatically. More worrisome are time limits, sanctions for non-compliant behavior, and categorical restrictions on eligibility, all of which drop cash assistance to zero. Some families hitting the limits or losing benefits when sanctioned for not following program rules will replace the lost welfare payments with income from work and other sources; others, perhaps as many as half, will see their incomes fall well below the poverty line. State-specific provisions that deny cash assistance to children born to underage, unmarried women will also lower dramatically the incomes of a subset of affected families.

Another major provision of the 1996 bill with implications for the well-being of children and youth is that requiring parents to be engaged in work or work-related activities in order to receive TANF. Parents not meeting their states' work requirements are to be sanctioned with a reduction or termination of benefits. What is likely to happen to sanctioned families?

Welfare recipients in Iowa, since 1993, have been required to help formulate and then follow a "family investment agreement." Failure to comply has led to a series of sanctions, including a six-month cutoff of all cash benefits. A follow-up study of sanctioned families found an almost equal split between those working immediately after cash benefits were terminated and those not working.[26] Nearly half enjoyed average monthly income increases of $500, but the rest suffered average decreases of nearly $400. As with welfare recipients in general, the heterogeneity of these Iowa families is key in understanding the consequences of sanctions and time limits: roughly half of recipients may indeed respond well to sanctions, but the other half will not.

Some Policy Implications

Research on the effects of poverty on child development suggests that policy should focus on situations involving deep poverty occurring in early childhood, a crucial indicator of the welfare of children.

In the case of welfare reform, time limits may be less deleterious than sanctions and categorical restrictions, especially in states that opt for the full five-year time limit. Unless additional children are born during the period of receipt, mothers accumulating five years of welfare receipt are not likely to have young children present in their households. In contrast, sanctions and many categorical provisions are much more likely to deny benefits to families with very young children. Not only do young children appear to be most vulnerable to the consequences of deep poverty, but mothers with very young children are least able to support themselves in the labor market.

An obvious recommendation is that states consider exempting families with young children from time limits, sanctions, and categorical restrictions. A minority of states currently exempt mothers of very young children from various provisions of their welfare reform, but in almost no state does the exemption extend beyond the child's first birthday, and in some cases only until the child is three months old. States without exemptions should consider granting them, and all states should consider extending the exemption to a child's second or third birthday. It would also be useful to gear universal programs, such as a child allowance or refundable tax credits, to children's ages. A problem with such provisions is that they may create incentives for mothers to bear more children, but evidence suggests, at most, weak links between fertility and generosity of welfare benefits.[27]

Several European countries gear time-limited benefits to the age of children in their assistance programs. In Germany, a modest parental allowance is available to a mother working fewer than twenty hours per week until her child is eighteen months old. France guarantees a modest minimum income to most of its citizens, including families with children of all ages. Supplementing this basic support for lone parents is the Allocation de Parent Isolé (API) program. Eligibility for generous income-tested API payments to families with children is limited to the period between the child's birth and it's third birthday, even if low-income status persists beyond that point. In effect, the API program acknowledges a special need for income support during this period, especially if a parent wishes to care for very young children and forgo income from work. The elaborate state-funded system in France for providing child care beginning at age three lessens the problems associated with the parent's transition into the labor force.

Yet another strategy is to liberate long-term recipients from welfare through a combination of cost-effective job-training and other skill-building programs; redoubling efforts to make work pay by increasing the after-tax family incomes of women who take low-wage jobs; and funding work-for-welfare jobs of last resort for those who are unable, despite effort, to find an employer to hire them.

If the goal is to promote the healthy development of children, it is important to go beyond cash transfer programs and consider service delivery programs, such as those providing nutrition supplements and education (Women, Infants, and Children), medical care (Medicaid), early childhood education (Head Start), and housing (Section 8 vouchers). The case for giving preference to such programs over income transfers is strongest for programs focused on health and behavior, since there is little evidence that outcomes in these domains are responsive to improvements in family living standards and considerably more evidence that these programs themselves are efficacious.[28]

The pathways through which poverty influences children also suggest some recommendations. Since about half of the effect of family income on tests of cognitive ability is mediated by the home environment, including learning experiences in the home, interventions might profitably focus on working with parents. An example is the Learninggames curriculum, which was developed by Joe Sparling and Isabelle Lewis at the Frank Porter Graham Center at the University of North Carolina at Chapel Hill. This program offers parents instruction, materials, and role-playing practice in providing learning experiences.

Programs that focus on teaching parenting skills and encouraging and modeling reading skills have been shown to alter parenting behavior and child language and school readiness.[29] At the same time, child language effects are only seen if programs are intensive. For example, home visits focusing on parenting skills have to be frequent (at least several times per month) and extensive (several years in duration) and have specific curricula focused on behaviors and interactions.[30] More generally, economic logic requires a comparison of the costs and benefits of the various programs directed at enhancing the development of disadvantaged children. In this context, expenditures on income transfer and service delivery programs should be judged by the benefits they produce relative to their costs.

It will be years before we have a definitive accounting of the long-run effects of increases in urban poverty and the 1996 welfare reforms. We argue that increases in poverty are likely to leave developmental scars on children and that welfare reforms will almost certainly increase both successful transitions from welfare to work and the number of severely economically disadvantaged children. Recent research suggests that economic deprivation early in a child's life is most harmful to his or her chances for achievement. Economic logic suggests that prevention of economic deprivation and its effects would be both profitable social investment.

3

Poverty as a Public Health Issue: Since the Kerner Report of 1968

Gary Sandefur, Molly Martin, and Thomas Wells

American society has changed in many ways since the Kerner Commission issued its report on March 1, 1968.[1] Our understanding of poverty, its dimensions, and possible ways of dealing with it is much different from the perceptions that underlay that report. In this chapter, we review trends in poverty and antipoverty policy since 1968. In part, it is an update of a report prepared on the occasion of the twentieth anniversary of the Kerner Report.[2]

One startling feature of poverty in the United States is that it is as prevalent now as it was in the late 1960s. This is in spite of the War on Poverty launched in the 1960s and subsequent efforts to make poverty policy more effective. Many have become disillusioned with government efforts to help the poor, given the failure of these efforts to reduce the level of poverty. Such a pessimistic view of government efforts ignores two essential aspects of poverty and government policy.

First, government efforts to help the poor do in fact raise substantial numbers of people above the poverty line, and these efforts also do a good deal to ameliorate the effects of the poverty.[3] Food stamps help feed those among the poor who would not otherwise eat, and Medicaid provides medical care to poor children who would not otherwise receive it. To criticize government programs that help the poor because they do not eliminate the problem of poverty is like criticizing aspirin because it does not eliminate the causes of headaches.

A medical analogy, more specifically a public health analogy, can also illustrate the second aspect of poverty ignored by the critics of govern-

ment programs. A certain level of poverty in our society is generated by
the nature of the American economy. In an economy in which 5 percent
or so of the population is unemployed in the best of times, and in which
millions of Americans have full-time jobs that do not pay enough to lift
them and their families above the poverty line, a substantial group of
people will be poor. Poverty in our society is, in effect, similar to the
common cold. Although people may engage in behavior that increases
or decreases their risk of catching a cold, it is naive to believe that no
one will catch a cold even if they do all the right things. The same is
true of poverty. People may behave in ways that increase or decrease
their risks of being poor or the length of time that they remain poor, but
it is foolish to believe that poverty is solely the fault of the poor.

If we accept the analogy of poverty as a public health problem, our
understanding of why poverty has not disappeared becomes dramatically
different. It will never disappear as long as our economy is characterized
by an unemployment rate of at least 5 percent and by millions of jobs
that do not pay above the poverty line. Given that these negative features of the economy are associated with positive features, such as low
inflation, we are not in a position to eliminate unemployment or pay
everyone a wage above the poverty line. What we need are government
programs that reduce the length of time that people are poor and ameliorate the effects of poverty. Recent policy changes do not move in this
direction. In fact, our current efforts are likely to generate more poverty
rather than reduce it.

As we revisit the Kerner Report, it is also important to note that
poverty is not just an inner-city phenomenon, nor does it involve only
blacks. In fact, levels of poverty in some nonmetropolitan areas exceed
those in inner cities. What is most distinctive about inner-city poverty
is the geographical concentration of large numbers of black and Hispanic
poor people. Many of the factors associated with poverty seem to be
similar whether we are talking about rural or urban poverty, or black,
white, Hispanic, Asian, or American Indian poverty.

Poverty was only one concern of the Kerner Commission. It set out
to understand the circumstances leading to the urban race riots of the
mid-1960s. In its investigation, the commission appropriately identified
the plight of poor urban blacks as one major factor in the riots. In 1992,
a large-scale race riot again raged in Los Angeles, yet this time the media,
social scientists, and politicians discussed more than just blacks and
whites. The 1960s riots involved predominantly blacks, while the 1992
riot involved Hispanics as well as blacks, with Korean-owned businesses

targeted for vandalism and looting. The change in the nature of the riots illustrates a fundamental change in America's urban poverty. Urban poverty can no longer be thought of as primarily a black issue: the urban poor have become increasingly diverse, as Asians and Hispanics have moved into urban areas. Further, racial issues in the United States can no longer be seen solely, or even predominantly, in black–white terms. The Hispanic population of the United States will soon surpass the black population in size, and the Asian population continues to grow at a much faster rate than either the black or white populations.

Below, we discuss the recent debate over defining and measuring poverty and the implications of using the definition of poverty proposed by the National Research Council (NRC) for understanding minority poverty. We also review trends in poverty since the 1960s, looking not only at inner cities but also at other geographical areas. We also follow trends for different racial and ethnic groups and different demographic groups. We then review trends in public policies for dealing with poverty, including the 1996 Personal Responsibility and Work Opportunity Reconciliation Act. We conclude with a call for viewing poverty as a public health issue rather than as a moral issue.

Measuring Poverty

In 1965, the U.S. government adopted an official poverty definition for use in national statistics. Under the definition, the poverty threshold equals the cost of a minimum diet multiplied by three and adjusted for the age of the household head and the number of persons in the family. Except for changes in poverty thresholds for different types of family and a change in the price index used to adjust for inflation, the official poverty definition has not been altered since its inception.[4]

Many have begun to wonder, however, whether a definition of poverty developed in the mid-1960s is applicable today. Observers have criticized the official poverty definition over the years. One issue has been the method of measuring household income. The official poverty definition compares a family's pretax income to the appropriate threshold, but some argue that government in-kind benefits (such as food stamps and Medicaid) should be included in income; others argue that income should be measured after taxes; and still others suggest that work-related expenses and child care costs should be deducted from income to better indicate the amount of resources a family has available.

Another criticism is that the poverty line does not take into account the different costs of living in various parts of the country.

Responding to these concerns, the Joint Economic Committee of Congress authorized an independent review of the official poverty measure. The NRC appointed a committee to conduct the review, and after much deliberation, the committee proposed several changes in the measure of poverty. One recommendation was that the threshold represent a budget for food, clothing, shelter, utilities, and a small amount for other needs, instead of simply a multiple of basic food costs. Another recommendation was that the threshold reflect the needs of different family types and geographical differences in housing costs. The committee also recommended that family resources be measured as the sum of all money income and near-money benefits (food stamps, free school lunches) from all sources minus expenses not included in the family budget of goods and services (taxes, child care, work-related expenses, and out-of-pocket medical costs).

This proposed definition of poverty is dramatically different from the official definition, and using it leads to a different estimated poverty rate for any given year. In 1992, for example, the official poverty rate was 14.5 percent, but under the NRC's proposed poverty measure the overall poverty rate would have been 18.1 percent.[5] In addition, the poverty rates for various groups of people differ under the two measures (see table 3.1). With the NRC's proposed poverty definition, the poverty rate for each racial and ethnic group increases. Whites have the lowest poverty rate under either definition. With the official poverty definition, blacks have the highest poverty rate, but with the alternative definition,

TABLE 3.1
Poverty Rates under Current Poverty Definition and Proposed National Research Council Poverty Definition, by Racial or Ethnic Group, 1992 (%)

		Poverty Rate	
Race	Total Population	Current Measure	NRC Measure
White	83.6	11.6	15.3
Black	12.5	33.2	35.6
Hispanic[a]	8.9	29.4	41.0

Source: National Research Council, *Measuring Poverty: A New Approach* (Washington, D.C.: National Academy Press, 1995), table 5.8.
a. Hispanics can be of either race.

Hispanics have the highest rate. The dramatic increase in the Hispanic poverty rate under the proposed definition is due mainly to the adjustment for housing costs in the alternative definition. By taking into account housing costs, the poverty rates for the Northeast and the West regions increased. Since Hispanics are concentrated in these two regions and whites and blacks are not, Hispanic poverty rates were greatly affected by this attention to differential housing costs.

While the investigation into the definition and limitations of the current official poverty measure proved valuable, the NRC's proposed measurement of poverty is not yet the national standard. Thus, in this chapter we use statistics based on the official poverty definition, even though these statistics may be underestimates of the actual poverty rate in the United States. Further, we are particularly interested in trends over time, and sufficient data do not exist for estimating poverty rates using the proposed NRC definition for the period from the late 1960s through the mid-1990s.

Poverty since the 1960s

We begin with a review of trends in poverty in general, without attention to geographical location. As other researchers note, "poverty in the early 1990s . . . is high relative to what it was in the early 1940s; it is high relative to what analysts expected given the economic recovery of the 1980s; it is high relative to what it is in other countries that have similar standards of living."[6] In 1968, the year of the Kerner Report, 12.8 percent of the U.S. population was poor. In 1995, 13.8 percent of the U.S. population was poor.[7] In sum, no progress was made in permanently reducing the overall rate of poverty in the United States between 1968 and 1995.

The pattern in poverty rates for all persons varies by racial and ethnic group. The poverty rate among whites declined in the 1960s and 1970s, but it has slowly increased since the 1980s. Despite this increase, the poverty rate among whites remains the lowest among all racial and ethnic groups. The black poverty rate has consistently declined since 1959, but it remains higher than that for most other racial and ethnic groups. The poverty rate among Hispanics fluctuated before the 1980s, but since then it increased to become the highest poverty rate among all racial and ethnic groups in 1995. The black and Hispanic poverty rates are still nearly three times that for whites. The American Indian poverty rate has fluctuated but has remained relatively high. In 1989, the poverty rate for American Indians was the highest for all reported racial and ethnic groups. The Asian poverty rate has remained relatively constant and relatively low throughout the 1979–95 period.[8]

Although the breakdown of poverty rates for individuals by racial and ethnic group illuminates differences in the time trends among groups, these rates also hide important changes in the composition of the poverty population. Since 1959, poverty rates for persons aged sixty-five and older dramatically decreased for most racial and ethnic groups (especially whites, blacks, and American Indians). Asians aged sixty-five and older are the only elderly group to remain at relatively the same poverty rate; black, Hispanic, and American Indian persons in this age group continue to experience the highest levels of poverty (see table 3.2). Children have had a much different experience than have older Americans. In general, children experienced a decline in poverty rates between 1959 and 1969, but since 1969 their poverty rates have increased. In 1959, the poverty rate for related children under eighteen years in families was 26.9 percent; by 1969, the poverty rate for these children had dropped to 13.8 percent; by 1995, their poverty rate had increased to 20.2 percent.[9] The pattern is similar across racial and ethnic groups, but the level of poverty differs. White and Asian children experience the lowest levels of poverty, while black, Hispanic, and American Indian children face poverty rates over twice those of white and Asian children.

At the time of the Kerner Commission Report, only 9.8 percent of all families in the United States were headed by a single female. By 1995, this had increased to 17.5 percent. Families headed by single females are much more likely to be poor than are families headed by two persons. For example, in 1995 the poverty rate for families headed by married couples was 4.5 percent, while the poverty rate for families headed by single females was 36.3 percent. The percentage of families headed by single women also differs by racial and ethnic group: 12.9 percent of white families, 47.3 percent of black families, 23.0 percent of Hispanic families, and 10.7 percent of Asian families are headed by single women.[10]

The percentage of poor individuals living in families headed by single females varies with race and ethnicity. Nearly half of American Indians, blacks, and Hispanics living in such families are poor. Less than a third of whites and Asians living in such families are poor. Over time, there have been declines in the poverty rates for persons in families headed by

TABLE 3.2
Poverty Rates, by Demographic Group and Race, 1959–1995,
Various Years (%)

Group and Race	1959	1969	1979	1989	1995
All persons					
White	18.1	9.5	9.0	10.0	11.2
Black	55.1	32.2	31.0	30.7	29.3
Hispanic		24.3[a]	21.8	26.2	30.3
American Indian		38.3	27.5	30.9	
Asian			13.1	14.1	14.6
Persons aged 65 and older					
White	33.1	23.3	13.3	9.6	9.0
Black	62.5	50.2	36.2	30.7	25.4
Hispanic		30.1[a]	26.8	20.6	23.5
American Indian		50.8	32.1	29.4	
Asian			14.5	7.4	14.3
Related Children under age 18					
White	20.6	9.7	11.4	14.1	15.5
Black	65.6	39.6	40.8	43.2	41.5
Hispanic			27.7	35.5	39.3
American Indian		44.9	32.2	38.3	
Asian			14.9	18.9	18.6
Persons in female-headed families					
White	40.2	29.5	24.7	28.1	29.9
Black	70.6	58.3	49.8	49.4	48.2
Hispanic		54.3[a]	50.7	50.6	52.8
American Indian		63.5[b]	49.0	50.4	
Asian			27.4	34.6	28.9

Sources: U.S. Bureau of the Census, Poverty in the United States: 1995 (Washington, D.C.: Government Printing Office, 1997), table C.2; Gary Sandefur, "Blacks, Hispanics, American Indians, and Poverty—and What Worked," in Fred R. Harris and Roger W. Wilkins, eds., Quiet Riots: Race and Poverty in the United States (New York: Pantheon, 1988), table 4.1; Bureau of the Census, Census of Population, 1990: Social and Economic Characteristics, United States (Washington, D.C.: Government Printing Office, 1993), table 49; Bureau of the Census, Census of Population, 1980: General Social and Economic Characteristics, United States Summary (Washington, D.C.: Government Printing Office, 1983), table 129; Bureau of the Census, Census of Population, 1970: Persons of Spanish Origin (Washington, D.C.: Government Printing Office, 1973), table 10; Bureau of the Census, Census of Population, 1970: American Indians (Washington, D.C.: Government Printing Office, 1973), table 9.

a. For persons in families with heads who are of Spanish heritage.

b. Includes only persons self-identified as American Indian, whereas later years also include those self-identified as Eskimo or Aleut.

single females, but these declines are not substantial. Thus, the experiences for many persons in these families are difficult.

Location and Poverty in the 1990s

Considering poverty rates by geographical area, the most notable pattern is that rates are lowest for all persons living in metropolitan areas but outside the inner cities (see table 3.3).[11] Most whites experience higher poverty rates in inner cities than in nonmetropolitan areas. However, for persons sixty-five years and older, whites face the highest poverty rates in nonmetropolitan areas. Blacks and Hispanics in all demographic groups experience their highest poverty rates in nonmetropolitan areas. These nonmetropolitan poverty rates, however,

TABLE 3.3
Poverty Rates, by Area, Demographic Group, and Race, 1992 (%)

	Metropolitan[a]			
		Outside		
	Inner	Inner	Non-	
Group and Race	City	City	metropolitan[a]	Total
All persons				
White	15.6	8.3	14.2	11.6
Black	35.2	25.4	40.8	33.3
Hispanic[b]	33.7	22.2	36.7	29.3
Persons aged 65 and older				
White	12.8	8.6	13.0	10.9
Black	34.0	29.0	35.3	33.3
Hispanic[b]	26.6	13.2	31.8	22.0
Related children under age 18				
White	23.4	11.5	18.3	16.0
Black	50.2	35.3	52.2	46.3
Hispanic[b]	44.9	29.4	45.6	38.8
Persons in female-headed families				
White	37.3	24.5	31.8	30.2
Black	54.5	46.1	61.8	53.7
Hispanic[b]	56.8	39.4	57.4	51.2

Source: U.S. Bureau of the Census, Poverty in the United States: 1992 (Washington, D.C.: Government Printing Office, 1994), tables 2, 3, 8.
   a. Metropolitan areas are those with a minimum population of 50,000 persons; nonmetropolitan areas are those with fewer than 50,000 persons.
   b. Hispanics can be of either race.

are still relatively close to inner-city rates. Therefore, a general pattern emerges, wherein the poverty rates of nonmetropolitan areas and inner cities are similar in magnitude and are higher than the rates in metropolitan areas outside the inner cities. In most cases, the nonmetropolitan poverty rate is higher than either metropolitan rate. Therefore, although urban poverty is more concentrated than nonmetropolitan poverty, we should not neglect nonmetropolitan poverty.

Close to one-third of the white poor lived in each location in both 1985 and 1992, while this was not the case for blacks and Hispanics (see table 3.4).[12] In 1992, the majority of poor whites lived outside the inner cities, and only a very small proportion (12.6 percent) lived in inner-city poverty areas.[13] Blacks and Hispanics are much more likely to experience concentrated poverty than are whites. Roughly 60 percent of poor blacks and poor Hispanics reside in inner cities. In addition, poor blacks and poor Hispanics are much more likely to be located in poverty areas, especially in inner-city poverty areas, than are poor whites. In 1985, only 28.4 percent of whites lived in poverty areas. The corresponding figure for blacks and Hispanics was 69.5 percent and 55.6 percent, re-

TABLE 3.4
Distribution of Poverty, by Area and Race, 1985 and 1992 (%)

Year and Race	Inner City	Metropolitan Area[a]	Nonmetropolitan Area	Inner-City Poverty Area	Metropolitan Poverty Area	Nonmetropolitan Poverty Area
1985						
White	35.5	32.0	32.6	14.2	4.5	9.7
Black	60.9	16.6	22.5	47.4	7.6	14.5
Hispanic[b]	64.2	24.8	11.0	41.7	9.0	4.9
Mexican-American	54.8	30.1	15.1	31.3	13.0	7.1
Puerto Rican	89.0	10.4		75.5	0.5	
Total	42.9	27.5	29.6	23.8	5.3	11.2
1992						
White	34.5	36.3	29.3	12.6	3.4	8.6
Black	59.8	21.6	18.6	38.4	7.1	11.8
Hispanic[b]	59.9	30.7	9.4	32.8	6.1	4.0
Total	42.4	31.8	25.8	20.5	4.5	9.6

Sources: Fred R. Harris and Roger W. Wilkins, eds., *Quiet Riots: Race and Poverty in the United States* (New York: Pantheon, 1988), table 4.4; U.S. Bureau of the Census, *Poverty in the United States: 1985* (Washington, D.C.: Government Printing Office, 1987), tables 6, 12, 16; Bureau of the Census, *Poverty in the United States, 1992* (Government Printing Office, 1994), table 9.
a. Outside inner city.
b. Hispanics may be of any race.

spectively. However, between 1985 and 1992, the percentage of poor blacks and poor Hispanics living in inner-city poverty areas declined substantially.

Another way to think about the distribution of poverty is to look at the racial composition of the various areas and the racial composition of the poor population in these areas. First, let us look at the racial composition of three types of area (see table 3.5). Whites are underrepresented in inner cities but still constitute the largest group in any area. Blacks and Hispanics are overrepresented in inner cities and underrepresented in nonmetropolitan areas and metropolitan areas outside the inner cities, which in 1980 and 1990 were close to 90 percent white.

Whites are underrepresented among the inner-city poverty population but still constitute the largest group of poor in the inner cities in terms of sheer numbers (see table 3.6). In 1990, 44.1 percent of the inner-city poor were white, versus 38.2 percent who were black. Hispanics constitute the other large segment of the inner-city poverty population.

TABLE 3.5
Composition of Population, by Area and Race, 1980 and 1990 (%)

Year and Race	Inner City	Metropolitan Area[a]	Nonmetropolitan Area
1980			
White	69.7	89.9	88.2
Black	22.5	6.1	8.8
Asian	2.5	1.6	0.6
American Indian	0.5	0.4	1.3
Hispanic[b]	10.8	5.4	3.2
1990			
White	66.2	86.6	87.2
Black	22.0	6.9	8.7
Asian	4.3	3.0	0.8
American Indian	0.6	0.5	1.8
Hispanic[b]	14.5	7.4	3.8
Mexican-American	8.2	4.7	2.9
Puerto Rican	2.4	0.6	0.2

Sources: U.S. Bureau of the Census, Census of Population, 1980 (Washington, D.C.: Government Printing Office, 1983), tables 140, 150; Bureau of the Census, Census of Population, 1990 (Washington, D.C.: Government Printing Office, 1993), table 5.
    a. Outside inner city.
    b. Hispanics may be of any race; thus columns do not add up to 100 percent.

TABLE 3.6
Composition of Poor Population, by Area and Race, 1980 and 1990 (%)

Year and Race	Inner City	Metropolitan Area[a]	Nonmetropolitan Area
1980			
White	46.7	75.8	72.5
Black	41.3	16.2	21.9
Asian	2.5	2.0	0.6
American Indian	0.7	1.0	2.9
Hispanic[b]	17.9	11.9	5.6
1990			
White	44.1	71.3	72.2
Black	38.2	16.0	19.8
Asian	4.6	3.3	0.7
American Indian	0.9	1.2	4.0
Hispanic[b]	23.3	17.4	7.2

Sources: U.S. Bureau of the Census, *Census of Population, 1980* (Washington, D.C.: Government Printing Office, 1983), tables 149, 159; Bureau of the Census, *Census of Population, 1990* (Washington, D.C.: Government Printing Office, 1993), tables 38 and 93–97.
    a. Outside inner city.
    b. Hispanics may be of any race; thus columns do not add up to 100 percent.

Blacks are overrepresented among the poverty population in each type of metropolitan area relative to their total population in each area. Hispanics and Asians demonstrate overrepresentation among the inner-city and metropolitan area poverty populations, with Hispanics increasing their proportional representation between 1980 and 1990. American Indians are highly overrepresented among the nonmetropolitan poverty population.

Characteristics of the Poor, 1980 and 1990

Another way to look at poverty is to examine the characteristics of individuals living in these different areas (see table 3.7). In 1980 about half of all whites lived in metropolitan areas outside inner cities, whereas the majority of blacks and Hispanics were located in inner cities. Asians were evenly distributed, and in very high proportions, between inner cities and metropolitan areas. Close to half of all American Indians resided in nonmetropolitan areas.

Across all racial and ethnic groups, inner-city and nonmetropolitan

TABLE 3.7
Population and Labor Market Characteristics, by Demographic Group, Race, and Area, 1980

Area	Distribution of Population (%)	Persons in Poverty (%)	Median Age (years)	Female-headed Families (%)	Labor Force 16 and Older (%)	Unemployed 16 and Older (%)	Population 25 and Older with Less Than High School Diploma (%)	Foreign Born (%)	Families with Children Younger Than 18 Years (%)
White									
Inner city	25.0	11.1	31.8	14.7	62.0	5.7	31.1	8.4	45.0
Metropolitan[a]	48.3	6.7	31.0	10.0	64.5	5.4	27.2	5.0	51.3
Nonmetropolitan	26.6	12.7	31.2	9.0	58.2	6.7	38.7	1.7	50.1
Black									
Inner city	57.8	30.0	25.4	41.6	59.2	12.8	46.5	3.8	61.4
Metropolitan[a]	23.3	22.1	24.6	30.2	64.9	9.6	41.3	3.1	64.5
Nonmetropolitan	18.9	39.0	23.9	31.8	53.2	11.6	65.7	0.8	57.7
Hispanic[b]									
Inner city	50.3	26.8	23.5	24.3	62.3	9.3	58.8	29.6	67.8
Metropolitan[a]	37.3	17.7	23.2	14.5	66.5	8.3	50.3	31.6	68.6
Nonmetropolitan	12.4	27.3	21.9	14.1	58.5	9.7	62.4	15.1	67.8
Asian									
Inner city	46.4	16.1	28.9	12.4	66.4	4.8	28.6	62.6	57.3
Metropolitan[a]	44.9	9.5	28.1	9.0	68.1	4.5	19.8	57.3	67.3
Nonmetropolitan	8.7	15.3	27.4	11.4	60.0	5.9	33.7	43.4	60.2
American Indian									
Inner city	21.7	24.5	24.9	28.9	62.9	12.3	36.4	5.0	64.6
Metropolitan[a]	29.4	18.8	24.8	18.6	64.0	11.0	37.7	3.0	65.0
Nonmetropolitan	48.9	34.0	21.5	22.4	52.7	15.3	53.3	1.1	67.5

Sources: Fred R. Harris and Roger W. Wilkins, eds., *Quiet Riots: Race and Poverty in the United States* (New York: Pantheon, 1988) table 4.5; U.S. Bureau of the Census, *Census of Population, 1980* (Washington, D.C.: Government Printing Office, 1983), tables 140–44, 149–53, 159.

a. Outside inner city.
b. Hispanics may be of any race.

residents demonstrated lower labor force participation rates, higher rates of unemployment, and higher rates of poverty than their metropolitan area counterparts. More than one explanation accounts for this. One researcher argues that more employment opportunities exist in the suburbs,[14] a situation that lessens metropolitan area unemployment and poverty rates. Labor force participation rates are highest among people in metropolitan areas outside the inner cities and lowest among people in nonmetropolitan areas, with the opposite pattern prevailing for unemployment rates. This pattern is consistent across all racial and ethnic groups, except for the unemployment rate of inner-city blacks. However, metropolitan area residents may possess human capital and demographic characteristics favorable for securing employment and avoiding poverty. People with the willingness and the financial ability to live in the suburbs are more likely to have high financial and human capital. For instance, the proportion of high school dropouts is generally lowest in metropolitan areas and highest in nonmetropolitan areas. The high school dropout rate is especially high among blacks, Hispanics, and American Indians living in nonmetropolitan areas. There is evidence for both arguments regarding employment in metropolitan areas and perhaps for an interaction between the two. Within each racial and ethnic group, residents of metropolitan areas display higher rates of high school graduation, encounter better labor market conditions, and not surprisingly also demonstrate lower rates of poverty than those living elsewhere. More foreign-born residents and female heads of families reside in inner cities, which may explain, in part, the high rate of poverty among inner-city residents.

However, low educational attainment, weak attachment to the labor market, and high rates of poverty are not unique to inner-city residents; these conditions also confront all racial and ethnic groups living in nonmetropolitan areas. With the exception of Asians, the poverty rate among all groups is highest in nonmetropolitan areas, with very high rates being found among American Indians and blacks. Nonmetropolitan blacks display higher rates of poverty than blacks in inner cities; however, because three times more blacks live in inner cities than in nonmetropolitan areas, the majority of poor blacks reside in inner cities.

Among each racial and ethnic group, the metropolitan distribution of the population in 1990 was similar to that in 1980 (see table 3.8). Poverty rates remained lowest in metropolitan areas and highest in nonmetropolitan areas, except for Asians. Poverty rates stayed relatively stable or increased somewhat among all groups, except for blacks in metropoli-

TABLE 3.8

Population and Labor Market Characteristics of Persons, by Geographical Area, 1990

Area	Distribution of Population (%)	Persons in Poverty (%)	Median Age (years)	Female-headed Families (%)	Labor Force 16 and Older (%)	Unemployed 16 and Older (%)	Population 25 and Over with Less Than High School Diploma (%)	Foreign Born (%)	Families with Children Younger Than 18 Years (%)
White									
Central city	25.8	12.0	34.0	16.0	65.2	5.7	21.9	8.6	43.7
Metropolitan[a]	49.8	6.6	34.4	11.1	67.8	4.5	19.0	4.9	46.5
Nonmetropolitan	24.4	13.9	35.0	10.7	60.8	6.1	28.6	1.4	46.7
Black									
Central city	57.3	31.1	28.5	48.0	61.9	14.4	36.6	5.7	55.7
Metropolitan	26.4	19.5	28.2	34.4	69.0	9.5	31.0	5.7	58.6
Nonmetropolitan	16.2	39.6	27.7	40.6	55.4	13.6	51.6	0.6	55.8
Hispanic[b]									
Central city	51.5	28.6	25.7	26.3	66.5	11.3	53.3	37.3	64.2
Metropolitan	38.9	19.1	25.7	16.4	70.2	8.9	45.3	37.6	64.6
Nonmetropolitan	9.6	32.7	24.4	16.7	61.5	12.0	53.7	20.6	65.7
Asian									
Central city	46.5	19.1	29.9	13.6	65.3	6.1	27.2	67.2	56.1
Metropolitan	47.4	9.0	30.5	10.0	70.3	4.6	17.3	61.5	62.6
Nonmetropolitan	6.2	16.0	28.3	12.9	63.0	5.6	26.1	44.2	58.9
American Indian									
Central city	23.3	28.2	27.8	33.0	65.9	13.2	29.4	5.4	60.1
Metropolitan	28.0	19.8	29.2	20.7	67.6	9.9	28.8	2.9	57.9
Nonmetropolitan	48.6	38.6	25.0	26.4	56.4	18.5	43.6	0.6	62.8

Source: U.S. Bureau of the Census, *Census of Population, 1990* (Washington, D.C.: Government Printing Office, 1993), tables 6–10, 51–55.

a. Outside inner city.

b. Hispanics may be of any race.

tan areas. They increased most notably among Hispanics, American Indians, and inner-city Asians. In both 1980 and 1990, blacks, Hispanics, and American Indians were two to three times more likely to be mired in poverty than whites living in the same type of metropolitan area. As in 1980, 1990 labor force participation was highest in metropolitan areas and lowest in nonmetropolitan areas, and unemployment rates were lowest in metropolitan areas and higher in nonmetropolitan areas than in inner cities, except among blacks and Asians. The percentage of families headed by females continued to be highest in inner cities. Finally, the percentage of high school dropouts was lowest among metropolitan residents and highest among nonmetropolitan residents, with inner-city Asians representing the only exception to this pattern.

Between 1980 and 1990, the percentage of female-headed families increased among all groups, although most notably among blacks living in inner-city and nonmetropolitan areas. Labor force participation rates increased among almost every group between 1980 and 1990, but so did unemployment rates, except among whites, non-Hispanic metropolitan residents, and Asians living in nonmetropolitan areas. The percentage of high school dropouts declined among all groups. Finally, the percentage of foreign-born residents increased over time among Asians and Hispanics. In 1990, 63 percent of Asians and 36 percent of Hispanics were foreign born.

Consider the characteristics of foreign-born Asians and Hispanics and their native-born counterparts (see table 3.9). The poverty rates of all Hispanics are quite high, and there is little difference between native born and foreign born. However, a sizable difference exists between foreign-born and native-born Asians, with respect to median age, unemployment rates, percentage of high school dropouts, and percentage of families with children. Perhaps not surprisingly, poverty rates also differ between these two groups. Among Hispanics, differences in median age, percentage of female-headed families, labor force participation rates, and the percentage of high school dropouts are related to nativity. However, unemployment rates are exactly the same and poverty rates are similar.

Poverty Trends by Group

The data presented in this chapter demonstrate that poverty assumes qualitatively different forms among various racial and ethnic groups. In 1990, American Indians displayed the highest poverty rate among all groups. Their poverty is largely a nonmetropolitan phenomenon. Al-

TABLE 3.9

Population and Labor Market Characteristics of Persons, Hispanic and Asian, by Nativity, 1990

Group	Percentage of Population	Percentage in Poverty	Median Age (years)	Female-headed Families (%)	Labor Force 16 and Older (%)	Unemployed 16 and Older (%)	Population 25 and Older with Less Than High School Diploma (%)	Families with Children Younger Than 18 Years (%)
Hispanic[a]								
Native born	64.2	25.1	19.6	25.2	65.6	10.4	39.2	62.4
Foreign born	35.8	25.7	32.1	17.5	69.7	10.4	61.6	66.9
Asian								
Native born	36.9	10.6	15.6	13.6	69.1	4.7	13.6	46.8
Foreign born	63.1	16.2	35.2	11.3	67.0	5.5	24.9	62.9

Sources: U.S. Bureau of the Census, *Census of Population, 1990: Persons of Hispanic Origin in the United States* (Washington, D.C.: Government Printing Office, 1993), tables 1–5; Bureau of the Census, *Census of Population, 1990: Asians and Pacific Islanders in the United States* (Washington, D.C.: Government Printing Office, 1993), tables 1–5.

Note: Because detailed data are available only for 1990, no cross-time comparisons can be made. In addition, nativity and metropolitan location are not cross-classified in the published census.

a. Hispanics may be of any race.

though the percentage of high school dropouts has declined among American Indians, those living in nonmetropolitan areas still experience high levels of high school dropouts. While the labor force participation rate of American Indians living in nonmetropolitan areas has increased slightly over time, it still remains relatively low. Among this group, unemployment rates hover around 20 percent, poverty rates around 40 percent.

The Hispanic poverty rate stood at 25.3 percent in 1990 but climbed to 30.3 percent in 1995. In many ways, patterns of Hispanic poverty have come to resemble those of black poverty. Hispanic poverty is concentrated in inner cities, in areas of concentrated poverty, and in inner-city poverty areas. By 1990, the poverty rate of inner-city Hispanics was almost comparable to that of inner-city blacks, and by 1994, the Hispanic poverty rate actually eclipsed the black rate.[15]

Inner-city Hispanics also have relatively high percentages of families headed by females, double-digit unemployment rates, and very high percentages of high school dropouts—more than 50 percent. Native-born Hispanics differ from foreign-born Hispanics across a number of labor market and demographic characteristics. Foreign birth alone, however, cannot explain high levels of inner-city Hispanic poverty, since foreign-born and native-born Hispanics display similar rates of poverty and since foreign-born Hispanics are as likely to live in inner cities as in other metropolitan areas.

White poverty is lower than for all other groups considered. At the same time, whites represent the single largest component of the poverty population overall and across each type of area. White poverty is distributed fairly evenly across metropolitan areas and is unlikely to be concentrated in poverty areas, especially in inner-city poverty areas. In 1992, only 24.6 percent of poor whites lived in areas of high poverty, compared to 57.3 percent of blacks and 42.9 percent of Hispanics.

Asian poverty is higher than white poverty, but like the white poverty rate, the Asian poverty rate is of much smaller magnitude, about half that of blacks, Hispanics, and American Indians. Asian poverty is higher among the foreign born and is more likely to exist in inner cities. In 1990, 64 percent of all poor Asians were living in inner cities, and the inner-city Asian poverty rate stood at 19.1 percent. However, like the Hispanic pattern, the high poverty rate for inner-city Asian residents cannot be attributed completely to larger proportions of foreign-born people. While foreign-born Asians are more likely to live in inner cities than in other metropolitan areas, the difference is relatively small.

Black poverty is multifaceted. Although concentrated in inner cities, it is not solely nor exclusively an inner-city phenomenon. In 1992, 60 percent of poor blacks lived in inner cities, and 38 percent of poor blacks lived in high-poverty inner-city areas. In addition, blacks are highly overrepresented among the inner-city poverty population. Only one in five poor blacks resides in nonmetropolitan areas, but black rural poverty runs deep. In 1990, the black nonmetropolitan poverty rate was just under 40 percent. Blacks constituted 8.7 percent of the nonmetropolitan population but 19.8 percent of the nonmetropolitan poverty population. The percentage of black female-headed families and the black unemployment rate are very high in both nonmetropolitan areas and inner cities, although higher in the latter. The percentage of high school graduates and labor force participation rates are low in both types of area but especially so in nonmetropolitan areas. The point is that poverty rates are high in both areas, as are all the factors just mentioned. High levels of poverty and the conditions leading to poverty are not unique to the inner city. In several inner-city neighborhoods, a majority of people are not working.[16]

Trends in poverty since the late 1960s suggest several conclusions. First, overall poverty in the mid-1990s was roughly the same as overall poverty in the late 1960s. Although the level has fluctuated during this period, we have made no progress in permanently reducing the rate of poverty since the Kerner Report. Second, poverty is more prevalent in nonmetropolitan areas and the inner cities than in metropolitan areas outside the inner cities. It is inaccurate to regard poverty as a solely urban problem. Third, Hispanics and American Indians, as well as African Americans, continue to experience much higher rates of poverty than do whites. Asian poverty rates are intermediate between those of whites and other minority groups. Poverty is not just a black problem, and urban poverty is not just a black problem. Finally, the factors associated with poverty seem to be similar across geographical areas and across racial and ethnic groups: low levels of education, low levels of labor force participation, high levels of unemployment, and high rates of single-headed families.

Fighting Poverty since 1968

The major lesson we have learned about poverty since 1968 is that permanently reducing poverty is more difficult than was anticipated during the 1960s. Some interpret this as evidence that the government cannot permanently reduce poverty, while others see this as evidence that the government has not done enough to reduce poverty.

It is instructive to review trends in poverty policy during this period. The years following President Lyndon Johnson's declaration of a War on Poverty in 1964 were characterized by an expansion of existing anti-poverty programs and the introduction of new ones.[17] Among the programs expanded or introduced during the War on Poverty era, and that continue to exist, are Medicare, Medicaid, food stamps, Head Start, elementary and secondary educational assistance, and manpower development (training) programs. Many of these programs have substantially improved the lives of the poor and the near-poor over what their lives would have been like in the absence of these programs. This era was characterized by great optimism about the ability of government to eliminate, or at least to substantially reduce, poverty in the United States.

This optimistic view of the government's ability to deal with poverty and to solve other difficult social problems was severely challenged by the oil shocks, slow economic growth, and high inflation of the 1970s. Pessimists began to argue that government had grown too large and had become a drag on economic growth and that government programs provided disincentives for Americans to work and save. By 1982, this pessimistic view of the ability of government to solve social problems had become official policy. During the 1980s, the government emphasized policies designed to promote economic growth, and antipoverty policy was not a priority. Legislated changes in unemployment insurance and welfare reduced the effectiveness of the federal safety net. In 1980, federal spending on employment and training programs amounted to $9.3 billion (in constant 1986 dollars), but by 1986 this had fallen to $3.7 billion and remained at roughly that level in the early 1990s. The 1980s witnessed a seven-year economic recovery, but this recovery did not lead to a substantial reduction in poverty. Indeed, instead of a period in which rising tides lifted all boats, this was a period of uneven tides.[18] The poor and the middle class hardly benefited from the recovery, and the gaps between the poor and the rich and between the middle class and the rich widened.

By the late 1980s, the national experience of high poverty rates during an economic recovery prompted a rejection of a hands-off approach to poverty and the adoption of several important pieces of legislation. These included the Tax Reform Act of 1986, the Family Support Act of 1988, and the budget summit agreement of 1990. This flurry of legislation reflected a bipartisan agreement to reform tax and welfare policies for the poor. The emphasis was on helping people work their way to a better life. The climate of antipoverty policy at the beginning of the 1990s viewed the elderly and the disabled as in need of expanded income support but expected the able-bodied low-income population as a group to work to overcome their poverty.

Although the country made major changes in its efforts to fight poverty in the late 1980s and early 1990s, the welfare reform train that left the station in the late 1980s had not yet reached its ultimate destination. Presidential candidate Bill Clinton campaigned on a platform that included the pledge to "end welfare as we know it." The Clinton welfare reform plan was never enacted, however, and was replaced by a bipartisan agreement that emphatically eliminated the major cash assistance program for the poor, Aid to Families with Dependent Children (AFDC). We are, indeed, in a completely new era of antipoverty policy, one that differs from the War on Poverty as dramatically as the War on Poverty differed from previous policy. Among the most startling differences are the discontinuation of the federal guarantee of support to poor children who are eligible for support and the devolution of responsibility for many antipoverty efforts from the federal level to the state level.

The current centerpiece of federal efforts to deal with poverty and its related problems is the 1996 Personal Responsibility and Work Opportunity Reconciliation Act (PRWORA). This legislation emphasizes the personal responsibility of poor people to confront their own problems and to behave in ways that enable them to deal with poverty by escaping it or living with it. Although the legislation was endorsed by many Democrats as well as most Republicans, and enthusiastically signed by President Clinton, it is closely related to the poverty agenda of the broader Contract with America.

The Contract with America, drafted in 1994 by Republican hopefuls running for seats in the U.S. House of Representatives, clearly presented a different direction for the role of government. The policies in the contract were designed to restrict and limit the role of the federal government rather than to expand it. They represented an attempt to scale back government programs, government involvement, and government spending and at the same time to emphasize individual responsibility. As a result, the contract included proposals for fewer government regulations, pared-down government programs, and reductions in taxes. The contract is based on five principles: individual liberty, economic opportunity, limited government, personal responsibility, and security at home and abroad.[19]

PRWORA attempts to address other social problems that disproportionately affect inner cities, namely illegitimacy and welfare dependency. First, AFDC, in existence since 1935, has been eliminated. States now have the primary responsibility for administering their own welfare and work training programs and are given block grants to fund them. This constitutes the essence of the Temporary Assistance for Needy Families (TANF) program. Under TANF, welfare receipt is now temporary and transitional in nature. Recipients are required to work within two years of originally receiving benefits or be dropped from the state's rolls. In addition to the two-year time limit, recipients are allowed to receive benefits for only five years over the course of their lives. It should be noted that additional federal money will be provided to states experiencing high unemployment and that exemptions to the time limits will be allowed for hardship cases and in the event that a recipient cannot find child care for a child under six years old.

In an attempt to discourage teenage pregnancy and illegitimacy, provisions were proposed to deny or restrict welfare benefits to mothers who had out-of-wedlock births. These provisions were not enacted, but most states are adopting programs that do not increase benefits for families that have additional children on welfare. This has the effect of reducing real benefits for children already in the family when a new child joins the family.

Alternative Assumptions

Our current approach to poverty emphasizes personal responsibility: we expect people to work if possible and to make responsible reproductive decisions. Unemployment and out-of-wedlock childbearing are significantly associated with poverty. Unfortunately, our current emphasis on personal responsibility ignores some important features of poverty, such as the fact that not all jobs enable people to support themselves and their families and the fact that much of out-of-wedlock childbearing is unintended. Over the next several years, it will become increasingly clear that our current approach to dealing with poverty may reduce the number of women with children who receive cash assistance but will not reduce the number of women with children who are poor. Further, it will do little to decrease poverty among individuals in other kinds of living arrangements.

Since 1968, social policy has repeatedly ignored a critical feature of poverty in our society, in spite of admonitions from those who study and work with the poor: our economy generates a large number of jobs that do not provide sufficient earnings to permit individuals to support themselves and their families. In the past, many women chose welfare over these jobs, or they illegally combined welfare with these jobs in order to make ends meet.[20] We are now forcing them to take these jobs, but they will not be substantially better off in either the short run or the long run. The initiatives proposed by President Clinton to expand child care and health insurance will help, but they cannot turn bad jobs into good jobs, nor can they substantially reduce the large numbers of the working poor in our society.

If we were to assume that most poor people are poor because the nature of the American economy generates a certain level of unemployment and poverty, we would try a different way of dealing with poverty. Recently, some have argued that two of the major problems intertwined with poverty—drugs and out-of-wedlock childbearing—should be considered primarily as public health issues rather than primarily as moral failures.[21] What if we broaden our public health focus and think of poverty itself as a public health issue? What kinds of policies would we then devise to replace the current efforts?

First, we must recognize that the American economy will always produce a certain level of unemployment and poverty. Individuals will have different risks of being poor at some points in their lives. We know a good deal about what the major risk factors are: too little education, few skills, and for women, single parenthood. Unemployment and poverty levels will vary with the overall health of the economy, but even in the best of times, some people will be without work and some people, unemployed and employed, will be poor. Second, most people will be poor for other short periods of time because of a job loss or changes in their family situation, while others will be poor for longer periods. The latter situation occurs largely because some families or heads of families have characteristics that make it difficult for the family head to earn enough money in the labor market to support a family at an income above the poverty line. Some people, in fact, are incapable of working much at all because of physical or emotional problems. In some cases, the past behaviors of these people, such as drug or alcohol abuse, have produced their problems. Their children, nonetheless, deserve a chance at a decent life.

President Clinton's recent proposals to expand funding for child care, to provide health insurance to children, and to restore food stamps to immigrants are notable steps in the right direction. In effect, we are already moving back in the direction of helping individuals fight their impoverished situations. Nonetheless, the myth that no one need be poor as long as they play by the rules continues to characterize much public discussion of poverty. Our economy produces poor people, and we have to give them more help than we are currently giving them so that they and their children have a real chance at a better life.

Conclusion

Although much has changed in the poverty picture since 1968, the level of poverty in our country has not permanently declined. The poverty rate is highest in inner cities, standing at 20.6 percent in 1995, well above the national rate of 13.8 percent. In 1992, 42 percent of all poor people resided in inner cities, although only 30 percent of all Americans lived in such areas. For these reasons, it is perhaps not surprising that urban poverty captures a large share of the public imagination. In addition to concentrated poverty, phenomena associated with the inner city, such as higher rates of violent crime, higher rates of welfare use, and episodes of violent unrest, tend to focus attention on urban areas and on urban poverty. Nonetheless, poverty in metropolitan areas and nonmetropolitan areas is also worthy of attention. The data show that poverty is not simply an inner-city phenomenon and that the majority of the poverty population actually lives outside the inner city, and only about 20 percent live in inner-city poverty areas: "about seven in eight poor persons [do] not live in ghettos and barrios (defined by poverty rates of 40 percent), contradicting the often implicit assumption that poverty is synonymous with the inner city."[22]

In 1990, poverty rates for whites, blacks, Hispanics, and American Indians were actually higher in nonmetropolitan areas than in inner cities. Extremely high levels of joblessness and poverty confront blacks and American Indians living in nonmetropolitan areas. Further, the socioeconomic conditions of groups other than whites and blacks are worthy of attention, especially given the growing racial diversification of the American population, a trend most apparent in inner cities. "A new

Kerner Commission would certainly agree, 25 years later, that poverty, employment problems, economic dislocation, and family instability are barriers at least as important as racism and discrimination to the exclusion, not only of blacks, but also of Hispanics, American Indians, and some Asians, from full and equal participation in American society."[23]

Although whites are underrepresented among the poverty population, they still are the largest racial group among the poor. Blacks and Hispanics represent a large proportion of the poverty population, but high rates of poverty are not the domain of a single racial or ethnic group. In 1990, blacks, Hispanics, and American Indians all experienced poverty rates in excess of 25 percent. The current composition of the population and the poverty population is much more complex than it was thirty years ago, and thus it is arguably no longer relevant to refer to the existence of "two societies, one black, one white."

Politicians and policy makers should shift their view of poverty from seeing it primarily as a personal failure to seeing it primarily as a creation of our economy. Poverty is, in effect, a public health issue. Further, poverty is in some ways the cost of the affluence that a substantial majority of the country enjoys. The cost of our affluence is borne disproportionately by the young, members of minority groups, and those in the inner cities and nonmetropolitan areas. Our focus should be on shortening the time that the poor remain poor and on ameliorating the effects of poverty.

At the time of the Kerner Report in 1968, the country had already committed itself to fight poverty, and many were optimistic about our chances to succeed. The battle turned out to be more difficult than anticipated, and the world has changed dramatically since then. Our current approach to poverty represents a failure of national will and political courage. We have simply given up at the federal level and thrown it to the states. Shame on us.

4

The New Urban Poverty: Consequences of the Economic and Social Decline of Inner-City Neighborhoods

William Julius Wilson, James M. Quane, and Bruce H. Rankin

The *Report of the National Advisory Commission on Civil Disorders* had some ominous predictions for the future of race relations in the nation.[1] The disparities between blacks and whites was growing, the report argued, and if allowed to continue unabated would undermine the fabric of the society. In addition, a dearth of real employment opportunities for black males was "the single most important source of poverty among Negroes." Widespread unemployment coupled with the spatial segregation of urban blacks would result in the dramatic upheaval of the black community and foster social dislocations, such as marital breakdown, crime, and feelings of disassociation. With blacks lacking opportunities for stable employment and shut off from mainstream society, the cycle would perpetuate itself, and the gap between the races would widen irreversibly.

Some authors contend that the commission was overly influenced by the riots that transfixed the nation earlier in the decade and that its members failed to include a frank discussion of the gains minorities, especially middle-class blacks, had made in the years leading up to the release of the report.[2] Indeed, during the 1950s and well into the 1960s, the extraordinary accomplishments of the civil rights movement garnered a great deal of public attention and significantly improved the social and economic conditions of blacks. Furthermore, the demonstrations that originated in Birmingham in 1963 and that spread north to Harlem in 1964 and west to the Watts region of Los Angeles in 1965 focused a considerable amount of national and international attention on the problem of ghetto poverty.[3] Undoubtedly, when the report was written, the commission was affected by these momentous events. But if anything, commission members sowed a deep commitment to tackling the root causes of racial unrest at a time when the mood of white America had soured toward civil rights in the aftermath of the riots.[4] The report's recommendations emphasized that the social integration of blacks required access to adequate jobs. By stressing this point, the commission underscored the fact that, although the social movement had made significant strides in providing blacks equal access to integrated schools, public housing, and welfare benefits, far fewer gains had been realized in creating jobs that would afford less-skilled families a decent standard of living.[5]

Welfare Policy and Employment Opportunities

Reforms of the welfare system in the late 1950s and early 1960s were clearly instrumental in lifting many poor families, black and white, out of destitution. Until then, blacks were underrepresented among the ranks of the welfare poor due to the dominant perceptions of what constituted a "deserving home."[6] Existing provisions greatly limited access by blacks and families with children born out-of-wedlock to welfare and, especially in southern states, ensured a constant source of cheap labor for the fields and homes of the gentry.[7] However, with the passing of the Social Security amendments in 1962 and the drive by the Office of Economic Opportunity, community action programs, and civil rights groups such as the National Welfare Rights Organization and the National Association for the Advancement of Colored People, minorities were better informed about their rights to public assistance, and application procedures became less discriminatory against blacks.

As restrictions were relaxed, the welfare rolls expanded from 3.1 million in 1960 to 11 million by 1972. Whereas 30 percent of those eligible for benefits in 1960 actually applied for and received benefits, by 1972 that figure stood at around 90 percent and constituted a 400 percent increase in federal, state, and local spending on AFDC.[8] Even though whites made up most of the additions to the welfare rolls and exceeded blacks in total numbers receiving benefits, blacks were overrepresented in proportion to their numbers in the general population.[9] Increasingly, the public came to view welfare as a subsidy for poor inner-city blacks.

The considerable expansion of social programs and greater access to public assistance cushioned some of the effects of inner-city blacks' lack of access to jobs that paid a living wage and their high rates of unemployment. Although officials recognized the importance of this thicker safety net, minority unemployment in the 1960s was generally perceived of as marginal to the national debate on economic well-being, since the country was experiencing significant prosperity at the time.[10] National policy aimed at alleviating black joblessness in the ghetto focused on job training and skills development and not on the macroeconomic forces that kept low-skilled blacks from entering the labor market. However, job training programs, which by 1967 were already being viewed with disfavor, never received the kind of political or financial support required to attain the goal of retraining an urban workforce. Thus, the Manpower Demonstration and Training Act of 1962, the Job Corps Act of 1964, and the Work Incentive Program of 1967 never came close to formulated goals and were ineffective in moving the unemployed, especially inner-city blacks, into the labor market.[11]

Ironically, while joblessness and welfare receipt expanded for some blacks after the mid-twentieth century, other blacks experienced greater job opportunity and increasing social mobility due to structural changes in the economy and political changes in the government.[12] On the one hand, the expansion of the economy facilitated black migration from the rural areas of the South to the industrial centers of the nation. This population shift combined with the liberalization of trade unions increased black job opportunities and resulted in greater occupational differentiation within the African American community. On the other hand, the government, instead of reinforcing or ignoring racial barriers created in earlier periods, began to move toward a policy of racial equality. Responding to the pressures of increased black political resources that accompanied the growing concentration of African Americans in large urban areas and the pressures of the black protest movements (partly a result of greater black political strength), the government consistently enacted and enforced antidiscrimination legislation. In short, a combination of economic and political changes increased economic opportunities for a substantial segment of the African American population.

The curious paradox, however, was that although economic expansion after the mid-twentieth century led to increased occupational mobility for many blacks, transformations in the economy after the late 1960s diminished mobility opportunities for others. Most of the increases in productivity were brought about by technological advances and a more skilled workforce. Although these changes in technology produced many new jobs, they made others, in particular jobs that depended on a manual workforce, obsolete. The gap between skilled and low-skilled workers widened, as education and skill specificity became more important. While the rapid pace of technological change benefited educated workers, lesser skilled workers faced the growing threat of job displacement and income stagnation.[13] This sharp decline in the relative demand for low-skilled labor had a more adverse effect on blacks than on whites. Burdened by cumulative experiences of racial restrictions, the proportion of blacks who were unskilled by the 1960s was extremely large, making them particularly vulnerable to a shift in the labor market in favor of skilled workers.[14]

Thus changes in the economy during the past several decades have resulted in a much more rapid rate of social mobility for the trained and educated, including blacks, than for the untrained and uneducated. And whereas antidiscrimination legislation has dislodged many racial barriers, not all blacks have benefited. Indeed, while the number of blacks in professional, technical, and administrative positions increased significantly during the 1970s and 1980s, and while progress was also evident in the growing number of African Americans in colleges and universities and in the increasing number of black homeowners, the position of the black poor actually deteriorated. Between 1977 and 1993, African Americans in the "poorest of the poor" category (those with incomes 50 percent less than the official poverty line) climbed from 9.3 percent of the black population to 16.7 percent.[15] In 1977, 29.9 percent of all poor blacks were in this "poorest of the poor" category, but by 1993, the proportion rose to 50.4 percent. Moreover, whereas poor African American families fell an average of $5,481 below the poverty line in 1977, after adjusting for inflation, they dropped an average of $6,818 below in 1993, "further below the poverty level than in any year since the Census Bureau started collecting such data in 1967."[16] And the condition of poor urban blacks has been made even worse by the changing demographics of inner-city neighborhoods.

The Changing Demographics of Inner-City Neighborhoods

Encouraged by technological advances, improvements in transportation, and increased employment opportunities outside of metropolitan areas, whites, by 1968, had already begun their outmigration from the inner cities. Recognizing this trend, and troubled by the dwindling taxation and revenue base that cities would have at their disposal to provide institutional support for the disadvantaged, the Kerner Report emphasized the need for a national policy to pursue a course of ghetto enrichment that would ensure inner cities a "greater share of national resources—sufficient to make a dramatic, visible impact on life in the urban Negro ghetto."[17] In response to a concern about how ghetto enrichment might disproportionately impact some residents, the commission expressed doubt that any gains realized by the black middle class would be large enough to promote an outmigration among them that might impede the social and economic betterment of the community as a whole. Rather, the commission reasoned, enrichment would proceed slowly, during which time educational opportunities and skills development would improve the economic and social condition of blacks and move the country toward the ultimate goal of racial and social class integration.

However, enrichment programs of the kind advocated by the commission never really received sustained support. By the late 1960s, the public and political focus, and consequently government appropriations, had shifted to the war in Vietnam and away from concerted action to bring about permanent improvement in the lives of ghetto dwellers. And although federal spending on the poor continued to rise throughout the decade of the 1970s, the increase was accounted for by changes in how services were doled out to recipients and not in the size of the cash assistance. In fact, while the cost of administering programs rose sharply, actual payments to the poor declined.[18]

With the nation lacking a policy to combat structural joblessness in the ghettos, the stagflation and labor market restructuring of the 1970s further eroded the economic condition of poor blacks. On the other hand, the hard-won victories of the civil rights movements in the two preceding decades had brought to educated and skilled blacks opportunities for higher paying and more desirable jobs. As a result, the black community polarized, as large numbers of the working and middle classes, no longer severely constrained by restrictive housing policies, began to leave ghetto neighborhoods in search of better housing, schools, and jobs.[19]

Up until the mid-1960s, inner-city neighborhoods were best categorized as mixed-income communities, featuring a vertical integration of social strata of the urban black population: working- and middle-class blacks were confined by restrictive covenants to neighborhoods also inhabited by the lower class. As significant numbers of nonpoor blacks relocated to more socioeconomically diverse neighborhoods throughout the 1970s and into the 1980s, many inner-city communities confronted the growth of two problems, the "concentration effects" of poverty and joblessness and the erosion of a social buffer that had long played a role in the stability of urban black communities.[20] Concentration effects are the constraints and opportunities embodied in an overwhelmingly socially disadvantaged neighborhood, including the ecological niches that the residents of these communities occupy in terms of access to jobs, availability of marriageable partners, and exposure to conventional role models. The presence of a sufficient number of working-class and middle-class professional families might cushion the effect or absorb the shock of uneven economic growth on an inner-city neighborhood, including decreased relative demand for low-skilled labor and periodic recessions.

However, the significant outmigration of these nonpoor black families eroded the social buffer, making it more difficult, especially in the face of prolonged joblessness, to sustain basic institutions such as schools, churches, stores, and recreational facilities in the inner city. As the basic institutions declined, the social organization of inner-city neighborhoods—positive neighborhood identification, including a sense of community, and explicit sanctions against aberrant behavior—declined as well. Stable working- and middle-class families once provided role models to reinforce mainstream values pertaining to education, employment, and family structure; what is more, given their greater economic and educational resources, especially during periods of an economic stagnation and heightened joblessness in poor urban areas, they provided institutional stability to their neighborhoods.

Furthermore, this outmigration along with increased joblessness significantly increased the proportion of inner-city poor blacks. During the 1980s, poor blacks living in ghettos doubled, from 21 percent to 41.6 percent.[21] But total blacks (both poor and nonpoor) residing in areas designated as ghettos also rose (from 15.7 percent to 24.2 percent)—not simply because of the increased number of poor blacks or because more people moved into them but mainly because the poverty spread to more and more neighborhoods.[22] In other words, areas that were not ghettos before 1980 became ghettos after 1980 because the proportion of residents who were poor increased to at least 40 percent. In the 1970s, the exodus of the nonpoor (working- and middle-class families) from mixed-income black areas was a major factor in the spread of ghettos.[23]

After 1980, the number of ghetto census tracts increased in a large majority of the metropolitan areas in the United States, including those that experienced depopulation. Nine new ghetto census tracts emerged in Philadelphia, even though the city experienced one of the largest declines in the proportion of people living in ghetto areas. "In a number of other cities, including Baltimore, Boston, and Washington, D.C., a smaller percentage of poor blacks lived in a larger number of ghettos census tracts. Chicago had a 61.5 percent increase in the number of ghetto census tracts from 1980 to 1990, even though the number of the poor residing in those areas increased only slightly."[24]

The spread of ghettos has important implications for both the social organization of poor neighborhoods and the life chances of those who reside in them. Social organization, which refers to the ability of a neighborhood to maintain effective social control and realize its common goals,[25] is attenuated in neighborhoods characterized by high levels of poverty and joblessness.[26] Ghetto neighborhoods have less effective institutions, weaker informal networks, and social milieus that discourage collective supervision and responsibility. Lacking these important social resources, high-poverty neighborhoods are more likely to experience a breakdown in public order, whereby crime, delinquency, and other forms of social disorder flourish. Thus, poor ghetto residents are doubly disadvantaged, first, by being poor and, second, by residing in neighborhoods characterized by low levels of social organization.

In addition, the individual experience of poverty is exacerbated by the social isolation brought on by residing in neighborhoods that offer few opportunities to interact with individuals and institutions representing mainstream society. Ghetto residents lack contact with regularly employed persons, who could provide social support (e.g., job networks) and reinforce normative orientations toward work.[27] In addition to the constraints on the life chances of adults, the behavior, expectations, and aspirations of youth from inner-city ghettos are directly affected by the joblessness and other social dislocations that pervade these communities. The overrepresentation of jobless adults and the lack of opportunities for gainful employment leads to reduced youth expectations about their future and a weaker commitment to education as a path to social mobility.[28] The developmental trajectories of ghetto youth are also threatened by the prevalence of criminal elements and deviant peer groups in ghetto neighborhoods, which provide attractive opportunities for involvement in illegal and other nonnormative and risky behavior.

Below, we explore the impact of inner-city ghetto life on families and children by highlighting comparative data on neighborhoods in the city of Chicago, which, like many other northern metropolises, has experienced considerable growth in its urban ghetto neighborhoods over the last three decades.[29]

The Economic and Social Transformation of Chicago's Neighborhoods

In most U.S. cities, racial minorities, especially African Americans, are much more likely to reside in poor neighborhoods,[30] and Chicago is no exception. In 1990, more than 87 percent of all non–Hispanic whites lived in neighborhoods of low poverty; 29 percent of the non–Hispanic black population of Chicago lived in neighborhoods of medium poverty; and 29 percent of this population lived in ghetto or high-poverty areas. The figures for the poor population are even more stark. Half of all poor blacks in Chicago lived in ghetto neighborhoods in 1990, compared to 15 percent of Hispanics and 4 percent of whites. Thus, poor blacks were more than three times as likely to reside in the ghetto neighborhoods as poor Hispanics and twelve times as likely as poor whites.

Looking at high-, medium-, and low-poverty neighborhoods in 1990, we get a sense of how dramatic the decline has been in some of these areas between 1970 and 1990 (see figure 4.1). Joblessness played a major role in the rise of poverty in Chicago's poorer neighborhoods in these two decades. Although the percentage of all adults who were employed who lived in low-poverty neighborhoods in 1990 remained relatively stable since 1970 (around 60 percent), rates for medium- and high-poverty neighborhoods significantly decreased. In 1990, around half of all adults (49 percent) in medium-poverty neighborhoods and only one-third of adults (33 percent) in high-poverty neighborhoods were employed. In 1970, the rate was 56 percent for medium-poverty and 47 percent for high-poverty neighborhoods.

High rates of joblessness, especially among males, have also fueled the growth of welfare-dependent and female-headed families in poor neighborhoods, largely by reducing the number of males in inner-city neighborhoods who can support a family.[31] The 1980s witnessed a sharp increase in the proportion of mother-only families across all neighborhoods, but the rates in poor neighborhoods were especially high (see figure 4.2). By 1990, six of ten households (64 percent) in the poorest neighborhoods of Chicago were headed by a single mother, compared

FIGURE 4.1
Working Adults in Chicago Neighborhoods, 1970–1990

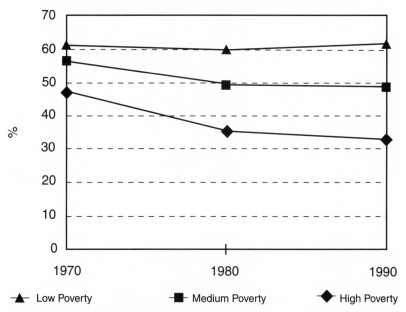

Source: U.S. Bureau of the Census, *Census of Population and Housing, 1970; 1980; 1990* (Washington, D.C.: Government Printing Office).
Note: Neighborhoods were defined as low, medium, and high poverty in 1990.

to 42 percent and 22 percent of the households in medium- and low-poverty neighborhoods, respectively.

Most of the growth in families on public assistance occurred in the 1970s, but welfare rolls remained at high levels twenty years later (see figure 4.3). Nearly half of all families in Chicago's ghetto neighborhoods and one-quarter in medium-poverty neighborhoods were receiving public assistance in 1990.

To examine the effects of poverty concentration on neighborhood social organization and the life chances of individual residents, we turn to data collected for the Youth Achievement and the Structure of Inner City Communities study, a project funded by the MacArthur Foundation Research Program on Successful Adolescent Development in High Risk Areas. It was completed in June 1991. A total of 546 African American mothers, as well as 830 of their adolescent children living in inner-city Chicago neighborhoods, were interviewed. The study found that, on average, African American mothers residing in low-poverty neigh-

FIGURE 4.2
Female-Headed Households in Chicago Neighborhoods, 1970–1990

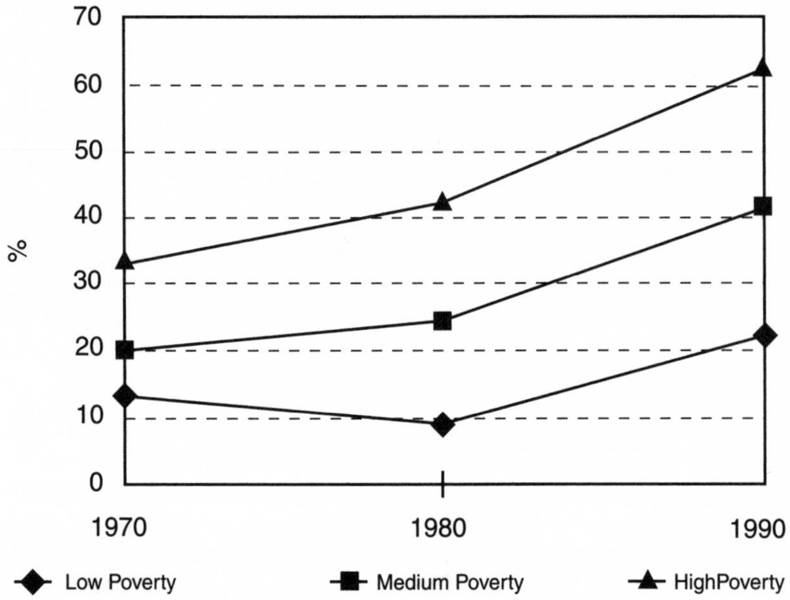

Source: See fig. 4.1.
Note: See fig. 4.1.

borhoods, compared to those living in ghetto neighborhoods, were more educated (with two years of college), less likely to be unemployed at the time of the interview (28 percent), and rarely received AFDC (4 percent), despite the low number of intact, or two-parent families (47 percent). The mothers residing in ghetto neighborhoods had, on average, slightly less than a high school education, were typically not working (74 percent), tended to receive public assistance (61 percent), and were rarely in intact families (12 percent). Mothers residing in medium-poverty neighborhoods typically fell somewhere in between, although the proportion representing families that were intact was similarly low (17 percent).

Data from the Chicago study neighborhoods include a comparison of low-, medium-, and high-poverty neighborhoods on social organization (based on mothers' responses to questions about neighborhood characteristics). Social organization is a multidimensional concept that encompasses both formal and informal institutional structures and social

FIGURE 4.3
Public Assistance in Chicago Neighborhoods, 1970–1990

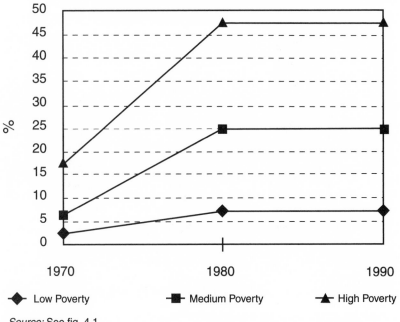

Source: See fig. 4.1.
Note: See fig. 4.1.

networks that facilitate individual community participation and responsibility. The key indicators of neighborhood social organization include informal social control, neighborhood cohesion, formal institutional effectiveness, neighborhood crime, and teen problems.

Informal social control represents the extent to which residents of a neighborhood seek to achieve common goals by monitoring activities in the neighborhoods, actively promoting normative behavior, and intervening if problems are encountered (see figure 4.4).[32] Empirical indicators of informal social control included the proportion of residents who indicated that a neighbor would "likely" or "very likely" intervene to help the respondent if he or she witnessed a break-in at their home, someone trying to sell drugs to their child, fighting in front of their house, or their kids getting into trouble. In a pattern repeated throughout the analyses presented here, the results show significant differences between respondents in the low-poverty neighborhoods and respondents in both the medium- and high-poverty neighborhoods. About 95

FIGURE 4.4
Informal Social Control in Chicago Study Neighborhoods

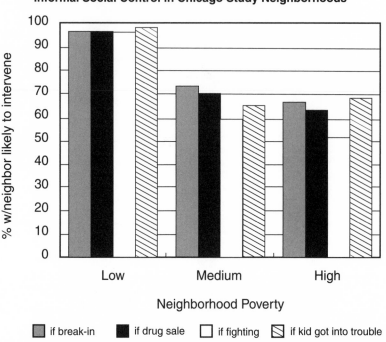

Source: Robert J. Bursik Jr. and Harold G. Grasonick, *Neighborhoods and Crime: The Dimensions of Effective Community Control* (New York: Lexington, 1993).

percent of all mothers residing in low-poverty neighborhoods reported that a neighbor was likely to intervene under each circumstance described. Informal social control is clearly less prevalent in medium- and high-poverty neighborhoods, where figures range from a low of 52 percent of the respondents in ghetto neighborhoods who believed that a neighbor would intervene to stop fights to 74 percent in medium-poverty areas who believed that a neighbor would respond to a break-in at the respondent's home.

Informal social control is much more likely to come into play when neighborhoods are cohesive.[33] Neighborhood cohesion refers to the degree to which neighbors feel a common interest and collective responsibility for activities in the neighborhood (see figure 4.5). What proportion of residents agreed or strongly agreed that neighbors got together to deal with problems in the neighborhood? Low-poverty neighborhoods were much more cohesive, with 76 percent of the respondents

FIGURE 4.5
Neighborhood Cohesion in Chicago Study Neighborhoods

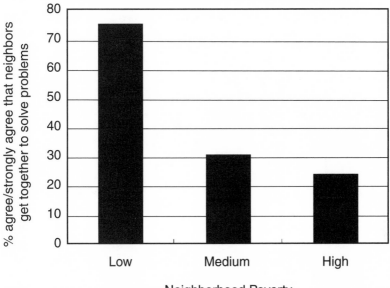

Neighborhood Poverty

Source: Frank Furstenberg, "How Families Manage Risk and Opportunity in Dangerous Neighborhoods," in William Julius Wilson, ed., *Sociology and the Public Agenda*
(Newbury Park, Calif.: Sage, 1992).

reporting that neighbors were likely or very likely to get together to
solve problems, in contrast to 32 percent in medium-poverty neighborhoods and only 24 percent in ghetto neighborhoods.

Formal institutional effectiveness refers to the degree to which formal
institutions responsible for public order and education are perceived by
residents as effective (see figure 4.6). What proportion of residents in
each neighborhoods indicated that police responsiveness, public safety,
and school quality were not a problem? Mothers in both medium-
poverty and ghetto neighborhoods reported significantly less satisfaction
with formal institutions. Whereas the proportion of mothers in these
neighborhoods who felt that the effectiveness of these community institutions was not a problem in their neighborhood ranged from 9 percent
to 28 percent, the figures for low-poverty residents were much higher
(71–87 percent).

Disadvantaged neighborhoods, particularly those with low levels of
social organization, tend to have more problems with crime and delin-

FIGURE 4.6
Institutional Effectiveness in Chicago Study Neighborhoods

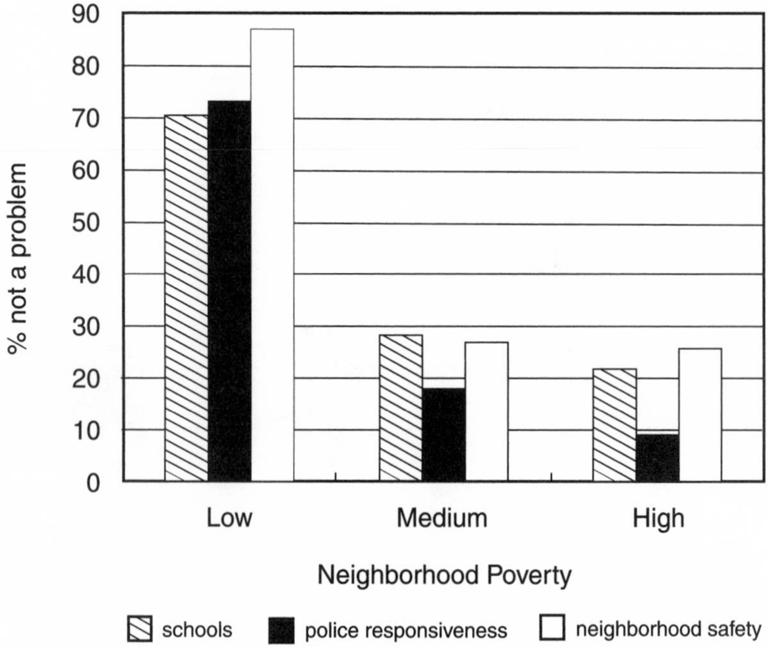

Source: See fig. 4.5.

quency.[34] Crime problems were measured by whether respondents indicated that assaults, vandalism, or drug sales were big problems in the neighborhood (see figure 4.7). Crime is a major concern for the residents of poorer neighborhoods. Residents in the medium-poor and ghetto neighborhoods were eleven or twelve times more likely than those who lived in low-poverty neighborhoods (33, 39, and 3 percent, respectively) to state that assaults were a big problem. Nearly 80 percent of residents in ghetto neighborhoods and 69 percent in medium-poverty neighborhoods indicated that drug sales were a major problem, in comparison to 13 percent in low-poverty neighborhoods. We also asked respondents to indicate the extent to which they felt that delinquency, in the form of "teen groups causing problems," was an issue. Only 10 percent of mothers in low-poverty neighborhoods reported such problems with teen groups, in contrast to 55 percent of those in medium-poverty neighborhood and 63 percent in ghetto neighborhoods.

The Chicago neighborhood data show that social organization was

FIGURE 4.7
Crime and Delinquency Problems in Chicago Study Neighborhoods

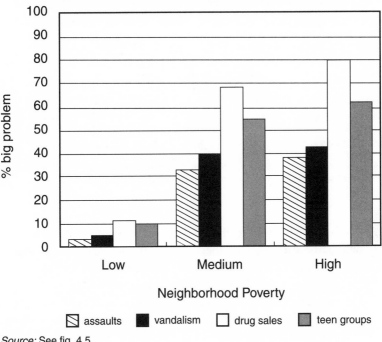

Source: See fig. 4.5.

significantly lower in both medium-poverty and ghetto neighborhoods than in low-poverty neighborhoods. Mothers in the poorer areas were less likely to feel that neighbors would intervene if they witnessed problems in the neighborhood or got together to deal with common neighborhood concerns. They also reported more problems with serious crime and more difficulty controlling teenagers. In contrast to the large differences between the low-poverty neighborhoods and the medium- and high-poverty neighborhoods on all measures, differences between medium- and high-poverty neighborhoods were minor, and only one, drug sales, was statistically significant.

A concept linking neighborhood disadvantage and the reduced life chances of poor inner-city residents is social isolation, which is defined as a lack of contact with individuals and institutions who represent mainstream society and who reinforce normative orientations, provide support, and help sustain neighborhood institutions (see table 4.1).[35] The extent to which mothers and their adolescent children are socially iso-

TABLE 4.1
Social Isolation in Chicago Study Neighborhoods, by Neighborhood Poverty and Socioeconomic Status (number of persons)

| | Neighborhood Poverty | | | | | |
| | Low | | Medium | | High | |
Measure	Low SES	High SES	Low SES	High SES	Low SES	High SES
Employed	4.8	7.2	4.8	7.0	3.1	6.2
College educated	1.5	4.0	1.0	2.4	0.8	2.2
On public assistance	0.7	0.3	1.8	0.7	3.2	0.9
Provide crisis support	5.0	6.1	4.3	4.9	4.1	5.2

Source: William Julius Wilson, *The Truly Disadvantaged: The Inner City, the Under Class and Public Policy* (Chicago: University of Chicago Press, 1987).

lated can be gauged by looking at the composition of the mother's social network, particularly the number of close friends or relatives with the following attributes: hold a steady job, graduated from college, receive public aid, and can be counted on in a major crisis. The data indicate that there is greater social isolation among residents of poorer neighborhoods, although the degree of social isolation varies by the socioeconomic status (SES) of the mother. Residents of poorer neighborhoods have fewer employed close friends or relatives in their networks, especially the low-SES residents of ghetto neighborhoods. While most residents of poorer neighborhoods reported fewer college-educated persons in their social networks, high-SES residents in both ghetto and medium-poverty neighborhoods had nearly two fewer college-educated friends than their low-poverty counterparts.

Low-SES residents of ghetto neighborhoods had nearly three more welfare recipients in their social network than those in low-poverty neighborhoods. The number of potential supporters in times of crisis was higher for mothers residing in low-poverty neighborhoods than their counterparts in poorer neighborhoods. On all the indicators of social isolation, low-SES mothers in ghetto neighborhoods fared worse than all other groups, both within and across neighborhood type. The data confirm that mothers who reside in neighborhoods with high levels of poverty have fewer community resources upon which to draw. These neighborhoods are less socially organized, less cohesive, and have less effective formal and informal social controls.

But what about the children who reside in these neighborhoods? Research indicates that youth in disadvantaged neighborhoods are less likely to interact with prosocial peers and are more likely to be exposed to and affected by any deviant activities that occur in their neighborhoods.[36] Empirical indicators of neighborhood peer group orientation included responses to two questions regarding the academic orientation of a youth's neighborhood friends—whether they got good grades and whether they attended school regularly. All neighborhood differences on peer group orientation were statistically significant (see figure 4.8). While 85 percent of all youth in low-poverty neighborhoods and 66 percent in medium-poverty neighborhoods stated that most of their friends got good grades in school, only about half (51 percent) did so in the ghetto neighborhoods. Perhaps more disconcerting, because it indicates high truancy and subsequent dropout rates, is the fact that only 61 percent of the youth in ghetto neighborhoods reported that most of their friends attended school regularly, compared to 73 percent and 89 percent in medium- and low-poverty neighborhoods, respectively. In

FIGURE 4.8
Neighborhood Peer Group Orientation in Chicago Study Neighborhoods

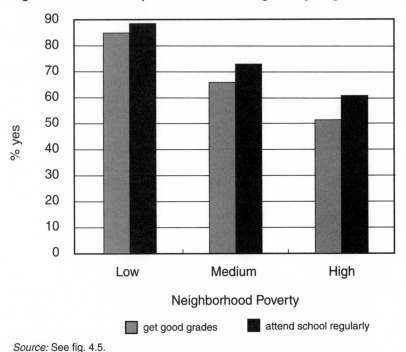

Source: See fig. 4.5.

short, youth residing in ghetto neighborhoods are much more likely to have friends who are not oriented toward academic achievement, and thus these youths are at greater risk of school failure.

Predictably, the combined effect of growing up in resource-depleted neighborhoods, where youth are exposed to peers who are disinterested in school, means reduced expectations of completing a successful course of adolescent development. Expectations about neighborhood youth was measured using two positive outcomes (graduating from high school and getting a good job as an adult) and two negative outcomes (becoming a teen parent and going on welfare). It was found that a large majority of the youth in low-poverty neighborhoods believed that the chances were high or very high that other youth in their neighborhood would graduate from high school (75 percent) and get a good job as an adult (63 percent) (see figure 4.9). Youths residing in ghetto neighborhoods were much more pessimistic: 42 percent felt that the chances were high that the youth in their neighborhoods would complete high school and just 24 percent felt that way about their chances of getting a good job. Nonnormative outcomes followed a similar pattern. Whereas just over 10 percent of the youth in low-poverty areas believed that the chances of youth in their neighborhoods going on welfare or becoming a teen parent were high, roughly half of the respondents residing in high-poverty neighborhoods felt that way. Overall, youth in poorer neighborhoods are more gloomy about the life course of their peers and acquaintances.

Discussion and Conclusion

The Kerner Report stressed the need for inclusionary approaches to remedy racial, spatial, and economic disparity. Concerned about the "polarization of the American community," the commission warned that if trends continued unabated the nation's largest cities would see greater spatial isolation of low-income blacks in the inner cities of the largest cities.[37] The report cautioned that family disruption and social problems would pervade neighborhoods in which the highly concentrated urban poor are cut off from employment opportunities and lack effective institutional resources. This prescient view of the rapid social and economic deterioration of the nation's metropolitan regions after the 1960s, in particular the older industrial cities of the Northeast and

FIGURE 4.9
Expectations about Neighborhood Youth in Chicago Study
Neighborhoods

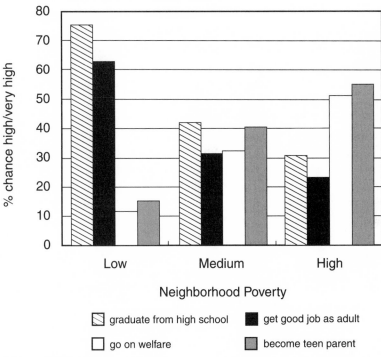

Source: See fig. 4.5.

Midwest, foretold the emergence of a new urban poverty, a poverty featuring chronic joblessness and related social dislocations.[38]

We have considered, here, the causes and consequences of the decline in inner-city neighborhoods and located this discussion in a historical context, highlighting some of the demographic shifts, economic trends, and political and social transformations that helped shape what we know today as ghetto neighborhoods. The explosion in the size of the urban black population in the 1950s and 1960s gave rise to a new pattern in local and national politics. The politicization of urban blacks, staunchly Democratic, helped to propel John F. Kennedy to victory in the 1961 presidential election. Realizing the importance of the black vote, politicians began to call attention to the plight of ghetto residents and to propose palliatives to alleviate the pernicious effects of persistent joblessness. The civil rights movement successfully challenged discriminatory

housing policies, brought about significant improvements in the education and the health and nutrition of children, and pushed for the expansion of social programs such as Head Start, Medicaid, and food stamps,
which benefited the ghetto poor.[39] However, labor market policies that
would have produced jobs for low-skilled workers did not get the kind
of support needed to effect a significant improvement in the rate of
poverty among minorities in the ghetto.[40]

The growing concentration of blacks in urban ghettos coincided with
a fundamental change in the structure of the labor market that greatly
affected the ability of low-skilled workers to provide for their families.
Technological advances increased industrial efficiency but also decreased
the need for workers in labor-intensive industries, especially manufacturing, which had been a mainstay for blue-collar jobs. At the same time,
the exodus of working- and middle-class blacks from core inner-city
neighborhoods enhanced the concentration effects of joblessness and
poverty and removed important economic and social buffers that had
softened the impact of macroeconomic changes in these vulnerable
communities.

During the 1970s and 1980s, conditions in inner-city ghettos went
from bad to worse. Rates of joblessness and concentrated poverty increased and so did the social dislocations associated with them, including
family breakups, welfare receipt, and crime. The Reagan and Bush administrations further aggravated conditions in the inner cities by sharply
cutting spending on direct aid to cities, including urban programs such
as public service jobs and job training, compensatory education, social
service block grants, and economic development assistance, designed to
alleviate some of the distress in these areas.[41]

The data for Chicago illustrate the increase in joblessness and concentrated poverty as well as the social dislocations associated with them.
They also highlight the multiple pathways by which the new urban
poverty impinges on the life chances of inner-city residents. While high-
poverty neighborhoods in Chicago include a disproportionate number
of jobless adults, welfare recipients, and single-parent families, they also
feature lower levels of social organization—that is, the extent to which
associations and relationships among neighborhood residents help to
maintain social norms and realize common goals.

Worsening the lack of informal social controls are weak formal institutions, notably schools and law enforcement. Moreover, these problems
are not unrelated, because when youth are unprepared to enter the
workforce, and without opportunities in the conventional world of

work, these youth may engage in illegal activities, creating problems for law enforcement. When we consider that mothers in high-poverty neighborhoods reported much higher rates of criminal activities and teen problems, we see that the continued weakness of these institutions can only heighten the disorder in many ghetto neighborhoods. Residence in poor neighborhoods also limits the social networks of adults, isolating them from mainstream individuals and institutions. Moreover, the unemployed friends and relatives of ghetto residents are less able to provide social and economic support in time of need. The data also confirm that the friends of youth residing in high-poverty neighborhoods are less committed to education and are at greater risk of dropping out. As the Kerner Report predicted, growing up in neighborhoods in which poverty and joblessness proliferate undermines the hopes and aspirations of inner-city youth and reinforces attitudes and behavior that reduce their chances of escaping poverty.

Social scientists and policy professionals concerned about the changing conditions in the inner city, especially in light of the new welfare legislation, would do well to reflect on the past as we debate the future. The Personal Responsibility and Work Opportunity Reconciliation Act, signed into law on August 22, 1996, by President Clinton, replaced the AFDC program and drastically alters how we deal with the poor. By emphasizing personal responsibility, this legislation makes the values and orientations of the poor a central issue and reignites decades of discussions on whether or not the poor deserve our help. With each change in national policy come renewed efforts to ensure accountability and a preoccupation with meeting institutional standards for compliance.

The other side of the equation, work opportunity, has not been well articulated, and after decades of lackluster attempts to define a national policy that would create jobs, it is still unclear how present policies will contribute to employment objectives. Indicators of the reform's successes have focused almost exclusively on caseload reductions, while data on job procurement by welfare recipients and terms of employment have been slow to materialize. Even more worrisome is the fact that little or no attention has been paid to male joblessness, which is inextricably tied to the welfare receipt of mothers and the well-being of children. Most low-income women date, marry, and have children with low-income men. Attempts to cut the welfare rolls without confronting the labor market opportunities of these men lessens the likelihood that poor urban families can be self-sufficient.

The social and economic conditions of the ghetto did not occur overnight. Thirty years have transpired since the Kerner Report called on the Johnson administration to approve massive government interventions to alleviate the conditions that fostered social disorder and despair in the ghetto. Since then, each subsequent administration has retooled the welfare system to make it more and more difficult for mothers to obtain public assistance while at the same time failing to mount a serious attack on chronic unemployment. We delude ourselves if we believe that we can continue along this worn path. The problems in the ghetto have compounded over the years as work has disappeared and the illegal economy has flourished. Consequently, the ominous predictions of the Kerner Report have become our urban reality.

5

Urban Poverty, Race, and the Inner City: The Bitter Fruit of Thirty Years of Neglect

Paul A. Jargowsky

The Kerner Report could be Exhibit A in defense of the American nation. Here was a nation, racked by racial violence, whose mainstream political establishment stood up and acknowledged the complicity of white racism in creating the conditions that led to the civil disorders, as they were euphemistically known. At the same time, the lackluster response of the nation to the bold agenda laid out by the Kerner Commission could be Exhibit A for the plaintiffs, proof that the nation has never accepted its responsibility for the conditions of black Americans and is not serious about redressing the racial divide in our society. Indeed, at least in part because of inaction and neglect, the conditions of the inner-city ghettos that spawned riots have grown worse. More blacks live in impoverished inner-city ghettos today than thirty years ago. Many more. These neighborhoods have grown larger and in some ways are more desperate and isolated from the social and economic mainstream than ever before.

In important ways, however, the situation is very different from that of the 1960s. Whereas ghettos were primarily formed and maintained by the inmigration of southern blacks and strict enforcement of racial segregation, the ghetto expansions of the last few decades were largely driven by the selective outmigration from the inner cities of both the white and black middle classes. This new urban dynamic explains the seeming conflict between the overall economic numbers for African

Americans, which have improved or at least not deteriorated, and the objective conditions of inner-city neighborhoods, which have for the most part continued to decline.

This chapter takes stock of the intersection of race and poverty in our nation's cities since the release of the Kerner Report in 1968. I examine the trends in black family income and changes over time in residential segregation by race. My primary focus, however, is the spatial organization of poverty within metropolitan areas, particularly the expansion of impoverished ghetto neighborhoods.

Family Income

The median income of African American families, like that of U.S. families in general, increased between 1970 and 1995, but only at a very slow rate. Median family income, after adjusting for inflation, rose from $23,170 to $25,970, for a meager annualized rate of increase of 0.5 percent. (White family incomes grew by about the same rate, rising from $37,772 to $42,646.) The poverty rate of black families dropped from 29.5 percent in 1970 to 26.4 percent in 1995. Yet the poverty rate of black *children*—in other words, the percentage of black children living in families classified as poor—did not change at all between 1970 and 1995, the rate being 41.5 percent in both those years. Keep in mind that the poverty level for a family of four in 1995 was only $15,569. With more than four in ten black children growing up in poverty, decade after decade, it is not surprising that so many black youth are troubled, do poorly in school, and have little commitment to mainstream institutions.

These numbers, however, miss a significant development. At least part of the black population has prospered: black family income distributions in 1970 and 1995 show a striking transition (see figure 5.1). By 1995, black income distribution had become substantially more skewed in the direction of higher incomes. A slightly larger percentage of black families were in the lowest income bracket (family income less than $10,000). Substantially more had higher incomes; in 1995, 21.3 percent of black families had incomes in excess of $50,000, compared to 12.4 percent in 1970. There were declines in all the income brackets between $10,000 and $50,000.

The implication is that there was a substantial increase in the inequality of black family income, primarily caused by an increase in the proportion of affluent families, but little change in the proportion of poor

FIGURE 5.1
Income Distribution of Black Families, 1970 and 1995

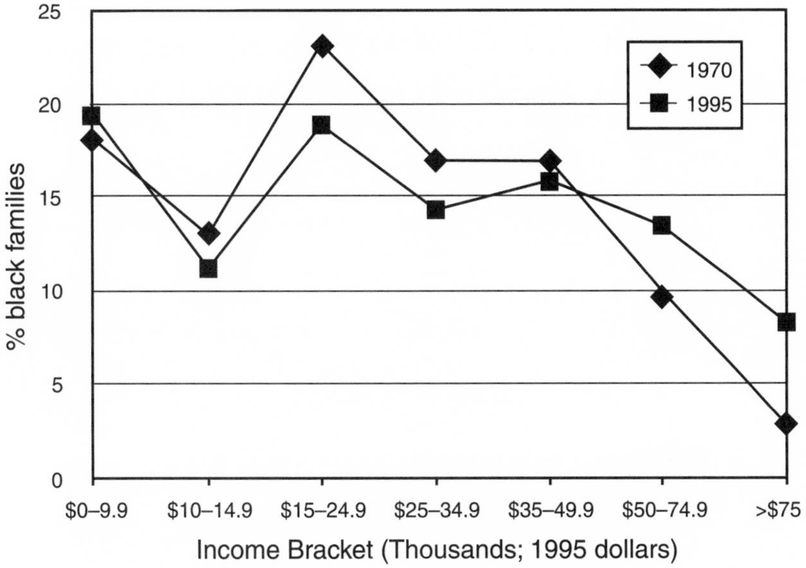

Income Bracket (Thousands; 1995 dollars)

families. While part of the black community was moving forward, another part was left behind, in spite of twenty-five years of economic growth and rising standards of living in the general population. For that part of the black community with growing incomes, the growth in inequality was the solution to their problem.

This growth in inequality of family income reflects a general trend in American society and is consistent with the trends for white families. While the full explanation of rising inequality in recent decades is the subject of much debate, most analysts agree that two major factors are a change in the technology of production and greater openness in the world economy.[1] Both factors lead to increasing demand for high-skilled labor and decreasing demand for low-skilled labor. For our purposes, however, it is important to note that the trends in black income distribution mirror the trends for whites: benefits to those at the upper end of the skill distribution and stagnation at best for the less well-off. This is quite a contrast to the decades leading up to the riots, when blacks were systematically excluded from participating in the robust economic growth enjoyed by white Americans, the children of earlier European immigrants.

Racial Segregation

The Kerner Commission identified racial segregation as one of the most pernicious legacies of white racism and a major contributing cause of the riots. In the South, of course, de jure segregation was the norm. Vast migrations of blacks from the rural South to the urban North resulted in heavy black concentration in areas of slum housing, following a pattern trod by generations of European immigrants. Unlike these earlier immigrants, however, blacks did not become residentially assimilated over time:

> Nowhere has the expansion of America's urban Negro population followed this pattern of dispersal. Thousands of Negro families have attained incomes, living standards, and cultural levels matching or surpassing those of whites who have "upgraded" themselves from distinctly ethnic neighborhoods. Yet most Negro families have remained within predominantly Negro neighborhoods, primarily because they have been effectively excluded from residential areas.[2]

The history of overt and covert forms of housing discrimination is well documented.[3] But the Kerner Commission was also careful to point out that housing segregation is a product not only of constraints on black families' choice of housing but also of choices made by whites to flee borderline or mixed areas. "Normal population turnover causes about 20 percent of the residents of average United States neighborhoods to move out every year because of income changes, job transfers, shifts in life-cycle position or deaths. . . . The refusal of whites to move into 'changing' areas when vacancies occur there from normal turnover means that most vacancies are eventually occupied by Negroes. An inexorable shift toward heavy Negro occupancy results."[4] Thus, white fear of racial transition becomes a self-fulfilling prophecy. The result is " 'massive racial transition' at the edges of existing all-Negro areas."

Three decades after the passage of landmark civil rights and fair housing legislation, racial segregation between blacks and whites remains extremely high.[5] The good news, however, is that racial segregation has been declining in most metropolitan areas since about the time of the Kerner Report.[6] Between 1980 and 1990, the Index of Dissimilarity measuring segregation by race declined in 260 of 318 metropolitan areas; falling on average from 0.70 to 0.66. Declines occurred in every region of the country and were by no means limited to cities with small numbers of blacks. Of the metropolitan areas in the top quartile in terms of the percentage of black population, sixty-six of eighty had declines in racial segregation, and the index declined from 0.75 to 0.72—still very high by historical standards and in comparison to other racial and ethnic groups but moving slowly in the right direction.[7] The number of neighborhoods (census tracts) with zero black residents has declined by 25 percent between 1980 and 1990, even as the number of census tracts was increasing and the vast majority of new census tracts were created in the suburbs.[8]

In terms of racial segregation, then, there has been progress since the 1970s. The key element in the turnaround was probably the passage of the Fair Housing Act (1968), despite little active enforcement of the measure. The Kerner Commission's recommendation for "programs designed to encourage integration of substantial numbers of Negroes" has been largely ignored.

Urban Ghettos

Central to the argument of the Kerner Commission was its analysis of the social and economic conditions of the black ghetto and the role of those conditions in sparking civil disorders. The term *ghetto* as used by the Kerner Commission referred to "an area within a city characterized by poverty and acute social disorganization, and inhabited by members of a racial or ethnic group under conditions of involuntary segregation."[9] With uncommon directness, the commission identified the "bitter fruits" of white racism as the primary cause of the "explosive mixture which has been accumulating in our cities since the end of World War II." In the ghetto, "segregation and poverty have intersected to destroy opportunity and hope and to enforce failure."[10]

The commission's emphasis on the spatial aspects of the poverty problem was a departure from traditional ways of viewing poverty, which emphasized economic convulsions, on the one hand, and the supposed character flaws of individual poor persons, on the other hand.[11] The spatial concentration of poverty, achieved through the interaction of racial segregation and employment discrimination, affected both internal and external relationships for those trapped in ghetto neighborhoods. Within ghettos, the concentration of disadvantage leads to "an environmental jungle characterized by personal insecurity and tension" and "a system of ruthless, exploitative relationships within the ghetto." Exter-

nally, entrapment in ghettos isolated blacks from the mainstream economy because "future jobs are being created primarily in the suburbs" so
that "this separation will make it more and more difficult for Negroes
to achieve anything like full employment."[12]

There is no reason to believe that the years since 1967 have lessened
the logic behind worrying about the spatial aspects of poverty. Social
isolation intensifies and exacerbates the effects of economic deprivation,
particularly as middle-class black institutions that once acted as social
buffers leave the inner city.[13] The predicted suburbanization of jobs has
occurred, and metropolitan areas have continued to sprawl and jobs have
continued to decentralize.[14]

How has the spatial organization of black poverty changed since the
Kerner Report? Black poverty has remained relatively constant since the
1960s, even as a black middle class has emerged and expanded. Since the
black poverty rate has not increased and segregation by race has actually
decreased, one might surmise that the ghetto problem would have diminished since the 1960s. Surprisingly, this is not the case. In fact, the
ghetto problem has become dramatically worse. High-poverty areas in
inner cities have expanded rapidly, more of the black population resides
in such neighborhoods, and the black poor are increasingly concentrated
within them and isolated from the social and economic mainstream.

Has the number of blacks living in impoverished ghettos grown or
diminished since the release of the Kerner Report? To answer this question, an operational definition of the term is needed. The Kerner Commission's use of the term *ghetto* had several elements, each of which must
be addressed.

First, a ghetto is "an area within a city." Thus I examine only neighborhoods within metropolitan areas. As a proxy for neighborhoods, I
use census tracts, which are small, relatively homogeneous areas deline-
ated by the Census Bureau throughout the country.[15]

Second, a ghetto is "characterized by poverty and acute social disorganization." Neighborhoods span the whole range of poverty in a continuous distribution from 0 to 100 percent. A clean division of neighborhoods into "slums" on the one hand and "good neighborhoods" on the
other is not possible. However, field research in a number of metropolitan areas indicates that areas in which the census tract poverty rate exceeds 40 percent correspond well to the neighborhoods of greatest concern to social service providers, neighborhood organizations, and other
individuals who are familiar with local neighborhood conditions.[16]

Third, a ghetto is "inhabited by members of a racial or ethnic group under conditions of involuntary segregation." Most neighborhoods contain some mixture of whites, blacks, and members of other race groups. There is no consensus about what constitutes a segregated neighborhood, but any such scheme must take into account the underlying proportion of blacks in the population.[17] In 1990, blacks were about 12 percent of the U.S. population. If perfect integration had prevailed, all neighborhoods would have been 12 percent black. Hence, even though such a neighborhood would be predominantly white, logic demands that it be considered integrated. At the same time, a neighborhood in which half the residents are black and half are white must also be considered racially integrated in view of the commonsense meaning of the word.

Thus, the category of integrated neighborhoods must include, at a minimum, neighborhoods in which the percentage black is in the range of 12–50 percent. For this analysis, I categorize census tracts as segregated nonblack neighborhoods if the percentage of residents who are non-Hispanic blacks is less than half the national average (less than 6 percent). I categorize neighborhoods as integrated if the percentage of residents who are non-Hispanic blacks is 6 percent or more but less than 60 percent. Census tracts in which at least six in ten residents are non-Hispanic blacks are categorized as segregated black neighborhoods. While this categorization scheme is arguable, the results are not particularly sensitive to the specification of the categories because the distribution of neighborhood percentage that is black is basically bimodal.[18]

In 1990, nearly half of all blacks lived in segregated, black, metropolitan neighborhoods (see table 5.1). Yet nearly as many (42.3 percent) lived in integrated neighborhoods, and a nontrivial number (8.3 percent) lived in segregated white neighborhoods. More than four million blacks lived in high-poverty neighborhoods. Of these, more than eight in ten lived in neighborhoods that were also segregated by race. In comparison, blacks living in neighborhoods with lower poverty rates were also much more likely to live in integrated neighborhoods, especially those who lived in neighborhoods in which fewer than one in five persons were poor.

For blacks, therefore, neighborhood poverty goes hand in hand with segregation. However, the converse is not true. Of blacks living in racially segregated neighborhoods, most were not also living in high-poverty neighborhoods. Of the twelve million blacks in segregated black neighborhoods, 42.4 percent lived in neighborhoods with intermediate poverty rates. The rest were almost equally divided between low-pov-

TABLE 5.1

**Distribution of U.S. Blacks, by Neighborhood Poverty Level
and Segregation Level, 1990**

Neighborhood	All Neighbor- hoods	Neighborhood Poverty Level		
		0–19.9%	20–39.9%	40% and Over
Non-Hispanic black (thousands)				
All neighborhoods	24,525	12,000	8,327	4,198
Segregated white or other	2,026	1,798	192	36
Integrated	10,377	6,619	2,999	759
Segregated black	12,122	3,583	5,136	3,403
Distribution by segregation level (%)				
All neighborhoods	100	100	100	100
Segregated white or other	8.3	15	2.3	0.9
Integrated	42.3	55.2	36	18.1
Segregated black	49.4	29.9	61.7	81.1
Distribution by neighborhood poverty level (%)				
All neighborhoods	100	48.9	34	17.1
Segregated white or other	100	88.7	9.5	1.8
Integrated	100	63.8	28.9	7.3
Segregated black	100	29.6	42.4	28.1

Source: U.S. Census, Summary Tape File 3A, tabulation by the author.
Note: Census tracts are proxies for neighborhoods; "Segregated white or other" are neighborhoods less than 6 percent non-Hispanic black; "Integrated" are neighborhoods 6–60 percent non-Hispanic black; "Segregated black" are neighborhoods more than 60 percent black.

erty neighborhoods and high-poverty ghettos. Not all racially segregated neighborhoods are ghettos, in the Kerner Commission's sense of that term. Fewer than one-third of the blacks in racially segregated neighborhoods lived in slum conditions.

Changes in the Spatial Organization of Poverty

Between 1970 and 1990, the black population of the United States grew by about a third (see table 5.2). The number of black poor also grew, but not as rapidly, so the poverty rate of blacks dropped from about 35 percent to about 30 percent. At the same time, the black population became more centralized in metropolitan areas. About two-thirds of

TABLE 5.2
Distribution of U.S. Blacks, by Neighborhood Poverty Level and Income Level, 1970–1990

Area	1970	1980	1990	Change (%), 1970–90
U.S. total (thousands)[a]				
All incomes	21,931	25,623	29,031	32.4
Incomes below poverty level	7,596	7,649	8,441	11.1
Poverty rate (%)	34.6	29.9	29.1	
Metropolitan areas				
All incomes	17,000	20,351	23,927	40.7
Incomes below poverty	4,785	5,485	6,320	32.1
Poverty rate (%)	28.1	27.0	26.4	
High-poverty neighborhoods[b]				
All incomes	2,447	3,097	4,152	69.7
Incomes below poverty	1,247	1,548	2,120	70.0
Poverty rate (%)	51.0	50.0	51.1	
Percent in high-poverty neighborhoods				
All incomes		14.4	15.2	17.4
Incomes below poverty		26.1	28.2	33.5

Source: Census tract data for 1970–90. For details of tabulations see Paul A. Jargowsky, *Poverty and Place* (New York: Russell Sage, 1997), app. A.
  a. High-poverty neighborhoods are census tracts in which the poverty rate is 40 percent or more.
  b. Includes 239 metropolitan areas, with geographic adjustments to improve comparability over time.

blacks resided in metropolitan areas in 1970. By 1990, about three-quarters of blacks lived in these areas. Thus, the migration of blacks from rural areas and small towns to metropolitan areas, noted by the Kerner Commission, has continued, albeit at a slower rate.

More important, a greater share of the blacks residing in metropolitan areas lives in high-poverty neighborhoods (census tracts with poverty rates of 40 percent and above). The black neighborhood poverty rate, that is, the proportion of persons living in these impoverished neighborhoods, rose from 14.4 percent in 1970 to 17.4 percent in 1990. In comparison, in 1990, 10.5 percent of Hispanics and only 1.4 percent of whites lived in high-poverty neighborhoods. Thus, a black resident of a metropolitan area was more than twelve times as likely to be a resident of a high-poverty neighborhood as a white resident.

The combination of population growth, increasing metropolitaniza-
tion, and increasing neighborhood poverty resulted in a 70 percent increase in the number of blacks residing in impoverished ghetto neighborhoods, rising from about 2.5 million in 1970 to more than 4 million
persons by 1990. While some of these blacks were in racially integrated
high-poverty neighborhoods, the vast majority were in ghettos (in the
Kerner Commission's sense of the term). This disturbing trend is the
starkest measure of our failure to heed the warnings or implement the
policies of the Kerner Commission.

Persons who live in poor families are disadvantaged because they do
not have the resources to obtain the goods and services that others take
for granted and that are necessary to take advantage of opportunities in
the economy: clothing, health care, telephone service, day care, transportation, and so on. Persons who live in poor neighborhoods are disadvantaged because of the lack of stable neighborhood institutions, established pathways to success, remoteness from areas of job growth, and in
some cases high crime rates. People from poor families who also live in
high-poverty neighborhoods obviously face the greatest difficulties.
Those who suffer poverty at both levels cannot use resources from the
community to hep offset family poverty and cannot use family resources
to buffer the effects of residing in a poor neighborhood. Each type of
disadvantage thus exacerbates the other.

Concentration of poverty is the proportion of people in poor families
who reside in poor neighborhoods. Among blacks, the concentration of
poverty rose from 26.1 percent to 33.5 percent in 1990. Thus, while the
overall poverty level of metropolitan blacks changed little since 1970,
there has been a notable change in the spatial organization of poverty.
And the spatial component of poverty is likely to be more important in
the 1990s than it was in the 1960s, because of the increasing suburbanization of job growth and the increasing importance of language and
skills in the modern economy.

Forces Driving Ghetto Expansion

While the nation as a whole shows a steady upward trend in neighborhood poverty, a great deal of variation is contained within that average.
Trends in neighborhood poverty rates for the nine census divisions (sub-
divisions of regions), as well as for selected cities within those areas, show
that ghetto poverty is very responsive to local and regional economic

conditions (see table 5.3). In the Mid-Atlantic region (New York, New Jersey, and Pennsylvania), ghetto poverty nearly tripled during the 1970s. After the long economic recovery of the 1980s, which was particularly strong in the Northeast, New York and Philadelphia actually showed small declines in ghetto poverty between 1980 and 1990, as did the average for the Mid-Atlantic states.

Pittsburgh and Buffalo, however, went against the regional trend, with large increases in ghetto poverty in the 1980s. In Buffalo, the share of blacks living in high-poverty areas rose from 21 to 40 percent. These two cities mirrored the pattern of the eastern portion of the Midwest (Illinois, Indiana, Michigan, Ohio, and Wisconsin), where ghetto poverty increased substantially over both decades. The economies of the West South Central Division (Arkansas, Louisiana, Oklahoma, and Texas) are closely linked to the price of oil; these states boomed in the 1970s and slumped in the 1980s. Ghetto poverty responded dramatically to these economic changes, falling by 1980 to nearly half the 1970 level and rising substantially by 1990.

Statistical analysis confirms what these regional trends suggest: that ghettoization is highly dependent on overall economic trends and that it changes rapidly in response to changing economic conditions. This contradicts the notion that the residents of ghettos are so enmeshed in a culture of poverty that they cannot take advantage of available opportunities. It also suggests that in the years since 1990, with a booming economy in most of the United States, levels of ghetto poverty may have fallen from 1990 levels. Indeed many cities report success in stabilizing neighborhoods, reducing crime, and rebuilding devastated areas. Low unemployment is a powerful weapon against poverty and neighborhood deterioration.

Unfortunately, despite the recent gains due to the booming economy, there are still reasons to be deeply concerned about the future prospects of cities. Metropolitan economies improved on average between 1970 and 1990, and yet the number of blacks residing in impoverished ghettos increased by 70 percent. This long-term increase in ghetto poverty is independent of the business cycle. Middle-class persons of all races move out of the inner cities to the inner ring of suburbs. More affluent persons move from inner suburbs to the outer ring. The result of this process is that borderline high-poverty areas on the edges of the ghetto become poorer, eventually reaching 40 percent poverty. Thus, the physical size of the ghetto grew rapidly as the census tracts in the ghetto lost population. However, the area of population loss is usually much larger than

TABLE 5.3
Black Neighborhood Poverty, by Census Division and Selected
Metropolitan Areas, 1970, 1980, 1990

	Number of MSAs[a]	Neighborhood Poverty Rate (%)		
		1970	1980	1990
U.S. total	239	14.4	15.2	17.4
Northeast				
New England	26	7.2	9.3	7.7
Boston		10.5	6.5	6.3
Mid-Atlantic	25	7.3	21.3	17.9
New York		6.8	26.5	21.0
Philadelphia		11.1	21.1	15.7
Newark		9.2	20.7	8.9
Pittsburgh		13.6	16.2	27.6
Buffalo		1.7	20.5	40.3
Midwest				
East North Central	48	9.0	16.2	26.2
Chicago		11.8	22.8	23.1
Detroit		5.1	10.9	35.4
Cleveland		16.3	18.5	21.1
West North Central	19	14.5	14.4	19.1
St. Louis		19.6	19.5	22.9
Kansas City		8.1	7.6	9.9
South				
South Atlantic	36	18.7	13.4	11.6
Washington		3.4	3.2	1.8
Baltimore		17.7	19.2	15.3
Atlanta		16.5	17.1	11.1
East South Central	14	34.9	22.0	25.3
Memphis		44.1	26.5	32.5
Birmingham		21.0	16.9	20.7
Mobile		45.8	30.9	41.8
West South Central	35	25.9	13.1	21.6
Houston		10.0	7.2	14.9
Dallas		17.5	11.0	12.8
New Orleans		35.0	23.5	33.7
West				
Mountain	13	13.9	4.9	8.8
Pacific	23	7.0	5.1	6.7
Los Angeles		7.8	6.7	8.0
San Francisco		4.3	4.3	5.3

Source: See table 5.2.
a. Metropolitan statistical area.

the ghetto area per se. The area of population gain is consistently at the periphery.

This process of ghetto expansion driven by differential outmigration of more affluent households is common across the country. Even in metropolitan areas in which there was a decline in the number or percentage of people living in high-poverty neighborhoods, the number of census tracts classified as ghettos often grew. Thus, the long-run trend in neighborhood poverty is driven by suburban sprawl, in which jobs and wealthier people move farther and farther from centers of metropolitan areas, leading to higher levels of economic segregation.

Virtually every metropolitan area in the United States is becoming more segregated by income.[19] The growth in high-poverty neighborhoods is only the most visible manifestation of much broader changes in the spatial organization of metropolitan areas. For example, outer-ring suburbs allow, even encourage, developers to build single-income developments for the upper-middle class while inner-city neighborhoods wither. Public resources go into providing new streets, schools, and sewers for these fringe developments while similar assets closer to downtown are underutilized and in need of repair.

Metropolitan areas are undergoing important sociodemographic changes. Foremost among these is a continuing trend toward decentralization. Between 1960 and 1990, inner cities' share of total metropolitan area population declined from 51 percent to 40 percent, despite annexation.[20] While a robust economy helps inner cities and the poor neighborhoods within them, the long-term trend underlying the ups and downs of the business cycle is that prosperity and job growth are moving to the metropolitan periphery, and poverty and joblessness are concentrated in the core of metropolitan areas.[21] The pooling of poor individuals in urban centers is hardly a new development; urban areas have always been a port of entry for immigrants and migrants.[22] But concentration in the inner city is no longer an effective way for poor individuals to become connected to the larger economy and, instead, subjects its residents to multiple disadvantages.

Unfortunately, the public policy response to the plight of the inner city has taken little account of the process by which such neighborhoods are created. Policies such as empowerment zones and community economic development are based on the premise that something is wrong with individual neighborhoods and that these neighborhoods can be "fixed" by neighborhood-level interventions. While not harmful, these programs are unlikely to have any impact on the way metropolitan areas develop. Indeed, current federal programs often replicate the fragmented political structure of metropolitan areas; for example, there are often separate public housing waiting lists for the inner city and for the suburbs.

In fact, federal government policies have encouraged the mad rush toward economic segregation, through highway construction, the tax code, and infrastructure development.[23] State governments also have contributed to decentralization by tolerating exclusionary zoning and "not in my backyard" attitudes on the part of local governments. In fairness, federal and state government policies did not create the desire of people to live in neighborhoods segregated by race and income, nor were they the driving forces behind metropolitan decentralization. But their policies have enabled and accelerated these underlying processes, in effect, throwing gasoline on the fire. In contrast, government policy provided a countervailing force against the desire of people to segregate by race and ethnicity. While racial discrimination in housing markets obviously persists, the situation would be far worse than it is today if for the past thirty years state and local governments had encouraged and subsidized racial segregation.

Conclusion

One of the most striking things about the Kerner Report is the elegance and brutal honesty of the writing. The text does not mince words. For example, in a section discussing the Black Power movement, provocatively titled "Old Wine in New Bottles," the commission wrote: "The Black Power advocates of today consciously feel that they are the most militant group in the Negro protest movement. Yet they have retreated from a direct confrontation with American Society on the issue of integration and, by preaching separatism, unconsciously function as an accommodation to white racism."[24] Whether or not the commission's scathing characterization of the Black Power movement is accurate or overstated, there is no denying that the position is stated clearly and directly. Nor were the attitudes and actions of whites treated lightly by the commission, which concluded that white racism was the fundamental cause of the civil disorders:

> The record before this Commission reveals that the causes of recent racial disorders are imbedded in . . . the historical pattern of Negro-white relations in America.

Race prejudice has shaped our history decisively in the past; it now threatens to do so again. White racism is essentially responsible for the explosive mixture which has been accumulating in our cities since the end of World War II. At the base of this mixture are the most bitter fruits of white racial attitudes: *Pervasive discrimination and segregation . . . Black migration and white exodus . . . Black ghettos.*[25]

The commission, composed mostly of moderates and members of the "establishment," nevertheless refused to let white society off the hook by focusing on the criminal aspects of the actions of rioters, protestors, and activists. "The central thrust of Negro protest," the commission stated, "has aimed at the inclusion of Negroes in American society on a basis of full equality rather than at a fundamental transformation of American institutions. . . . Negro protest, for the most part, has been firmly rooted in the basic values of American society, seeking not their destruction by their fulfillment."

In the 1960s, blacks were systematically excluded from all important and desirable aspects of economic, social, and political life. As long as blacks expected no better, this situation was tolerated. Anger requires expectations, and blacks in America had none. But the civil rights movement changed all that by reaffirming that the American Dream was the birthright of all Americans, regardless of skin color. When de jure equality turned out to be a fraud and America continued to deny blacks real citizenship, the inner cities erupted in a spasm of protest and violence.

The urban crises of the 1960s can be summed up in just one word: race. Today, one word is not enough. A rough approximation of equality of opportunity has been achieved for blacks fortunate enough not to have been too badly disadvantaged by America's three-hundred-year legacy of slavery and racism. But a significant segment of the black population is unable to take advantage of that narrowly opened door. They live in impoverished ghettos that isolate them geographically, educationally, and socially from the possibility of living the American Dream.

Today's urban crisis can be summed up, awkwardly at best, as increasing economic segregation interacting with rising inequality in the context of the aftermath of three hundred years of poverty and racism. We are no longer moving toward two societies, one white and one black, and that is a change that should not be taken lightly. But we are moving in the direction of the kind of society that builds walls topped by broken glass, a society with permanent, deep, and bitter class divisions. By fulfilling only the easy and cheap parts of the Kerner Commission's mandate, we have traded one problem for another, and I fear it is a more complex and intractable one.

In the thirty years since the release of the report, much progress has been made in eradicating the racial basis of oppression. Unfortunately, our failure to deal with the geography of opportunity has resulted in an increasingly fragmented society. The spatial differentiation within metropolises now results in a profound inequality of access to the American Dream. The increasing concentration of poverty has given even more urgency to the commission's urgent plea not to stumble into the future through inaction: "We cannot escape the responsibility for choosing the future of our metropolitan areas and the human relations which develop within them. It is a responsibility so critical that even an unconscious choice to continue present policies has the gravest implications."[26] If the nation pursues policies that raise incomes, reduce inequality, and slow the momentum of metropolitan sprawl, the concentration of poverty can be significantly reduced and its affects ameliorated. The alternative is to continue blundering down the futile path of letting our cities become hollow shells and allowing our society to divide into two distinct groups, one with access to good neighborhoods and schools and the other warehoused in urban wastelands.

History and current events suggest that a strong nation, even one with no significant external threat, may decline because of internal racial and ethnic conflicts. Such conflicts are especially acute when there are large economic disparities among groups and when the groups are geographically and socially isolated. Although the ethnic conflicts in places like Somalia, Rwanda, and Bosnia may seem beyond anything that could happen in the United States, we should learn the lessons of those tragedies. And a persistent, low-level political conflict, on the order of the Quebec separatist movement, is not an impossibility in the United States. It can happen here. Indeed, scattered groups of disenfranchised rural whites have already renounced the United States, challenged its laws and institutions, and taken violent action against federal officials.

The inner cities of our metropolitan areas could well become crucibles for the radical rejection of American institutions. This is exactly the fear embodied in the Kerner Commission's warning that we were becoming "two societies . . . separate and unequal." In the post–Cold War era, this prospect now poses the greatest threat to the long-term economic and political stability of the country.

6

Race, Violence, and Justice since Kerner

Elliott Currie

Chapter 13 of the Kerner Report is titled "The Administration of Justice under Emergency Conditions." The commission was referring to the "emergency" of the urban disorders themselves, but there is a broader sense in which many commentators at the time regarded the high levels of urban violence in the late sixties as an emergency condition—and one that, given intelligent and sustained intervention, could be substantially relieved.

That didn't happen. Instead, since the late 1960s urban violence has become a kind of permanent emergency, an ongoing part of the background of American life. The high levels of violence that prompted the massive reports of the Katzenbach crime commission, the Kerner riot commission, and the Eisenhower violence commission have not only stubbornly persisted but also, for a several-year period of the late 1980s and early 1990s, reached heights that, in many cities, were worse than they had ever been in American history.

Since then, the welcome news is that the worst of that epidemic of violence has passed, at least for the moment. But we are left with a level of epidemic violence that remains the worst in the advanced industrial world, despite a massive "experiment" in incarceration that is unprecedented in this country or in any other advanced society and that has transformed America's criminal justice system into a permanent holding ground for a large segment of the minority poor.

This permanent crisis has been worse for some people, and for some communities, than for others: worse for the young than the old, worse by far for some cities than for others. But the broad outlines are starkly clear. Minorities—especially blacks but also, and increasingly, Hispanics, some Asian/Pacific Islanders, and Native Americans—suffer far more victimization by violence than their non-Hispanic white counterparts, who themselves are far more likely to be victims of violence than the citizens of most other advanced industrial countries. In most cases, these disparities have increased, often dramatically, in recent years. And they have increased simultaneously with the growing reach of the criminal justice system into minority communities.

Thus there are two reinforcing sides to this crisis. On the one hand, minority violence remains a public health disaster of staggering proportions in America. At the same time, the attempt to restore order in minority communities through a massive expansion of the prison system has compounded the tragedy, as ever greater numbers of the minority poor are swept up into the justice system and, all too often, crippled in their chances for a stable or successful future.

In this chapter, I sketch the dimensions of this permanent emergency, tracing recent patterns and trends in violence, especially homicide, in the "two societies"; examining the parallel explosion in minority incarceration; considering what an expanding body of research tells us about the role of racial discrimination in the criminal justice system itself in creating those disparities; and pointing to some possible long-range consequences of our current policies.

Recent "Two-Societies" Trends in Violence

Since the publication of the Kerner Report, over a quarter of a million black Americans have died by homicide. To put the figure into human perspective, consider that it is roughly equivalent to the entire population of a substantial midsized American city, like, Newark, New Jersey, Birmingham, Alabama, or Louisville, Kentucky. For further perspective, consider that the total number killed in the "troubles" in Northern Ireland on all sides of the conflict during roughly the same thirty-year period is slightly above three thousand.[1]

What is most startling, however, is not the sheer numbers but the disparity in the risks of violent death between black and white Americans. Although they make up only roughly 12 percent of the nation's population, blacks are almost half of the victims of homicide. And although the disparities are less glaring for other minorities, they are pervasive—and increasing. When it comes to the risks of violence, America is not two societies, but many societies. And especially since the mid-1980s, the fortunes of one of those societies—non-Hispanic whites—have increasingly diverged from all the others.

The differences are especially stark when we consider the trends in homicide deaths among young men (ages fifteen to twenty-four) in all racial groups. They are most prone to victimization by violence, but black, Hispanic, Native American, and some Asian youths are far more likely to die by violence than their Anglo counterparts, so much so that fundamental gender and age differences in the risks of violent death are often overcome by the effects of race.

To place these disparities in context, it is important to bear in mind that the risks of dying by violence are high in the United States for *all* races, especially among the young, when compared to every other advanced industrial nation. In 1994, the U.S. homicide death rate for non-Hispanic white youths was roughly eight times the overall rate for youths that age in England.[2] When we say that minority rates of homicide are far higher than those for whites, therefore, we are working from a base of comparison that is already remarkably high by world standards.

Among white, non-Hispanic youths, the homicide death rate in 1995 was 7.3 per 100,000. It ranged from 19.4 for Asian/Pacific Islanders to 32 for Native Americans, 64 for Hispanics, and a stunning 132 for blacks. Thus, the minority risk of violent death exceeded that of non-Hispanic white youth by almost three to one in the case of Asian/Pacific youths, better than four to one for Native Americans, almost nine to one for Hispanics, and fully eighteen to one for blacks. Moreover, every one of these disparities increased, sometimes spectacularly, over the previous decade, for the homicide death rate rose for every group *except* non-Hispanic whites in those years. In 1985, black youths' risk of homicide death was not quite nine times that of non-Hispanic whites, meaning that the racial disparity more than doubled by 1995. In 1985, the homicide death rate of Asian/Pacific youth was only fractionally higher than that of non-Hispanic whites; by 1995 it was nearly three times higher. Overall, the rate of change in homicide death rates from 1985 to 1995 ranged from a slight *decline* of 5 percent for non-Hispanic whites to a nearly 50 percent increase for Hispanics, a 100 percent increase for blacks, and a devastating 126 percent increase for Asian/Pacific Islanders.[3]

The Asian/Pacific Island figures, it should be noted, are somewhat misleading by themselves, because the category covers such a broad range of groups, with widely different risks of violence. Homicide death rates among Chinese and Japanese youths are especially low, for example; but those for Southeast Asian and Pacific Island youth are very high. Homicide is the leading cause of death among Vietnamese and Pacific Islander youths of both sexes in the United States—as it is also for blacks.[4]

Strikingly, the racial disparities in the risks of homicide are so large that they sometimes overwhelm the effects of two of the most important predictors of violence: gender and age. Men are everywhere more likely to die by violence than women, other things equal, and people in their volatile late teens and early twenties more likely to die by violence than the middle-aged and the elderly. But in the United States, race twists and upends these constants. The homicide death rate for young black women, for example, exceeds that for white non-Hispanic youth by 2.3 to 1. The death rate among young Hispanic women almost matches that for non-Hispanic white youth, though they are only one-ninth as likely to die by violence as a Hispanic youth.

At the other end of the age scale, another part of the racial disparity in violence appears: minority citizens remain at relatively high risk of violent death well into middle age (ages forty-five to sixty-four) and beyond. Among middle-aged blacks and Hispanics, homicide remains among the top ten causes of death (eighth for Hispanics, tenth for blacks), while it falls off that scale for middle-aged whites. Middle-aged Hispanics are more than half again as likely to be murdered as non-Hispanic white youths. On average, during the 1990s, an older (sixty-five or older) black American man was three to four times more likely to be murdered than an Anglo youth. Indeed, for black Americans, race overcomes the effects of both age and gender at once: during the first half of the 1990s, an older black woman was as likely to be murdered as a non-Hispanic white youth.[5]

Another way to illustrate these differences is to calculate what proportion of overall deaths that occur in a given racial or ethnic group are the result of deliberate violence. Thus, in 1995, among non-Hispanic white youths and young women, roughly 1 of every 14 deaths was a homicide. But among Hispanic youths, 1 of every 3 deaths was a homicide. And among black youths, almost half—1 of 2.2—of deaths resulted from deliberate violence. For black youths, the figure is slightly over half. We can see the same tragically disproportionate toll of violence in the patterns of death among small children. In 1995, 1 of 22 Anglo children aged one to four years old died of homicide; but so did one of twelve

Hispanic children and one of ten black children. The rate of child death—measured against the overall child population—is almost twice as high among Hispanics as among non-Hispanic whites and nearly five times as high among blacks.[6]

The extraordinary levels of violence among minority youth have eased off from their early 1990s peaks, but they remain staggeringly high—and staggeringly disproportionate—because their rise in the preceding several years was so rapid: so rapid, indeed, that they reversed the historical upward trend in life expectancy for black men. The overall death rate among black youths increased at an annual average of about 7 percent during the 1980s, the result of sharply rising homicide deaths coupled with less spectacular rises in suicide and other firearm injuries. Rising deaths from these causes countered the beneficial effects of a decline in car accidents, which would otherwise have caused death rates among black youth to fall, as they did for other ethnic and racial groups.[7]

Between 1984 and 1989, the overall life expectancy at birth among black men in the United States actually fell by roughly a full year, while white men gained about eight months of life.[8] Homicide was not the only contributor to this unusual reversal of progress in life expectancy; it was joined by rapidly rising deaths from HIV infection and, to a lesser extent, from drug-related causes. When we put these (often related) causes together, what we see is a public health disaster unprecedented in American history—and one that helps explain why the life expectancy of American black men in the 1990s was slightly higher than that of men in Romania.[9]

Disaster is heavily concentrated among the young. For though it is true that older minority men and women are still far more likely to be the victims of violence than their Anglo counterparts, their rate of death by homicide has fallen, often substantially, in recent years. Among middle-aged black men, the homicide death rate was about forty-five per thousand in 1960, rose sharply in the late sixties, and remained at more than seventy in 1980. It then fell to forty-six in 1985 and continued to fall, more or less steadily, to about thirty-five in 1995. But that decline was more than counterbalanced by the extraordinary rises, beginning in the last half of the 1980s, among black youths, especially those under twenty-five years. A somewhat similar, though less sharp, decline has occurred among middle-aged men of most racial groups since the mid-1980s, but with the clear exception of middle-aged Asian/ Pacific Island men, among whom homicide death rates were considerably higher in 1995 than a decade earlier.[10]

The result of this sharp shift in the relative risk of violent death from older to younger people has, in an important sense, been to dramatically increase the social cost of homicide. We can measure the extent of this tragedy through what public health researchers call "years of potential life lost," or YPLL. Obviously, the YPLL is greater when a fifteen-year-old dies than when a fifty-year-old does (measured against an estimate of their normal life expectancy). And the increasing proportion of minority young people among victims of homicide means that the YPLL for people of color has increased dramatically since the mid-1980s, especially among black men. In 1985, the YPLL due to homicide among black men stood at 1,956 per 100,000 population. By 1993, it had risen to 2,676—an increase of 37 percent (and 20 percent above its already high 1970 level). Years of life lost by black women rose from 400 to 518 per 100,000, or about 30 percent.

The impact of these rises is all the more telling because they have taken place simultaneously with falling loss of years of life for most other causes of death, notably heart disease and other ills in which medical advances have substantially improved life chances for people of all races. As a result, death by violence has become a far greater proportion of total life lost by people of color during the past generation. In 1970, 11 percent of the total YPLL among black men was due to homicide (and legal intervention). In 1985, the figure had risen to 15 percent, and with the explosion of black youth violence after the mid-1980s, rose to 19 percent by 1993. Unlike the sheer rate of deaths, then, the proportion of YPLL due to violence has increased steadily since 1970—a little-remarked escalation in the overall social cost of violence in the black community.[11]

The depth of the impact of violence on minority communities, more-over, is obscured when we concentrate on trends in homicide for the country as a whole. For the crisis of violence in minority communities has been far more concentrated in some areas and some social strata than in others. We can see some of the broad outlines of that concentration when we look at the startling rise of homicide rates in some cities, especially those with a high proportion of minorities in their population. This pattern remains starkly visible despite the much-celebrated drop in violent crime since the early 1990s.

We can compare reported homicide rates in 1968, at the time of the Kerner Report, with those for 1996—several years after we had suppos-edly "turned the corner" on crime in the cities—by looking first at cities with very large black populations. In 1968, for example, there were 195 reported homicides in Washington, D.C. By 1996 there were 397. In the meantime, Washington's population had declined considerably, meaning that the rate of homicide increased even faster than the absolute numbers by better than 175 percent. Washington's population, according to the 1990 census, was about 66 percent black.

In Detroit, which is 76 percent black, the homicide rate rose by about two-thirds between 1968 and 1996; in Baltimore, which is 59 percent black, the rate rose by three-quarters. It nearly doubled in Birmingham (63 percent black) and more than doubled in Memphis (55 percent black) and Philadelphia (40 percent black). It rose by more than 105 percent in Richmond, Virginia (55 percent black) and Jackson, Mississippi (56 percent black). It more than quadrupled in Gary, Indiana (81 percent black) and New Orleans (62 percent black). The increases were, astonishingly, even higher in some smaller cities with widespread poverty and very large black populations—more than quintupling, for example, in Camden, New Jersey, and Inglewood, California. Homicide rates also skyrocketed in a few cities with relatively small black populations, where violence was increasingly concentrated in compact, poverty-stricken communities, like Milwaukee, Wisconsin, where homicide rates tripled from 1968; and Minneapolis, where the increase was roughly 150 percent.[12]

These trends point to an even higher concentration of violence in inner cities, especially those with large concentrations of persistently poor minorities, than the national figures—bad enough in themselves—suggest. Studies of the types of homicide that grew the fastest in the inner cities—notably gang-related killings—drive the point home. In a study of drive-by shootings in Los Angeles in 1991, for example, a team of researchers from the University of Southern California found that almost all of the injuries and all of the deaths from drive-by shootings were among Hispanic and black youths (78 percent and 22 percent, respectively). Of 429 children and youths injured in drive-by shootings that year, only one was white and non-Hispanic. The incidence of injuries related to drive-by shootings among Hispanic girls was almost five times that among white Anglo boys.[13]

As this suggests, the racial disparities in the risks of violence apply not only to homicide. They also appear, only slightly less starkly, in other forms of violent crime. Measuring the extent of victimization by these crimes is harder than it is for homicide, and indeed all of the measures we have understate both the prevalence of nonfatal victimization by violence and its disproportionate impact on minorities. But even these imperfect measures show a distinctly troubling pattern.

Once source of evidence on these disparities, for example, is the National Criminal Victimization Survey (NCVS), published annually by the U.S. Bureau of Justice Statistics. The NCVS, based on a survey of sixty thousand households across the country, finds significant differences in the likelihood of victimization by what it calls "serious" violent crime, including robbery, rape, and aggravated assault. On average, in the three years from 1992 through 1994, 1 in 30 blacks, 1 in 35 Hispanics, and 1 in 58 whites were victims of a serious violent offense. Measured against their share of the population, the black rate of victimization was 2 times that of whites, and the Hispanic rate was about 1.7 times that of non-Hispanic whites. The disparities were sharper for robbery specifically; thus 1 in 48 blacks, 1 in 57 Hispanics, but only 1 in 101 whites were robbery victims during this period.[14]

These gaps are troubling enough, but they are clearly underestimated in this survey. That is mainly because the NCVS, as a household survey, leaves out important segments of the population who are among those at the highest risk of victimization by violence and who are also disproportionately black or Hispanic, including the homeless, people in institutions (jails, prisons, juvenile facilities), and anyone who lacks a stable connection to a household (or a telephone). Studies that adopt more direct methods of assessing the prevalence of violence, therefore, unsurprisingly find both higher levels of victimization overall and wider racial and ethnic gaps. A recent study of patients admitted to hospital emergency rooms for treatment of violence-related injuries points to the dimensions of this difference.[15] The Survey of Injured Victims of Violence (SIVV), carried out by the Bureau of Justice Statistics in 1994, found that the number of victims of violence actually treated in emergency rooms was roughly 2.5 times the number in the NCVS who reported being treated for violence in a hospital. And the racial disparity in rates of victimization was much greater. In the NCVS "aggravated assault" rates among blacks were about 1.7 times higher than for whites; in the SIVV, which did not restrict its population to those who were in stable households and also willing to report their victimization, the black rate of emergency room treatment for violent assaults in 1994—just over ten per thousand—was triple the "white" rate, which in this case included most Hispanics.

But even that figure—disturbing enough, especially when compared to the "white" figure—still understates the extraordinary devastation that violence has wrought in poorer minority communities. The SIVV surveys hospitals in all kinds of community, from inner cities to suburbs and rural areas. Studies that have focused on levels of victimization in the inner city alone have come up with figures that are considerably higher. A study of inner-city residents treated at hospital emergency rooms in poor neighborhoods in Philadelphia, for example, found that fully 40 percent of young black men had sustained a violent assault serious enough to send them to an emergency room in the four years, 1987–90.[16]

In a society in which high levels of violence are endemic across every racial and ethnic group, then, the risks of violent death or injury are far higher for minorities, especially blacks, and the disparities are increasing. The risks remain high, moreover, despite some developments that should have reduced them, notably, a smaller proportion of youth in the population and medical advances that have significantly improved our ability to keep the victims of violence alive. And what makes the devastating level of violence even more startling is that it persists in the face of our massive national investment in incarceration, which has been justified on the ground that it would sharply reduce violent crime.

An Explosion in Minority Incarceration

The toll of death and injury continues only modestly abated in minority communities despite the fact that vastly more minority men and women are behind bars. The basic patterns are unequivocal. By far the majority of prison inmates in the United States today are people of color, and their proportion of the prison population has grown. In 1995, according to the standard figures from the U.S. Bureau of Justice Statistics, the proportion of inmates in state and federal prisons who were white and non-Hispanic was about 36 percent. That is generally believed to be something of an overestimate, since a significant but unknown proportion of Hispanic inmates may be miscounted as "white" in many jurisdictions.

The figure, in any case, represents a decrease from 38 percent non-Hispanic whites in 1990 and roughly 41 percent in 1985. From 1985 to 1995, the number of Hispanic inmates rose by 219 percent, that of blacks by 146 percent, and that of whites (here including Hispanics) by 107 percent. (The number of prisoners of "other races," including Asian/Pacific Islanders and Native Americans, while it remains under 3 percent

of the total, has undergone the sharpest increase since 1985, nearly quad-
rupling in the course of a decade.) Adjusted to account for different rates
of increase in the general population, the incarceration rate for white
males rose by about 87 percent from 1985 to 1995; for black males, by
108 percent; and for Hispanic males, by 117 percent. There is some
roughness to these estimates, again, because of uncertainties about the
accuracy of the counts of Hispanic inmates, especially in the earlier years.
But there is no question about the general direction of this shift.[17]

Indeed, the magnitude of the shift is stronger, and the disparities even
sharper, if we focus on the state prison population alone; the overall
prison incarceration figure for non-Hispanic whites is brought up somewhat because they are a higher than usual proportion—about 44 percent
in 1995—of federal prisoners. That too may be partly the result of un-
dercounting, however, as substantial numbers of Hispanics are thought
to be unreported in federal prison statistics.[18] Among state prisoners in
1995, just 35 percent were non-Hispanic whites in 1995—down from
38 percent only five years earlier. Fully 49 percent—essentially half—of
state prisoners were non-Hispanic blacks. The situation in America's
local jails is only slightly less glaring: about 40 percent of jail inmates are
non-Hispanic whites, 44 percent are non-Hispanic blacks.

It is important to keep in mind, moreover, that the increasing proportion of prisoners of color does not reflect a fall in the absolute numbers
of white inmates; rather, that at a time when growing numbers of
Americans of all races were being put behind bars, the numbers grew
fastest for minorities. Between 1990 and 1995 alone, the number of
non-Hispanic white inmates in state prisons grew by a third. But it rose
by 45 percent for black non-Hispanics, 64 percent for Hispanics, and a
stunning 84 percent for "other" races.

Moving a little farther back in time—closer to the era of the Kerner
Report—the numbers become somewhat less reliable, but the trend is
nevertheless even clearer. In 1974, the non-Hispanic white proportion
of the state prison population was 45 percent—nearly half—versus just
over one-third today. Meanwhile, the Hispanic proportion shot from 6
percent to 14 percent. In local jails, similarly, Hispanics were 6 percent
of inmates in 1970, 10 percent in 1978, and an estimated 15 percent in
1995.[19]

One result is that an extraordinary proportion of minority men—
especially black, but increasingly Hispanic as well—are expected to
spend time behind bars. About 29 percent of black men will spend some
time in a state or federal prison (not counting local jails or juvenile

facilities) during their lives; the figure is 16 percent for Hispanic men and 4.4 percent for white men.[20] In the country as a whole, the incarceration rate for black males at any given time—here measured as the number behind bars in federal, state, and local institutions per thousand adult residents—reached close to seven thousand as we entered the latter part of the 1990s. The disparity between the black male incarceration rate and that for "white" males—here even including most Hispanic prisoners—was about 7.5 to 1, up from 6.7 to 1 as recently as 1990.[21] That figure represents only the tip of the iceberg, moreover, because it fails to count the even greater numbers who either left prison, were waiting to get in, or were otherwise "under the supervision" of criminal justice authorities. The Washington-based Sentencing Project, which pioneered these estimates, calculated that, as of 1995, about one in three young black men between ages twenty and twenty-nine are under criminal justice control nationally. In California, the figure is two in five; in Baltimore, Maryland, the figure is 56 percent.[22]

And though these numbers are for men, the pace of incarceration is even more astonishing for minority women. Largely as a result of the war on drugs, women of all races—great numbers of them low-level offenders—have been swept up into the nation's correctional system, often for long mandatory sentences. Among white (including most Hispanic) women, the incarceration rate since 1985 has risen twice as fast as it has for men, and the imbalance is only a little less for black women.[23] A black man was nineteen times as likely as a black woman to be behind bars in 1985 but only fifteen times as likely in 1995. It is still true that men of all races are far more likely than women of all races to be imprisoned. Such is the impact of the combination of race and gender in recent years, however, that, as recently as 1980, the incarceration rate for black women exceeded that for white men. Black women's incarceration rate is also higher than the rate of all incarceration in every advanced country in Western Europe.

These national averages, moreover, mask even more glaring—and surprising—differences in some states. The sheer number of black Americans in prison is greatest in big states like New York or California and in some southern states, including not very large ones. But the rate of black incarceration is higher in some states with smaller black populations, notably in New England and the Midwest, where the burden of imprisonment falls very disproportionately on black communities—and where relatively small proportions of whites go behind bars. In Alabama, there were more than 13,000 blacks in state prison in 1995, but blacks made up over a quarter of the state's overall population. In Wisconsin, there were fewer than 6,000 blacks in state prison, but blacks were only about 5 percent of the state's population. The result is that Wisconsin's black incarceration rate is nearly twice that of Alabama (about 2,050 versus 1,250 per 100,000 in 1995). Put another way, the ratio between blacks' share of the prison population and their share of the general state population is a relatively low 2.5 to 1 in Alabama and a startling 9 to 1 in Wisconsin. That is, blacks in Wisconsin are nine times as likely to be in prison as we would expect on the basis of their population alone. The figure is 10 to 1 in New Hampshire, and a mind-boggling 13 to 1 in Iowa and Minnesota. By the same token, these are also states in which the disparity between black and white imprisonment rates is the most gaping. In some southern states, the large numbers of blacks in prison are counterbalanced, to some extent, by the fact that there are also large numbers of whites in prison. The white incarceration rate in Alabama, for example, is twice that in Wisconsin and four times the rate in Minnesota. As a result, the disparity between the black and white rates of imprisonment in Alabama, while still glaring, is far less so than in the northern states: about 5 to 1, versus 18 to 1 in Wisconsin (and Iowa) and 25 to 1 in Minnesota.[24]

This is by no means to suggest that the racial policies in these northern states are necessarily harsher than those in southern states with long histories of segregation. What these figures most clearly point to is the pervasive white poverty in many southern states and its predictable impact on correctional populations. The northern states with very high racial disparities in incarceration tend to be the states in which social and economic disadvantage is heavily concentrated among a relatively small minority population and in which severe white poverty is relatively rare.

Nationally, what has most driven the rising proportion of minority inmates since the mid-eighties has been the war on drugs. Of the roughly 537,000 more inmates in state prisons in 1995 than in 1985, 117,000 (about 22 percent) were black drug offenders. Overall, the number of black state prison inmates grew by 132 percent during those years, while the number of "white" inmates (here, including most Hispanics) rose by 109 percent. That difference is significant, but it pales beside the difference in rates of growth of inmates sent to prison for drug offenses. "White" prisoners sentenced for drug offenses increased by slightly more than 300 percent during the decade, but among blacks the increase was a stunning 700 percent. Keep in mind that this is within the space of about a decade. Put another way, as recently as 1985 only one in twenty-seven state prisoners was a black sentenced for a drug offense. By 1995, one in seven was.[25]

But though drug offenses are the key factor in the shifting racial proportions in the prisons, they are not the only one. In California, for example, blacks are 7 percent of the state's general population but 44 percent of inmates sentenced on a "third strike" under the state's 1994 "three strikes and you're out" law. A 1996 analysis found that blacks were being imprisoned under the three strikes law at thirteen times the rate for whites.[26]

The Role of Discrimination in the Criminal Justice System

In the face of numbers like these, no one seriously denies that the racial and ethnic disparities in American prisons have reached devastating, and unprecedented, levels. But there is much less agreement on what these disparities mean, on why the prison population has become steadily darker and the prisons and jails have come to loom over minority communities to an extent unparalleled in our history.

Since the 1960s, there have been three waves of explanation of the why of minority overrepresentation in the justice system. The differences among these explanations revolve around the question of how much the racial disparities reflect the fact that minorities commit more of the kinds of offenses that get people incarcerated and how much reflect systematic differences in the way black (or more rarely, Hispanic) offenders are treated within the justice system.

There is no real disagreement at the extremes of this argument. No one seriously denies that the relative level of violent offending (for street crimes) is higher among blacks than among whites. And given what we know about the connections between social exclusion, family disintegration, and violence, we could hardly expect otherwise. Likewise, no one seriously denies that plain racism—even of the most blatant kind—still exists, at least some of the time, in some jurisdictions around the country. The serious question is how much of the minority disproportion can be explained by the higher levels (and greater seriousness) of minority offending and how much can be explained by extralegal factors, including discrimination.

The distinction is not just an abstract one, for how we answer this question powerfully influences how we think about policies to combat the problem of racial disparity in the justice system. If the root of the problem is simply that black people are committing more violent crimes, then reducing the disparity means reducing the factors that cause blacks to offend at higher rates in the first place. The implication—sometimes explicit—is that we should largely forget about addressing racial disparities by making the justice system operate in less biased ways. If, on the other hand, the racial disparities reflect both structural forces that push more blacks into serious crime and systematic discriminatory practices— deliberate or otherwise—within the criminal justice system, then focused efforts to right the wrongs within the system itself, whatever they may be, remain crucial.

Roughly speaking, the three waves of explanation since the time of the Kerner Report have moved from an emphasis on the pervasiveness of discrimination in the justice system, to a denial of discrimination's significance, to a more balanced assessment that reaffirms the importance of institutional discrimination while acknowledging the reality of higher rates of minority crime. Through the sixties, it was widely agreed that overt racial discrimination pervaded American criminal justice, a position expressed in landmark studies like Gunnar Myrdal's *American Dilemma* and in the (relatively few) empirical studies of the processing of minorities in the criminal justice system.[27] At that time, overt discrimination—especially in the South—was impossible to hide, and some studies backed up anecdotal observation with hard numbers. Few, however, controlled for the effect of legal factors on the apparent racial disparities they found; few studies, that is, adjusted the ratio of blacks to whites at various stages of the justice system to account for the type of offense, prior record, and other legally relevant factors that might explain some of the disproportion.

Accordingly, more sophisticated studies, mainly appearing since the 1970s, tried to do just that. Criticizing the methodological inadequacies of the earlier studies, they often found that, when the seriousness of offense and other legal factors were taken into account, little if any of the racial disparity at various levels of justice processing remained "unexplained." The result, even for those strongly critical of racial disproportion in the criminal justice system, was to focus attention away from bias in the system itself. As one researcher put it, "From every available data source . . . the evidence seems clear that the main reason that black incarceration rates are substantially higher than those for whites is that black crime rates for imprisonable crimes are substantially higher than those for whites." Accordingly, focusing on the conditions that promote high black crime rates was more constructive than trying to "ferret out a willful and pervasive bias in a criminal justice system in which most officials and participants believe in racial equality and worry about the racial patterns they see every day."[28]

But a third wave of research, mostly produced since the beginning of the 1990s, suggests a more complicated picture. It does so for several reasons. Much of the research finding little racial discrimination in criminal justice was, as it turns out, also burdened by methodological weaknesses. Sometimes, the problem was that it focused on only one stage of the justice process rather than on the process as a whole, in all of its multiple decision points; sometimes, that it overaggregated the evidence—that is, it lumped together the experience of every state, when in fact different states (or jurisdictions within them) may vary enormously in the way they deal with offenders of different races. And the distinction between intrinsic, or legal, factors affecting the treatment of minorities in the system versus overt, or willful, bias may itself have been misleadingly simplistic, obscuring patterns of institutional racism, which, while not necessarily reflecting willful racial hostilities on the part of people working in the criminal justice system nevertheless fosters policies that systematically work to the disadvantage of black or Hispanic offenders. The conduct of the drug war, especially since the mid-1980s, has been an example of this pattern—especially the emphasis on open street drug sales and the gaping disparity in sentencing between powder and crack cocaine—but it is by no means the only example.

The Research

The second wave view of racial disparities in imprisonment—that they are almost wholly explainable by higher rates of serious criminality among minorities—was based on a few influential studies done in the 1980s. Comparing black arrest rates for violent crimes with black imprisonment rates across the country, one study concluded that roughly 80 percent of the racial disparity between black and white rates of incarceration was explainable by higher rates of black violence.[29] Using somewhat different methods, a second study compared incarceration rates with crime rates based on victim reports and concluded that an even higher proportion (roughly 85 percent) of the racial disparity in imprisonment could be explained by the higher rates of black violence.[30]

The key problem with this kind of conclusion, however, has been sharply illuminated in a third study, which points out that even if we ignore the (very important) issue of potential racial bias in the arrest rates themselves, using national data may mask the existence of far sharper racial disparities in some states (not to mention specific jurisdictions within them).[31] If we compare racial arrest rates with imprisonment rates for each state separately, a very different, and more troubling, picture emerges: some states actually imprison fewer blacks than would be expected given the proportion of blacks arrested for violent crimes. Those states, moreover, are not easily predictable; they included (in 1981–82) Indiana, Wisconsin, Missouri—and Mississippi!

At the other extreme, the racial disparity in imprisonment in many other states was only weakly explained by higher black arrest rates. Again, the states with large unexplained racial differences in imprisonment are not predictable and are not confined to one region of the country. High black arrest rates explained considerably less than half of the racial imbalance in imprisonment in Massachusetts, for example, and even less in New Hampshire. Just 54 percent of the disparity in imprisonment in Alabama was explained by higher black arrests and 40 percent in Washington State. This study convincingly demonstrates that some states, and even some jurisdictions within states, deliver justice with greater equality than others.[32] It also suggests one of the key reasons that earlier research found only equivocal evidence of systematic racial discrimination.

The effect of discrimination may even be stronger in jail populations than in state prisons. That is one conclusion of a study of the sentencing of minor felony offenders and misdemeanants in New York State during the early 1990s.[33] Controlling for a wide range of legal considerations, including gender, offense type, seriousness of the charge, and county of jurisdiction, roughly one of three black defendants sentenced to a jail term would have received a more lenient sentence had they been treated the same as comparable white offenders. Disparities in the treatment of offenders of different races annually sent four thousand black defendants to jail who would not have gone behind bars had they been treated the same as similarly situated whites. The effects were less powerful in explaining disparities in the state prison population but still accounted for three hundred extra sentences to state prison for blacks every year.

For many years, research on racial disparities has been less ambivalent about treatment of juveniles than treatment of adults. On balance, most of the research on juveniles since the 1960s has leaned toward the finding that, in many jurisdictions, a pattern of discrimination exists, especially for blacks, and that it seems to focus on several levels of the juvenile justice system—from differences in the way police respond to youths of different races to differences in the severity of sentences. The most recent and sophisticated research bears out the earlier findings and sheds additional light on what explains them.

A study of the processing of delinquency cases in Florida in the late eighties found that nonwhite youth were disadvantaged at "each successive stage" of juvenile justice processing; as a result, the population became increasingly darker as youths moved through the juvenile justice system.[34] Nonwhite youths were 21 percent of the population between the ages of ten and seventeen years, but were 29 percent of youths referred to intake and 44 percent of those incarcerated or transferred to adult court. Controlling for other factors, including the seriousness of the youths' current offenses and their prior records, reduced the racial disparities somewhat but not entirely; at the end stage of the process, for example, the chance of being committed to a juvenile institution or transferred to adult court was almost twice as high for nonwhite as for white youths. Indeed, what the researchers describe as a "consistent pattern of unequal treatment" occurred at every stage of the juvenile justice process, though more glaringly at some stages than others. Nonwhite youths referred for delinquent acts were more likely to be held in preadjudicatory detention, to be formally processed in juvenile court, and to receive the most formal or most restrictive judicial dispositions.

This pattern, troubling in itself, is even more so because it is likely to represent the stages of what will become a long-term career for all too many of the youths thus processed. What happens to them in the juvenile justice system will powerfully affect what happens to them later in adult courts and prisons. Interviews with juvenile justice personnel suggest some of the most likely explanations for the different outcomes for nonwhite youths. There is widespread agreement, for example, that nonwhite youths "penetrate" more deeply into the system because their families are seen as uncooperative or are deemed incapable of providing sufficient support or control. Officials often believe, too, that the only way to get minority youths the services they need (like drug treatment or psychiatric help) is to commit them to the formal juvenile system, since their families cannot afford private ones. But though these strategies may be well intended, they result in a greater likelihood that nonwhite youths will be institutionalized and, accordingly, add to the "baggage" that black or Hispanic youths carry with them, as their early incarceration becomes part of their record that will be considered when they next encounter the criminal justice system. "What may begin with good intentions at an earlier stage ultimately becomes a self-fulfilling prophecy. The influence of race is obscured as decisions to formally prosecute and detain in the past are used to justify more severe sanctions for youths returning to the system."[35]

These findings are backed by other recent studies of the role of race and ethnicity in juvenile justice processing. A study of juvenile justice in five counties in a midwestern state found that although legal factors—including the seriousness of the offense, carrying a weapon, and prior record—were indeed important, they did not by themselves explain the fate of minority juveniles.[36] Looking specifically at the decision to detain or not detain youths at three stages—arrest, juvenile justice intake, and the preliminary hearing—they found that when all of the key legal factors were accounted for, youths who were black or Hispanic "were consistently more likely to be placed in secure detention." Moreover, this remained true even when a range of social factors was also taken into account.

Thus, consistent with earlier research, this study found that poor youths from single-parent families, other things equal, were more likely to be securely detained. That tendency worked to the disadvantage of minority youths, but even when family structure and economic status were controlled, black and Hispanic youths were still more likely to be detained by authorities than their Anglo counterparts. The researchers concluded that minority youths were systematically disadvantaged both indirectly—because they were more often from the kinds of social strata and the types of family most likely to face severe sanctions—and directly, in some way not clearly explainable from the evidence. What might that be? The researchers found some evidence that minority offenders may have been charged with more serious offenses in the first place, in part because of a tendency on the part of authorities to stereotype minority youths as more dangerous. And once the first decision to treat a youth as dangerous and in need of detention had been made by police, it may have a cumulative effect in later decisions to detain.

Another potential explanation for the unexplained disparities in black and white outcomes in juvenile justice is offered in a study of counties in several states across the country.[37] Counties with higher levels of "underclass poverty," as well as a greater degree of racial inequality, were likely to make greater use of more severe sanctions for juvenile offenders, including secure detention before disposition and out-of-home placement. The effects were strongest for blacks, a pattern "consistent with the idea that underclass black males are viewed as a threatening group to middle-class populations and thus will be subjected to increased formal social control by the juvenile justice system."[38]

Research that focuses on sentencing outcomes, for that matter, may already stack the deck against a finding of systematic discrimination, because it takes the higher arrest rate of certain minorities as a given—as a reflection, that is, of higher actual rates of offending. But the most careful research we have since the sixties points to considerable discrimination at the stage of police encounters with people of color, especially young people. This research shows some of the ways in which this process takes place at the arrest stage or even before, in strategic decisions by police about how and where to deploy resources and in their attitudes toward youths of different ethnic and racial groups.[39] The study found wide agreement among both police and community residents that black and Hispanic neighborhoods were routinely under heavier police surveillance and that in some communities at some times police engaged in especially aggressive surveillance of youths of color known to be gang members.

There has been relatively little research exploring the sources of the disproportionate involvement of Hispanics in the criminal justice system. Yet what we know generally parallels the findings for blacks: while much of the disproportion in imprisonment reflects a pattern of widespread social disadvantage, which breeds relatively high rates of street crime, some of it reflects criminal justice practices that are "unexplained' by legal factors. Thus, one study found that, controlling for such factors as the seriousness of the offenses and the offender's prior record, Hispanic drug offenders in Miami received longer sentences than non-Hispanic whites.[40] Another found that Hispanic defendants with prior records tended to receive considerably harsher sentences than whites.[41] A third study found that the treatment of Hispanic defendants varied enormously depending on the jurisdiction.[42] In Tucson, Hispanic offenders fared no worse than their Anglo counterparts in the late 1970s and, in some respects, were treated more leniently. In El Paso, on the other hand, Hispanics were less likely to be released at pretrial, more likely to be convicted in jury trials, and, if found guilty, likely to receive harsher sentences than Anglos.

Summarizing the Research: Policy Choices

It seems clear that the enormous racial disparities in incarceration result from a mix of deep social factors and systematic, if sometimes indirect, justice system policies that work to the disadvantage of minorities. Whatever the balance of those factors, what is undeniable is that the relationship between minority communities and the criminal justice system has been radically transformed since the time of the Kerner Report. We have barely begun to measure the long-range impact of the vast increases in minority incarceration. But the evidence we do have suggests that the impact on the hardest-hit minority communities will be profound. Rapid rises in incarceration, for example, have created a large, floating population of ex-inmates, who flow from poverty-stricken neighborhoods to the jails and prisons and back again and who have only bleak chances of economic success of contributing to the stability of their communities. Going to prison reduces the chances that young black men will be employed at reasonable wages, making their return to prison more likely, in a vicious circle. At the same time, it means they are also more likely to be drawn into illegal labor markets, especially drug sales; and in turn, the persistence of a widespread and volatile drug trade undercuts the community's capacity for economic viability and social control.[43]

Massive rises in minority incarceration can also have direct and destructive effects on families. The long-term consequences of these effects may haunt us well into the future. Removing hundreds of thousands of men from the community destabilizes families, makes the formation of new families far less likely, and removes what is at least a potential source of support for many low-income women. Even more directly, the still-faster rise in incarceration of women has left many minority communities with a growing population of parentless children, who are increasingly dependent on public support or the uncertain care of relatives. We do not yet know what the consequences—either economic and developmental—will be. But the possibilities are alarming.[44]

The huge investment in incarceration in many states has caused a dramatic shift of resources away from constructive social expenditure, including public spending that could have a long-term preventive impact on violent crime. The current economic boom has improved the fiscal condition of most states, at least for the moment, but many are still suffering deeply from years of starving other public spending in favor of building prisons. Nowhere is this more true than in public higher education. In California, where four times as many black men are "enrolled" in the state's prisons as in its public universities, only one new state college—but twenty-one new state prisons—have been built since the mid-1980s. Among other things, that has meant that at least 200,000 young Californians—mostly of low to modest income—are effectively excluded from public higher education in the state.[45]

More subtly, the great increases in minority imprisonment have served to mask the broader social crisis in urban America and to deflect serious efforts to deal with it. In a sense, prison expansion has become a replacement for constructive social policies we failed to launch. The prisons are what we have *instead* of an antipoverty policy, *instead* of a public housing policy, *instead* of effective drug treatment or mental health policies. Employment rates perhaps are most telling: in 1995, 762,000 black men were unemployed and another 511,000 were in prison. Adding the imprisoned to the unemployment count would raise the black male unemployment rate in that year by two-thirds, from just under 11 percent to almost 18 percent. One of the reasons the "compassionate, massive, and sustained" national effort to resolve the urban crisis, which the Kerner Report called for, was never realized may be that we instead hid a good part of that crisis behind prison walls.

That choice may be the most troubling aspect of today's situation with respect to race and criminal justice. In the face of the tragic mixture of endemic minority violence and mass incarceration, the country remains complacent. There is little sustained outcry and no articulate policy, and therein lies the challenge for the next century.

7

Racism and the Poor: Integration and Affirmative Action as Mobility Strategies

William L. Taylor

In March 1968, the Kerner Commission issued its report warning of the dangers of a nation divided into two societies, separate and unequal.[1] Less than a month later, Dr. Martin Luther King Jr., the most eloquent and persuasive voice in the effort to break down walls of segregation and establish racial and social justice, was struck down by an assassin.

Ever since, those who have sought to keep Dr. King's dream alive have had to wage a difficult battle to overcome new rationalizations for the existence of inequality and increasing calls for separatism. It is striking, in reviewing the three decades since the Kerner Commission Report and King's death, to realize that almost all of the major legislative and judicial initiatives that have sustained the effort for equal opportunity—the Supreme Court's decision in *Brown v. Board of Education,* the Civil Rights Act of 1964, the Head Start program, the Elementary and Secondary Education Act of 1965, and other elements of the War on Poverty—were in place *before* the events of 1968.[2]

Several other important policy events occurred in the five years that followed. The Civil Rights Act of 1968 barred discriminatory practices in housing.[3] In the *Green, Swann,* and *Keyes* cases, the Supreme Court prescribed effective school desegregation remedies in the South and set forth rules against intentional segregation in the school districts of the North and West.[4] Further, the Court's unanimous decision in *Griggs v. Duke Power Co.* broadly interpreted fair employment law to bar unintentional job discrimination practices that harmed minorities and could not be justified by business necessity.[5]

Over the last two decades, the most notable positive developments have been the extensions of civil rights guarantees to members of other groups that have been victims of systemic discrimination, particularly women, Hispanic Americans, and people with disabilities;[6] and the legislative restoration of rights and remedies that had been limited by the restrictive interpretation of civil rights laws on the part of an increasingly conservative Supreme Court.[7] Only in rare instances did statutes or court decisions seek to remove barriers to equal opportunity faced by the minority poor.

In a sense then, the drive for equality has been running on empty for a quarter of a century, sustained by laws and moral authority whose origins are remembered only dimly by millions of Americans. Although the officially sanctioned caste system that replaced slavery in the South and the sanction of racism throughout the nation are gone, racial animosity and fear still lie just beneath the surface and have erupted in recent years with frightening regularity in places such as Miami, Florida; Forsythe County, Georgia; and Howard Beach, Bensonhurst, and Crown Heights in New York City. The 1992 uprisings in Los Angeles, spurred by the acquittal of police officers accused of beating Rodney King, had a far more devastating impact in the minority community than the counterpart events in the 1960s that gave rise to the Kerner Commission.[8]

More daunting still are the combination of race and poverty and the seemingly impersonal structures and institutions that deprive the minority poor of opportunities for advancement. When the Kerner Commission wrote its report in 1968, many cities were still great centers of employment and economic activity. Now, employment and economic wealth have shifted to suburbs and to "new cities," while the movement of middle-class citizens (including the minority middle class) out of cities has intensified.[9] The growing wealth of suburbs has brought superior education and other public services, often financed without great difficulty out of local property and income taxes. For the minority poor in cities, services have declined. Today, cities face a form of triage in seeking to meet a host of health, social, housing, and education needs.[10]

In the face of these difficulties, what is surprising is not that the movement for equality has faltered but that it persists and that people continue to move out of the shadows of deprivation and discrimination to lead productive lives. The longevity of the movement is a tribute to the power of the idea of equality embodied in the Fourteenth Amendment and to a recognition during the 1960s that implementation required affirmative effort to undo the effects of past wrongs. The staying power of the movement is due also to the ability of so many minority citizens to use *Brown* and other decisions as a means of empowering themselves through education, employment, and political and community action and to the fact that race continues to be the central dilemma of our society.

This chapter is premised on a belief that the relevant test for racial justice in contemporary America is how well we serve those who are worst off in our society, focusing almost exclusively on conditions affecting the life chances of people who live in concentrated poverty in our nation's cities. While poverty remains a problem that transcends color lines, those who live in *concentrated* poverty are almost exclusively African Americans and Hispanic Americans.[11] This situation did not come about accidentally. Discrimination on account of race and skin color has not only limited the economic opportunities of minorities but also has kept them confined geographically to urban ghettos and barrios, usually densely populated, where they face barriers that are greater than those encountered by other poor people.

It is beyond the scope of this chapter to propose comprehensive policies for dealing with minority poverty. Rather I examine the utility of two long-standing national policies—desegregation and affirmative action—in providing opportunity for the minority poor. My thesis is that the two policies, often reviled these days as out of fashion or as serving only the needs of the middle class, have in fact been mainstays of what little antipoverty policy the nation has had over the past three decades.

Pursuit of desegregation and affirmative action has helped to create conditions in which many minority citizens have been able to lift themselves out of poverty and join the swelling ranks of the black and Latino middle class. Clearly, neither policy is sufficient as an antipoverty strategy. But they remain necessary policies, and abandonment of either would leave the minority poor more bereft of hope than they already are.

Desegregation as an Antipoverty Strategy

When the Supreme Court in the 1954 *Brown* decision struck down the laws of southern and border states commanding racial segregation in public schools, its unanimous opinion stressed the social science evidence of harm to black children, stating that segregation affects the "hearts and minds [of children] in a way unlikely ever to be undone."[12] There ensued a debate on whether the decision was grounded in equal protection jurisprudence (the right of black people to "exemption from unfriendly legislation against them distinctively as colored")[13] or whether it was based not on law but on the shifting sands of social science evidence. I count myself in the ranks of people who believe that the decision was solidly grounded in law and that Chief Justice Earl Warren stressed the social science evidence in an effort to persuade people that this far-reaching change in their lives had to be mandated because of the damage that was being done to little children. But most interesting and even surprising is that in more than four decades the sands have not shifted: the social science evidence on the *Brown* issues remains remarkably consistent, if not stronger.

In 1964, Congress mandated in the Civil Rights Act what became the largest education study ever conducted, an inquiry into the status of some 600,000 students in public schools. The Coleman Report concluded that socioeconomic and racial isolation are harmful to minority students and that the socioeconomic composition of classrooms (along with teacher competence) is one of the most important variables in determining educational outcomes.[14]

In 1997, another large congressionally mandated report was issued, an evaluation of the effectiveness of Title I of the Elementary and Secondary Education Act (the $7 billion program of federal aid to disadvantaged children). After studying the progress of thousands of students over several years, researchers found results very similar to those of the Coleman Report.[15] Specifically, the report found that poor children attending schools that were 75 percent or more nonpoor did far better on test of reading ability than their counterparts who attended schools that were 75 percent or more poor in student composition.[16]

The efficacy of school desegregation as an antipoverty strategy is bolstered by other important studies and data. Striking evidence of progress in the performance of black children over the years is found in the scores of thirteen- and seventeen-year-olds on reading tests conducted by the widely respected National Assessment of Educational Progress (NAEP).[17] According to one analysis, "by conservative estimates [the scores] indicate a reduction in the gap between African Americans and White students over the past 20 years of roughly 50 percent when the students are 17 years old."[18] Another analysis of the NAEP data concluded that, while gains made by white students between 1970 and 1990 were about as great as expected, the scores of black and Latino students increased by about *two-thirds more than predicted.*[19]

There is evidence that desegregation played an important role in this progress. Black elementary students in the Southeast recorded the greatest gains in reading on the NAEP assessments during the 1970s, the gains taking place during the period when school desegregation was occurring all across the region for the first time.[20] This strong indication of a link between desegregation and academic achievement is reinforced by case studies of particular communities that desegregated during the 1970s. These studies reveal that in many cases where the desegregation process was begun early in a child's career, the scores of minority students increased, in some cases modestly and in others significantly.[21] But the benefits to poor minority children flowing from desegregation are not simply a matter of better achievement scores. Other studies show that, in the long term, black students attending desegregated schools are more likely to complete high school, to enroll in and graduate from four-year desegregated colleges, and to major in subjects that lead to remunerative jobs and professions.[22]

From my own experience in representing a class of black children in school litigation in St. Louis, I can testify about the positive results stemming from desegregation. In 1983 a settlement was reached in that case that resulted in the largest voluntary metropolitan school desegregation program in the nation, with some thirteen thousand black youngsters from the city enrolled in sixteen predominantly white systems in the suburbs. Three of every four transfer students are poor; yet they complete high school at about twice the rate of their counterparts in racially isolated city schools and attend college at a rate that is three times the national average for black high school graduates.[23]

The reasons for these striking contrasts are not difficult to discern and have nothing to do with the canard that desegregation advocates hold the patronizing opinion that there is some magic for black children in sitting next to white children. First of all, in schools dominated by a middle-class or affluent population, parents are practiced in holding the school accountable for results, in ensuring that the curriculum and resources are up-to-date and adequate, and in securing the replacement of principals and teachers who are not performing adequately. Low-income schools also have concerned parents, but they generally lack the clout to bring about change.

Second, the hallmark of more affluent schools is high expectations of all students, a creed that is spread by principals, teachers, and parents and that is internalized by students. (High expectations are not extended automatically to minority and low-income students who transfer in, however. Educational leadership is needed to ensure that these students do not become victims of a dual standard.) High schools are places in which "students instruct each other how to live in America."[24] Once, in hearings held by the U.S. Commission on Civil Rights in the 1960s, I asked a black high school student to describe the differences between her old inner-city school and the more affluent, desegregated school to which she had transferred. "In my old school," she replied, "a student might ask another whether she planned to go to college; in my new school they ask 'which college are you going to.'" Nor is peer influence restricted to the matter of high expectations. Minority and low-income students gain access not only to better counseling but also to a host of informal lessons in how to get ahead in American society.

None of this is intended to suggest that substantial educational improvement cannot take place in racially and socioeconomically isolated schools. In every big city in the nation there are a handful of such schools that are producing results, usually through a combination of strong educational leadership, high standards and expectations, capable and dedicated teachers, and the development of school-parent ties. But these success stories have proven difficult to replicate, especially in an era when the once-captive pool of talented women and minority teachers has other opportunities, and inner-city schools have difficulty in attracting and retaining capable teachers.

The virtue of the St. Louis metropolitan initiative and other desegregation programs is that students who are minority and poor become participants in systems that are already successful in producing positive educational outcomes. While care must be taken that the minority students are treated equitably and derive the maximum benefit for their learning environments, that effort is less challenging than trying to rebuild an unsuccessful system from the ground up. Indeed, the danger now is that a conservative Supreme Court will draw the curtain on the *Brown* era and sanction a return to more segregated schools and a racially divided society. In the nineties, for the first time, the overall trend is toward resegregation,[25] and coincidentally or not, the gap between the performance of minority and white students, which had been narrowing for two decades, has begun to widen.[26]

On the occasion of the fortieth anniversary of the entry of black students into Central High School in Little Rock, President Bill Clinton said that "the alternative to integration is . . . disintegration."[27] He was speaking of the tendency of racial isolation to breed fear, mistrust, and division. It is equally clear that a return to segregation will cut off avenues of opportunity that have provided mobility for the minority poor. It will take acts of strong and courageous leadership to avert these results.

Affirmative Action as a Mobility Strategy

Affirmative action, a policy born in the 1960s, has evolved to meet the practical need of applying civil rights law in ways that provide real opportunity for people who have been denied it in the past. Affirmative action first appeared as a federal policy in President John Kennedy's executive order prohibiting discrimination by government contractors. The policy was initially applied to require corporations employing few minority workers to engage in affirmative outreach, for example, advertising in minority media and recruiting at black colleges, in an effort to stimulate more applications. After several years, there were few gains to report; institutional inertia was strong in many industries, and hiring through the grapevine, using current employees (almost all white), worked against change. Moreover, in some areas like the construction trades, the preference of dominant white groups to work with "their own kind" was so deeply entrenched as to resist effective affirmative action.

In response, the administrations of Lyndon Johnson and Richard Nixon developed the concept of goals and timetables. The notion was to achieve civil rights objectives by applying techniques familiar to the business world. The goals were not rigid and employers were not called upon to hire unqualified applicants, but by adopting a results-oriented approach, it was hoped that real progress could be made. In fact, these hopes were not disappointed. Goals and timetables became the basis of broad consent agreements that the government entered into in the seventies with AT&T and the steel industry, both to end discrimination and to establish processes for the future hiring and promotion of minorities and women.[28] Affirmative action also tempered the increasing tendency of employers to mechanically apply the results of tests (most of them invalidated) to select employees.

Contrary to the claims of critics, affirmative action policies have not been designed or implemented primarily to benefit middle-class people. In fact, the most striking gains have occurred in occupations and trades not usually associated with advantaged status, such as law enforcement, fire fighting, over-the-road trucking, and skilled construction work. In law enforcement, for example, the numbers of black police officers nearly doubled from 1970 to 1980 as a result of affirmative action litigation and enforcement efforts. In Philadelphia, after the initiation of goals and timetables for federal contractors, the proportion of skilled minority construction workers rose from less than 1 percent to more than 12 percent.[29]

Affirmative action policies in higher education have evolved in ways similar to their development in the employment field. Just as affirmative action in employment is applied mainly at the entry level, affirmative action in higher education is applied at the admission stage. Once applicants pass the gateways, they must succeed by dint of their own efforts. Affirmative action does not guarantee success—only an opportunity to compete. As in employment, critics have charged that the beneficiaries of affirmative action in higher education are already advantaged. This view is contradicted by studies showing, for example, that of the increased enrollment of minorities in medical schools in the 1970s, significant numbers were from families of low income and job status.[30]

Perhaps the most encouraging story to come out of the civil rights revolution is the emergence of a large, strong, black middle class, not totally freed from the wounds of racism but able to participate more fully in American society. Surprisingly little scholarly attention has been given to the dynamics of this change—how victories won in the courts and Congress have been translated into tangible opportunities for people to make changes in their own lives. But clues emerge from some of the research. A study that explored the potential explanations for the major gains made by black teenagers in reading proficiency—gains that cut the gap with whites almost in half—found that, among the factors contributing to these gains is the fact that the number of black parents with college degrees or experience quadrupled during the two decades, reaching 25 percent in the 1990s.[31] What accounts for this tremendous change? Certainly, opportunities for a better education from kindergarten through high school, provided through desegregation, were one factor. Surely, too, the affirmative action policies adopted by many colleges and universities provided opportunities to students of color who had been denied opportunities in the past. Many took full advantage of the opportunity, worked hard, got their degrees, found better and more remunerative jobs than their predecessors, married, and formed stable families. All of this created an environment in which their children could achieve, as reflected on the NAEP assessments.

The positive dynamic, while receiving little attention, is a counter to the well-publicized negative cycle of unemployment, poor education, and social pathology, yet the attack on affirmative action in the courts and by political leaders threatens one of the key elements of this dynamic. Affirmative action is no substitute for other policies designed to produce jobs and education, to rebuild communities, and to strengthen families, but in a nation that has not demonstrated a readiness to make the investments needed to effectuate these other policies, it would be folly to discard affirmative action, a policy that has made practical contributions toward achieving the same goal.

Judicial rulings against affirmative action in California and Texas have resulted in a dramatic drop in the enrollment of students of color in undergraduate and professional programs at colleges and universities. This should send a shudder through all of us. Unless countered, the ultimate result will be a halt in the progress of the last three decades and a swelling of the ranks of those who, lacking opportunity, sink into poverty and dependency.

Conclusion

America in 1998 is in many ways afflicted by the same racial schizophrenia that prevailed when the Kerner Report was published thirty years ago.

We see images of racial harmony on our television screens, in advertisements and shows, even while some scholarly books explicitly or implicitly endorse theories of white supremacy.[32] In many ways, the undeniable progress that has been made hinders efforts to extirpate the substantial vestiges of racism that remain: middle-class white Americans may feel that their acceptance of people of color who are most like them gives them permission to reject and even demonize people of color who appear to be different. Stereotypes that in the past have been used to impugn the character, intelligence, industry, and morals of people of color have been replaced by almost identical stereotypes applied to poor people. While open racial stereotyping is no longer acceptable, bashing the poor occurs without restraint on the floor of Congress and in other public places.

This schizophrenia is reflected in public policy making as well. In

1994, Congress adopted bold education reform legislation premised on the finding that "research clearly shows that children, including low-achieving children, can succeed when expectations are high and all children are given the opportunity to learn challenging material."[33] At the very same time, lawyers for the State of Missouri and other states that had until recently deliberately segregated their schools were arguing that public schools could not be expected to close the gap between white and black students because of the poverty of the latter. Demography is destiny, they argue in effect, and it is not reasonable to ask public schools to continue to perform their historic role of helping poor people to become educated enough to lift themselves out of poverty.

There is comfort to be found in the fact that in endorsing desegregation and affirmative action and in launching his race initiative, President Clinton is embracing the values and legacy of Dr. Martin Luther King Jr., Justice Thurgood Marshall, Chief Justice Earl Warren, and President Lyndon Johnson. But in the 1960s, oratory was accompanied by policy and action, and there is concern about whether that is happening today.

I offer two modest suggestions here. While the days of major school desegregation litigation in the federal courts may be ending, there is every reason to embrace the success that desegregation has brought in other forums of public policy making. For example, federal education law now identifies as a potential remedy for failing schools an option for students trapped in those schools to transfer to successful schools, either in their own school districts or in the region. Such an option, while not framed as a desegregation remedy, would enable the successful metropolitan desegregation program in St. Louis to be replicated elsewhere. But for the remedy to become a reality, national leadership is needed, and states will have to establish the mechanisms, including transportation assistance, to make the programs accessible to poor families.[34]

Similarly, the future of federal and state affirmative action policies hangs in the balance and will ultimately be determined by a closely divided Supreme Court. For years, under the guiding hand of Justice William Brennan, the Court took a measured approach, weighing the need to redress past discrimination against the settled interests of incumbent white workers. Under the present Rehnquist Court, the scales have shifted, and challenged affirmative action policies are required to meet a heavy burden of justification.

Critics of affirmative action say facilely that using race as a factor could be replaced by the use of socioeconomic status. But such a change would render affirmative action harder to administer and less effective in providing opportunities to those who need them. Rather, the leaders of universities should be thinking hard these days about the undue weight given to standardized tests as the primary factor in the admissions process. They should be thinking, too, about clearly articulating the mission of universities, including such questions as whether there is a place for students whose ability to excel in one or two areas is not reflected in general tests of aptitude or ability. Government officials, too, should be thinking about whether tests that disproportionately screen out minority applicants can be justified as educationally necessary, a standard required by the civil rights laws.

In 1998, the measuring rod for racial justice and equality—and for averting the Kerner Report fear of two societies, separate and unequal—is the one offered by President Franklin Roosevelt during the Great Depression: "The test of our progress is not whether we add more to the abundance of those who have much; it is whether we provide enough for those who have too little."[35] In the civil rights policies of the last three decades we have the foundation for meeting that test. The question is whether the nation will build on those policies or discard them.

8

Policy for the New Millennium

Lynn A. Curtis

Chapter 8 presents a policy framework for the new millennium that is complementary to the vision of the Kerner Commission but updated to address developments over the last thirty years.[1] To create the framework, I answer these questions:

- What are the facts on which to build an inner-city policy for the truly disadvantaged?
- What policy doesn't work?
- What policy works?
- What is the cost of replicating what works to scale and how can it be financed?
- What are the major political obstacles against replicating to scale?
- What is the political feasibility of a policy based on what works?
- What political alliance is needed to generate political will?

What Are the Facts?

The reversal of progress in the late 1970s and especially the 1980s[2] has left the United States with an unemployment rate today that former Secretary of Labor Ray Marshall has estimated at 15 percent.[3] This is far higher than the official "full employment" that pundits and politicians claim. The Center for Community Change in Washington, D.C., estimates the "jobs gap" to amount to more than 4.4 million persons needing work; a high proportion of them (I estimate well over 2 million) are

129

in the inner city.[4] For the first time in the twentieth century, most adults in many inner-city neighborhoods are not working in a typical week.[5]

Since the Kerner Report was issued thirty years ago, there have been other important trends:

- From 1977 to 1988, the incomes of the richest 1 percent in the United States increased by 120 percent, and the incomes of the poorest 20 percent in the United States decreased by 10 percent—all during a time of supply-side tax breaks for the rich and against the poor.[6]
- In the words of conservative analyst Kevin Phillips, this means that the rich got richer and the poor got poorer. The working class also got poorer. The middle class stayed about the same in absolute terms, so it, also, lost ground relative to the rich.[7]
- During the 1980s, child poverty increased by more than 20 percent, with racial minorities suffering disproportionately. Today, the child poverty rate in the United States is four times the average of Western European countries.[8]
- In the words of conservative scholar Glenn Loury, citing data from the President's Council of Economic Advisors (emphasis added): "The poverty rate of blacks, at just under a third, is still more than 3 times that of whites. In 1997, the median black family had . . . just three-fifths as much income as the median white family. This family-income ratio was actually a bit lower in 1997 than it had been in 1967. *Contrary to what conservatives claim, the growth in the number of single-parent black families explains only one-fifth of the racial gap in family incomes and poverty rates.*"[9]
- According to Loury, in 1997 the median African American family had one-tenth as much wealth at its disposal as the median white family.[10] Based on *New York Times* accounts, in terms of wealth and income, the United States is the most unequal industrialized country in the world, and is growing more unequal faster than any other industrialized country.[11]
- Twenty years ago, a corporate CEO made 35 times more than the average worker in the United States. Now the CEO's salary is 187 times higher. European and Japanese manufacturing workers now make 25 percent more in hourly wages than their American counterparts. Since the Kerner Report, the United States has had the most rapid growth in wage inequality in the Western world.[12]
- America's neighborhoods and schools are resegregating. Two-thirds

of African American students and three-fourths of Hispanic students now attend predominantly minority schools, one-third of each group in intensely segregated schools.[13]

- In urban public schools in poor neighborhoods, more than two-thirds of children fail to reach even the "basic" level on national tests.[14]
- America's housing policy for the poor and minorities has become prison building. During the 1980s and early 1990s, we tripled the number of prison cells at the same time that we reduced housing appropriations for the poor by more than 80 percent. Only one in four poor families can now get housing.[15]
- States now spend more per year on prisons than on higher education, while ten years ago spending priorities were just the opposite.[16]
- In the early 1990s, one of four young African American men was in prison, on probation, or on parole. By the late 1990s, this figure was one in three.[17]
- Today, according to the conservative economist Milton Friedman, the rate of incarceration of African American men in the United States is four times higher than the rate of incarceration of black men in South Africa during the pre-Nelson Mandela apartheid government.[18]
- Sentences for crack cocaine, used disproportionately by minorities, are much longer than sentences for powder cocaine, used disproportionately by whites.[19]
- Prisons disproportionately incarcerate minorities, but prison building has become a growth industry for whites in rural areas.[20]
- In the most prestigious study of the impact of prison building, a panel of the National Academy of Sciences concluded that "by itself the criminal justice response to violence could accomplish no more than running in place."[21]

Based on these data, it is fair to conclude that today, as we begin the new millennium, at least two breaches have continued or opened in America. These breaches are consistent with the Kerner Commission's prophesy thirty years ago on separate and unequal societies. The first breach is between those left behind in the inner city, who are disproportionately minorities, and Americans outside the inner city with more income, better education, and solid employment.[22] The second breach is between the poor, working class and middle class (for all races, urban and rural), on the one hand, and the rich, on the other.

What Doesn't Work?

The preceding data document the failure of our urban policy of the 1980s—much of which consisted of trickle-down supply-side tax breaks and affirmative action for the rich, welfare for corporations and prison building for the poor. Careful scientific evaluations[23] and assessments by *Business Week* and the conservative *Economist*[24] also have shown that enterprise zones have failed in their attempt to use tax breaks to lure corporations into inner cities to generate jobs for the truly disadvantaged. The main federal supply-side job training program of the 1980s, the Job Training Partnership Act, has failed out-of-school youth, according to the U.S. Labor Department and careful evaluations.[25] Boot camps have failed, based on the most comprehensive evaluations.[26]

These failed policies, and the accompanying disinvestment from the cities in the 1980s, often were presented to the public with political spin words like "volunteerism," "self-sufficiency," and "empowerment." Such political buzzwords remain in vogue today. With appropriate recognition of their strengths, weaknesses, and limitations, we have found that words as this have a role to play in national policy. However, used to excess, cynically, as public relations vehicles and without an understanding of what happens on the street, buzzwords like volunteerism, self-sufficiency, and empowerment can be used to cover up budget decisions against investing to scale in the children, youth, families, and neighborhoods of the inner city.

Some of this false political rhetoric is meant to camouflage a double standard when it comes to resources. We are told that corporate executives need high salaries, competent and full-time support staff, and the latest high-tech equipment. In the early 1990s, the Gulf War successfully was carried out with well-trained, salaried staff and cutting-edge equipment. Staff and equipment cost money. Yet, when it comes to the poor and the inner city, we often are told by naysayers that adequate resources don't matter that much. That is not true. *Scientific evidence now is available that shows what common sense suggests: adequate, sustained funding of paid, full-time staff and the support infrastructure of an organization make a big difference—if the funding is targeted on the replication of proven programs and is well managed.*[27]

We also need to expose the lack of morality and democracy in the policy of the 1980s, which lingers today. Giving to the rich and taking from the poor is not just failed economics but also failed morality. So is a policy of spending more on prison building than on higher education. The "free market," "open competition" ideology of supply-side naysayers is a purposeful lie. In practice, corporations today try to maximize market share, acquire the competition, and use their profits to hire lobbyists who buy votes in legislatures and during campaigns. The result is a "one dollar, one vote" democracy consonant with Al Capone's morality, not the traditional American concepts of fair play and "one person, one vote."

What Policy Works?

Yet much *does work*—and it *is* moral and democratic. If the nation will not carry out a practical policy of replicating what does work for the truly disadvantaged now, with a robust economy (for some), and projected federal budget surpluses, will we ever carry out such a policy?

A national policy can be based on scientifically evaluated successes and should be implemented as much as is feasible by the indigenous inner-city nonprofit organizations that are responsible for much of what works. Such organizations also are neighborhood centers of moral influence. Based on what evaluations show to yield the highest long-term cost-benefit ratios, the priority should be on reform of the urban public education system, a full employment policy for the inner city, and complementary reform to create more racial and criminal justice. This framework builds on new technical knowledge for *how* to replicate what works and for *how* to build nonprofit institutional capacity at the grassroots that we have acquired since the original Kerner Report.[28] Specifically, we need to:

Fully Fund Head Start

Dramatic new biological and chemical research findings have demonstrated that attention to children in their earliest years determines the way their brains are wired, which provides the basis for social, emotional, and intellectual development. The need for greater investment in early childhood development was pointed up by a report of the Committee for Economic Development, composed of corporate executives, which concluded: "It would be hard to imagine that society could find a higher yield for a dollar of investment than that found in preschool programs for its high-risk children. Every $1 spent on early prevention and intervention can save $4.75 in the costs of remedial education, welfare, and crime further down the road."[29] Yet, today, only about one-third of all eligible lower-income children aged three to five are served by Head Start, and most eligible children are in Head Start for only a year. The enrollment rates for three-year-olds is especially low. Accordingly, I recommend full funding for all eligible poor children.

Create a New Nonprofit Corporation for Youth Investment

Naysayers assert that the effects of Head Start diminish over time. Of course. After inner-city kids leave Head Start at age five or six, they are back on the mean streets. Evaluations by Columbia University, the Eisenhower Foundation, and others have shown that boys-and-girls-club type safe havens after school for kids six to sixteen work—as logical continuations of Head Start, to provide help with homework, direction by responsible adults, and safe passage through adolescence in a risky society. Some nonprofit grassroots successes—like the Dorchester Youth Collaborative in Boston; Koban, Inc., in Columbia, South Carolina; and Centro Sister Isolina Ferré in San Juan, Puerto Rico—combine paid civilian staff with police mentors, who also stabilize neighborhoods through community-based problem-oriented policing.[30] For teenagers, a Brandeis University evaluation has shown that the Ford Foundation's Quantum Opportunities adult mentoring program keeps high-risk high schoolers out of trouble and on track to jobs and college.[31]

There are many local nonprofit programs that claim success, but the ones just illustrated can show scientific proof of success based on control group or comparison group designs. Some of the evaluated successes are secular; some are part of the outreach of religious organizations. (Just to focus on one group or another, as do some naysayers, or to identify groups based on political ideology, misses our primary criterion for identifying a model to be replicated: statistically significant pre-postevaluation outcomes using valid comparison or control groups.) All the evaluated youth development successes identified here also are centers of moral influence.

A new national nonprofit Corporation for Youth Investment needs to be created to assist such proven nonprofit youth development organizations in replicating themselves, supply technical assistance, and finance replications with federal funds—while sidestepping much of the federal bureaucracy.

Replicate Successful Urban Public School Reform

Evaluations of the School Development Plan created and replicated widely by Dr. James Comer of Yale University,[32] the *Turning Points* plan for middle schools by the Carnegie Council on Adolescent Development that successfully has been tested,[33] and other school reforms documented comprehensively in her recent book, *Safe Passages*,[34] by independent researcher Joy Dryfoos, show that we need to

- Restructure academic programs to focus on a core of common knowledge and skills.
- Place policy for each inner-city school in the hands of a local management team, led by the principal and including teachers, parents, counselors, and other school staff.
- Dramatically increase the involvement of and assistance to inner-city parents.
- Provide focused intervention by a mental health team for children with emotional, behavioral, or academic problems.
- Create safe environments during the school day and supportive nonprofit safe havens after school.
- Create full-service community schools, in which nonprofit organizations are located in the buildings to provide health, family, community, cultural, and recreational initiatives and to ensure security.
- Reduce classroom size.

An example of a school that is implementing these principles is the Academy for Peace and Justice, operated by El Puente, a Brooklyn community-based organization. The school is open from 8:00 A.M. to 9:00 P.M., twelve months of the year.[35]

Another example is the Salome Arena Middle Academy, operated jointly by the Children's Aid Society and Community School District 6 in New York City. Located in a new building in Washington Heights, it offers students a choice of four self-contained "academies"—Business, Community Service, Expressive Arts, and Mathematics, Science, and Technology. The school opens at 7:00 A.M. each morning, year-round, and stays open after school, into the evening.[36]

To replicate such models, we need to establish the kind of quasi-governmental Safe Passage Commission recommended by Joy Dry-foos.[37] It would target federal funds and matching grants to schools and nonprofit organization partners in high-poverty inner-city neighborhoods.

Priority should be given to reforming urban schools and school bureaucracy, reinforcing the importance of a *public* education system as a national moral responsibility, and respecting the analysis of Jonathan Kozol:[38]

> [T]he children in poor rural schools in Mississippi and Ohio will continue to get education funded at less than $4,000 yearly and children in the South Bronx will get less than $7,000, while children in the richest suburbs will continue to receive up to $18,000 yearly. But they'll be told they must be held to the same standards and they'll all be judged, of course, by their performance on the same exams.
>
> Slogans, standards and exams do not teach reading. Only well-paid and proficient teachers do, and only if they work under conditions that do not degrade their spirits and demean their students. . . . Money, as the rich and powerful repeatedly remind us, may not be "the only way" to upgrade education, but it seems to be the way that they have chosen for their own kids, and if it is good for them . . . it is not clear why it is not of equal worth to children of poor people.

Reform the National Job Training System

One reason that the supply-side Job Training Partnership Act (JTPA) failed as the nation's primary job training system for out-of-school youth was that it offered little training before placement.[39] Current welfare reform, with its "work first" requirement that prevents training before an inexperienced person starts work, repeats the same mistake. It may become an extremely costly repetition for the American taxpayer.

Based on existing scientific evaluation evidence, one of the most promising job training models for both out-of-school youth and for the amendment of welfare reform is the Argus Community in the South Bronx. Argus is based on an understanding that there can be no political quick fixes and simplistic solutions (like "work first"). Argus gives priority to the development of character and a moral value system in participants; socialization and counseling in a drug- and violence-free environment; a life skills curriculum to prepare youth to be functioning adults who can handle conflicts and manage themselves well on the job; on-site education and remedial education (including general educational diploma high school courses in an alternative educational setting); on-site job training before job placement; job placement for jobs in demand and with upward mobility, not dead-end jobs; and follow-up to ensure better job retention.[40]

Sufficient funds need to be appropriated to replace JTPA with an Argus-like model and to provide Argus-type training for all unemployed persons in inner cities who need the training.

Generate One Million Private Sector Inner-City Jobs

Of the two million-plus jobs we need to create full employment in the inner city, our target is one million new private sector jobs—filled by inner-city residents who have had Argus-like training. Toward this goal, the regulations for HUD Community Development Block Grants, HUD housing grants, Commerce Department Economic Development Administration grants, Transportation Department Urban Mass Transit grants, and other federal, state, and local economic development grants need to be revised to require much more priority on the reduction of poverty and the generation of private jobs for inner-city unemployment. A more efficient federal interagency coordinating mechanism than presently exists is needed to cotarget these reformed grants to places of greatest need. Federal regulations need to require that localities employ the truly disadvantaged in local growth industries, following the model of the Target Industries and Employment Program of the Portland (Oregon) Development Commission.[41]

Match funds generated from local tax bases need to be encouraged. Given the loss of tax bases from the central city to the suburbs in many places, the federal government needs to condition grants to states and localities on local agreements to share across the entire metropolitan area (including suburbs) the value of commercial property, as well as to share other elements of the area-wide tax base—following the successful plan, for example, of Minneapolis/St. Paul.[42] The federal government needs, as well, to closely monitor the school finance plans in Michigan and other states that transition from property taxes to other forms of taxes that allow for more equitable expenditures in inner cities and the suburbs.[43]

Modeled on the successes of the South Shore Bank in Chicago, which already has been replicated elsewhere, a semi-independent National Community Development Bank, removed from the federal bureaucracy, needs to be capitalized as part of a comprehensive plan to generate more private jobs in the inner city. The South Shore Bank has pioneered in reinvesting the savings of inner-city residents back into their own neighborhoods—for example, to help capitalize new inner-city businesses.[44]

The capitalization of community development banks and businesses should be linked to tougher enforcement by HUD of the Community Reinvestment Act of 1977, which requires banks to invest in their communities. Over the last two decades, naysayers and well-paid lobbyists for the rich have tried to decimate the Act.[45]

Generate One Million Two Hundred Fifty Thousand Public Sector Inner-City Jobs

Past experience suggests that, given traditional private sector resistance to employing the truly disadvantaged, and given the failure of enterprise zones in South Central Los Angeles after the 1992 riots there, one million new private inner-city jobs is a very ambitious goal. And it still falls far short of the two million-plus jobs needed for a full-employment policy in the inner city.

Public jobs therefore need to be generated by federal dollars. The jobs should be implemented locally by groups like the nonprofit Youth Build USA (created by Dorothy Stoneman to teach construction to inner-city youth),[46] nonprofit community development corporations (like the New Community Corporation model created by Father William Linder after the 1967 Newark riots),[47] nonprofit youth development and youth employment organizations, for-profit entities with a social conscience (like the Washington, D.C.-based Telesis Corporation),[48] and local government. Our plan creates 250,000 public urban construction and infrastructure repair jobs and one million public service jobs.

Public infrastructure investment has shaped America's future. Early on, public investments built canals and subsidized the railroads to settle the West. Government financed the first assembly lines. The federal Interstate highway system was built in the 1950s and 1960s. Federal investments developed the jet engine, began the exploration of space, and helped develop the computer and the Internet.[49] Yet public infrastructure investment declined precipitously in the 1980s, as a result of supply-side economics and its associated urban disinvestment. The 1990s have not reversed this public disinvestment. In 1980, more than 4 percent of all federal outlays were for infrastructure. By 1990, that share had fallen to under 3 percent. As of 1997, public investment in infrastructure was

36 percent of its 1970s levels, and on our current budget trajectory it will drop another 37 percent. The United States is the only major industrial society that is not currently renewing and expanding its infrastructure.[50] Nowhere is public infrastructure more in need of repair and reinvestment than in our cities and inner cities.

Similarly, there is an enormous need for public service employment. To amend welfare reform, we need a great many qualified child care workers. With Argus-type training first, child care potentially can be a major employment sector for persons coming off welfare. Drivers and support staff workers are needed to create a transportation system that will allow persons coming off welfare and other unemployed people to get to jobs in the suburbs. Teachers in inner-city schools desperately need adequately trained support staff. Community-based nonprofit youth development and community development organizations need paid staff to work with supervisors. Housing shelters are in great need of staff. As the Argus Community has shown, there is a considerable demand for drug abuse counselors. Major cities no longer have enough telephone operators to answer 911 emergency calls in a timely way. Because there are so many unmet jobs, it will be easy enough to create safeguards that ensure that existing employees are not displaced. In many cases, qualified existing employees must become supervisors.

In support of these job investments, the nation needs a macroeconomic policy that more honestly recognizes how trickle-down economic growth does not eliminate poverty in specific locations; a fiscal policy that separates long-term investments from short-term operating expenses; a monetary policy that gives first priority to full employment for the poor, working class, and middle class; and a trade policy that raises labor and human rights standards.[51]

Replicate Complementary Investments in Racial and Criminal Justice

A commitment to reform of preschool and public urban education, combined with a policy of full employment in the inner city, are big first steps in bridging the millennium breaches of race and class that divide America.

However, given the racial biases documented in this book, we also need policy that more directly addresses race:[52]

- Replication of successful models of school integration (as in St. Louis) and housing integration (like the Gatreaux program begun in Chicago).[53]
- Continuation of affirmative action (justified by Rand Corporation and other studies that have measured success).[54]
- Creation of a Presidential Commission to review the "concrete ceiling" and hiring practices of Wall Street and major corporations, followed by a Presidential commitment to break through that ceiling.
- Creation of web sites that provide universal access to reliable and relevant information on race and models of successful racial dialogue.
- Elimination of the racial disparity in drug sentencing.
- Reallocation of spending by the failed "war on drugs" from 70 percent law enforcement and 30 percent treatment to a ratio closer to 50:50, including reduced prison building and more inner-city–based drug treatment.

What Is the Cost of Replicating What Works to Scale and How Can It Be Financed?

Table 8.1 summarizes the total cost of our proposed investments—which address the Kerner Commission's recommendation that we replicate "on a scale equal to the dimensions of the problem."[55] As much as possible, we encourage financing by the private sector and by state and local government. Yet experience has shown these sources to be unwilling or unable to invest at anything close to scale. *To be pragmatic, we need to recognize that only the federal government potentially has the resources to replicate to scale. At the same time, we recommend that these public dollars be implemented day to day as much as possible by private nonprofit grassroots organizations in concert with for-profits with records of inner city success, and with local government.*

We recommend financing primarily by reallocating a fraction of the $100B–plus paid by taxpayers annually for wealthfare, affirmative action for the rich, and corporate welfare. Table 8.2 illustrates some of these subsidies and tax breaks for the rich.

As former Secretary of Labor Robert Reich has concluded after reviewing such subsidies and tax breaks as assembled by conservative, moderate, and liberal nonprofit organizations:

TABLE 8.1
Summary of Federal Investments Proposed

Investment	Federal Cost Per Year (in billions)
Replication of Head Start Preschool for all Eligible Poor Children.	$ 7
Replication of the Comer School Development, Carnegie *Turning Points,* Dryfoos Full Service Community School, and Project Prepare Models in Urban Public School Systems.	$15
Creation of a Corporation for Youth Investment to Replicate After School Safe Haven Prevention Models, Quantum Opportunities Prevention Models and Related Successes.	$ 1
Reform of Job Training Modeled after the Argus Community.	$ 4.5
Creation of 1,000,000 Private Sector Jobs for the Inner City through Better Targeting Existing Economic Development Grants on Poverty Reduction.	$ 0
Creation of a National Community Development Bank Modeled after the South Shore Bank.	$ 1
Generation of 250,000 Public Construction and Rehabilitation Jobs for the Inner City That Are Targeted on Housing and Urban Infrastructure Development.	$ 5
Generation of 1,000,000 Public Service Jobs for the Inner City That Are Targeted on Public Service Employment in Day Care, Transportation Services, Urban School Staff Support, and Nonprofit Community Organization Support.	$20
Replication of School Desegregation and Housing Desegregation Models That Work and Affirmative Action. Upgraded Civil Rights Enforcement. Replication of Presidential Race Initiative Models That Work. Creation of an On-Line Database of Facts and Solutions.	$ .1
Replication of Successful Drug Treatment and Reintegration Programs. Replication of Community and Treatment-Oriented Drug Courts. Implementation of Sentencing and Drug Treatment Commission Recommendations.	$ 2.4
TOTAL	$56

The list contains all sorts of breathlessly ridiculous items, like $2B a year going to oil, gas, and mining companies for no reason whatsoever, $4B a year to pharmaceutical companies that create offices in Puerto Rico, $400M to Christmas-tree growers, windmill makers, and shipbuilders, and $500M a year to corn-based–ethanol refiners.

Also on the list is the $2B-a-year tax break for life insurance companies,

TABLE 8.2
Examples of Current Welfare Subsidies and Tax Breaks to Corporations and the Rich

Wealthfare Category and Illustration	Annual Cost to Taxpayers (in billions)
Taxes That Have Been Lowered on Capital Gains for the Rich	$ 37
Depreciation That Has Been Accelerated for the Rich	$ 37
Agribusiness Subsidies (Including Tobacco Subsidies)	$ 18
Tax Avoidance by Transnational Corporations	$ 12
Media Handouts, Like Free Corporate Use of the Airwaves	$ 8
Tax Loopholes Given to the Insurance Industry	$ 7.2
Business Meal and Entertainment Deductions as Part of Corporate Welfare	$ 5.5
Subsidies to the Nuclear Power Industry	$ 7.1
Subsidies to the Airline Industry	$ 5.5
Subsidies to the Mining Industry	$ 3.5
Tax Breaks to the Oil and Gas Industry	$ 2.4
Export Subsidies to Transnational Corporations	$ 2
TOTAL	$145.2

Source: Mark Zepezauer and Arthur Naiman, *Take the Rich Off Welfare* (Tucson, Ariz.: Odonian Press, 1996).

$900M for timber companies, $700M for the dairy industry, and $100M a year to companies like Sunkist, Gallo, M&M, McDonald's, and Campbell Soup to advertise abroad. On top of that are billions of dollars of special breaks for multinationals that make their products outside the United States. Some well-connected companies like Archer-Daniels-Midland (ADM, a giant Midwestern corn processor) triple-dip: ADM benefits from a sugar program that bars imports and sets sugar prices higher than world levels (so ADM can sell a high-cost sugar substitute), a tax break for corn-based ethanol, and the direct subsidy to ethanol refiners. Taxpayers and consumers pay dearly for the welfare flowing to this single company.

And that's just the beginning: If TV networks had to bid for extra space on the broadcast spectrum instead of getting it free, they'd pay $4B a year. If private corporate jets had to pay landing fees at airports, as commercial jets have to do, they'd pay $200M a year. If wealthy ranchers had to pay the full cost of grazing their cattle on public lands, they'd pony up $55 million a year. If corporations couldn't deduct the costs of entertaining their clients—skyboxes at sports arenas, theaters and concerts, golf resorts—they'd pay $2B more each year in taxes.

Imagine if even a portion of this money could be used instead for education, job training, and helping the poor and the near-poor get the jobs they need.[56]

Well-paid lobbyists will argue that the rich need affirmative action and corporate welfare to assure a robust economy. Yet this claim is disputed by the econometric forecasts made by Richard McGahey, then at the Center for Community Change. The Center has proposed one million new public service jobs, just as we have. McGahey analyzed the impact on the economy of these one million jobs if their total cost was financed by reducing corporate welfare by an equal amount. Using FAIRMO-DEL, a widely regarded econometric model based on 131 equations that is continually updated and reestimated, McGahey compared the current econometric forecast produced by the model five years into the future to an alternative forecast with the public service job program financed by the corporate welfare cuts. Compared to the current forecast, the forecast with the proposed change "has a higher level of real and nominal economic growth, stable private sector employment, and a lower national unemployment rate. Real wage increases and inflation are virtually the same in the two scenarios."[57]

In other words, a shift in some resources from corporate subsidies to public service jobs does not hurt the economy. It can help the economy.

In addition to eliminating corporate welfare, we should redirect some funds being spent on the military to our more serious domestic needs. Current federal plans call for military spending to be as much in the year 2000, in real terms, as it was in 1975, in the midst of the Cold War, when the Soviet Union still existed and was heavily armed. Many well-qualified experts support military cuts, including William W. Kaufman, a defense analyst for several U.S. Defense Department secretaries.[58] Kaufman concludes in a study for the Brookings Institution that the United States could reduce the defense budget to less than $200 billion per year over the next ten years without undermining its global security commitments or its position in arms control negotiations. Similarly, the Center for Defense Information, founded by retired admirals and generals, has proposed a reduction in military personnel from 1.4 million to 1 million and an annual Pentagon budget of $200 billion.[59]

We recommend, as well, that the table 8.1 budget be financed by eliminating other programs that don't work (like JTPA), allocating funds from any future budget surpluses, and directing funds from any tobacco settlement.

What Are the Major Obstacles to Replicating to Scale?

Without real political campaign finance reform, and without a citizen campaign to communicate to the public what works, only limited progress is possible. Money talks in our present political system, especially for those who support tax breaks for the rich and prison building for the poor. Today, the economic system runs the political system. The stranglehold of big money on the American political system and the public agenda is illustrated by the following practices:[60]

- lavish corporate subsidies to our two major political parties
- the contribution of as much as $1 million to national campaigns by individual foreign interests
- the virtual elimination of competition by congressional incumbents whose huge campaign war chests have ensured them a reelection rate of over 90 percent
- corporate sponsorship of the carefully scripted, plastic, made-for-television national conventions of the two major parties
- ongoing mobilization of special-interest money by members of Congress and shakedowns of fat cats by elected officials dialing for dollars
- the purchase of legislative and regulatory "relief," to use Washington Beltway jargon, by lobbyists who represent the interests that get the politicians elected and reelected

In many ways, clean money campaign reform, as pioneered in Maine and as advocated at the national level by Public Campaign,[61] is the reform that makes all the other reforms possible. Strictly limiting campaign contributions and expenditures and providing a system of public financing for congressional campaigns, like that available for presidential campaigns, would not guarantee replication of what works to scale. But it would level the political playing field to allow campaigns to be based more on issues than on money and to take into account the interests of the poor, the working class, and the middle class, not just those of the rich and the big corporations.

It will be easier to overcome the obstacle of "one dollar, one vote" if we overcome the obstacle of inadequate communication of what works. Foundations and corporations that support the position of supply-side naysayers generously have funded communications and media operations in naysaying think tanks and related organizations over the last twenty years. The naysaying think tanks have been extremely effective in communicating an ideology that little works except failed programs like supply-side tax breaks for the rich and prison building. On the other hand, foundations that support the development and replication of the kind of child, youth, family, community, and economic development policy in chapter 8, and that support policy based on scientific evaluation, have tended to view communications and media policy as outside of their mission.[62]

In some ways, the media conspire with the naysayers. Most media in America are controlled by a few giant multinational corporations, like General Electric, Time Warner, Disney, and Rupert Murdoch's News Corporation. There is unremitting pressure for profits. Most Americans prefer to get their news on local television. To maximize ratings and profits, local managers tend to follow a policy of, "if it bleeds, it leads." Crime and violence on the 5 p.m., 6 p.m., 10 p.m., and 11 p.m. local television news are thought to be the best way to maximize ratings, profits from commercials, and the television manager's job security. The resulting high frequency of bloody and sensational stories also often targets young minority males, who are demonized as offenders, and "welfare mothers," who are portrayed as inadequate parents. As George Gerbner, Dean Emeritus of the Annenberg School of Communications at the University of Pennsylvania, has observed, the result of the present violent and negative programming can be the "mean world syndrome." Day in and day out, the average, middle-class, suburban American viewer is left with the feeling that nothing works. This may increase the likelihood that the middle-class viewer will conclude that policies like naysaying and prison building are the answer, not replication of programs that do work.[63]

The consequent need is for a communicating what works movement that is both "top down" and "bubble up." From the top, national nonprofit organizations need to encourage more foundations to make media and communications grants. Reports on what works need to be more frequently published and more widely distributed to private and public decision makers. A set of what works web sites needs to summarize what works in specific locations and for specific groups (for example, mentoring for six- to sixteen-year-olds), summarize the technology for how to replicate what works, and encourage interaction between model programs, and those that want to become models. To help educate the public and decision makers, we need celebrities like Whoopi Goldberg, Robin Williams, and Billy Crystal illustrating what works on *Comic Relief*-type programs. We need a new generation of public service announcements showing, for example, Patrick Ewing at Argus in the South Bronx, Oprah Winfrey at the Comer School Development program in Chicago, and Bill Cosby at Delancey Street in Los Angeles.

In terms of bubble up, thousands of grassroots community-based inner-city nonprofit organizations need to become a coordinated force, based on their being trained in communications and media, as is done in the Eisenhower Foundation's television school for nonprofit organizations. Grassroots nonprofits need to be assisted to bring on their own communications directors (few have them) and to generate strategic communications plans. Inner-city groups should learn to communicate to the public what their own programs are about and, through this public education, help raise funds and become more self-sufficient. They can communicate what works in the local media. They can push for more local electronic media news and talk shows that embrace more of what works, less of what doesn't work, and less of a bleeds/leads philosophy. Nonprofits also can try local, cost-effective, alternatives to conventional television, radio, and print news. Such alternatives include Internet venues, cable programs, more word of mouth street organizing and pamphleteering (as suggested by Bill Moyers), town meetings, and public service announcements crafted by the nonprofit organization itself. For example, such announcements can be modeled after the youth media enterprises at the Dorchester Youth Collaborative in Boston. There is great potential for replicating youth media enterprises. They can communicate very effective messages, involve youth in popular and constructive activity in safe havens after school, and even lead to income generation.[64]

What Is the Political Feasibility of a Policy Based on What Works?

To what extent is public opinion supportive of the policy set forth in this chapter? One measure of public opinion is the response of the media to the Eisenhower Foundation's thirty-year update of the Kerner Report upon which this chapter is based. Released on March 1, 1998 (thirty years to the exact day of the release of the original Kerner Report), the update received saturation media coverage—for example, on ABC, BBC, BET, CBS, CNN, NBC, NBC Today, NPR, the *News Hour with Jim Lehrer,* scores of radio talk shows in big cities, *Newsweek,* the Associated Press, and almost every major and minor newspaper in the country. Of course, the naysayers whom we criticized, in turn, criticized the update. But news stories were "framed" by print and electronic media in a way that was favorable to the update.[65] The naysaying was superficial and could easily and effectively be dismissed.[66] Among editorials, feature columns, and op eds, we found a network of supportive opinion in every region in the nation, in towns large and small.[67] It is a network upon which a communicating what works movement can build.

Considerable support for the priorities proposed here also can be found in the results of public opinion polls. For example, national surveys conducted from 1988 to 1994 by the National Opinion Research Center at the University of Chicago show that a substantial majority of Americans want to see more money spent on improving the nation's educational system and on reducing crime and drug addiction.[68]

Similarly, in 1992, immediately after the Los Angeles riots, the *New York Times* and CBS News asked Americans in a nationwide poll: "Are we spending too much money, too little money, or about the right amount of money on problems of the big cities, on improving the conditions of blacks, and on the poor?" Sixty percent of respondents said that too little was being spent on urban problems, 61 percent said that too little was being spent on improving the conditions of African Americans, and 64 percent said that too little was being spent on problems of the poor. The pollsters also asked: "To reduce racial tension and prevent riots, would more jobs and job training help a lot, help a little, or not make any difference?" Seventy-eight percent of respondents said that more jobs and training would help a lot.[69]

Complementary findings come from a 1996 poll of voters sponsored by the Children's Partnership, the American Academy of Pediatrics, the Coalition for America's Children, the National Association of Children's Hospitals, and the National Parent-Teacher Association. Seventy-six percent of the voters polled in that survey said that they would be more likely to vote for a candidate who supported increased spending for children's programs. Sixty-five percent favored proposals for children and families, even if this would mean slowing down deficit reduction. Sixty-four percent said that government should play a large role in solving problems facing children. Sixty-two percent said that they would oppose a balanced budget amendment if it required cuts in children's programs.[70]

In 1998, in the first national sampling of attitudes on surpluses after a federal fiscal year 1999 budget surplus was projected, a *USA Today/* CNN/Gallup Poll found that the biggest group of respondents, 43 percent, called for using any extra money to invest in Social Security, Medicare, and education. (Thirty percent backed paying down the debt, and 22 percent favored tax cuts.)[71]

What Political Alliance Is Needed?

In spite of evidence of public support, the political will does not at present exist nationally to carry out the budget priorities in table 8.1 as we enter the new millennium. How can we create the political will?

We need a new political alliance with a broad constituency. The heart of our recommended policy—investing in education and employment to provide opportunity—needs to embrace not only the truly disadvantaged, and not only those in the inner cities, but also the working class and the middle class.

The alliance should include those in core cities and older suburbs who are already forming common fronts in places like Minneapolis/St. Paul and Cleveland against losing their resources to new exurbs. The goal of the alliance should be to recapture some of the national mood that existed after World War II, when Americans sought to build a more inclusive, equitable society, one in which everyone had a fair chance of "making it."[72]

What story, or message, might update that post–World War II American feeling and build the new political alliance for the coming millennium? We need words around which to rally, and these might include some of the following:[73]

You, the average citizen, are not alone in your search for a safe niche in the I-win-you-lose world. The very rich have profited at the expense of the families of salaried and working people of America. It is not fair for the rich to get richer at the expense of the rest of us. Power has shifted so significantly toward those at the top of the income and wealth pyramid that the majority of Americans who are struggling must mobilize to force the rich and the elites back to the bargaining table. We must close the income, wage, and job gaps.

The way to do this is to invest in education, training, and retraining, so that Americans have the opportunity for jobs—and for better jobs. Among the middle class, working class, and the truly disadvantaged, and among different racial and ethnic groups, this policy can be win-win. None of these groups needs to gain at the expense of the others. We can succeed with a full-employment policy that eliminates the economic marginality of the poor and at the same time reduces the anxiety of the working and middle classes.

Americans deserve a higher quality of life. We must invest in the human capital of all of our citizens, so all can deal successfully with technological change and the global economy. The role of the federal government must be to make investments that serve the interests of the salaried and working classes, along with the poor.

Does this story, this message, have sufficient appeal to sufficient numbers of Americans? There is no doubt the potential exists. The majority of Americans seem to know that they are not necessarily winners in today's economy. For example, a 1996 *New York Times* poll reported that the share of the electorate that identifies itself as "working class" now outnumbers those who consider themselves "middle class"—55 percent to 36 percent. If to this 55 percent we add those who identify themselves as "poor," the total becomes 61 percent of the electorate. National polls also show that, despite a higher level of education, young people often say that they expect to do worse than their parents. This is a likely group, too, for recruitment into the new alliance.[74]

In terms of policy, the common ground among the poor, working class, and middle class can be job training and retraining, to make all more productive. For example, building and repairing low-tech urban infrastructure (like roads and buildings) can generate jobs, both for the truly disadvantaged and for working-class family breadwinners. New high-tech industries for which working- and middle-class persons can be trained and retrained include, for example, computer-smart urban transit systems, computer networking, electronic digital imaging, ceramics, advanced composites, sensors, photonics, artificial intelligence, robotics, computer-aided manufacturing, biotechnology, and research and development to find the cure for cancer, Parkinson's disease, AIDS, other serious diseases, and the common cold. Additional examples include research and development to allow a shift to renewable energy as well as research and development to reduce environmental deterioration and pollution.

Leadership

The most that we can expect for now is that grassroots, citywide and statewide versions of our recommendations—the funding priorities, the what works agenda, and the new alliance—will emerge with greater frequency, gaining strength and local momentum from one another. We can work toward a kind of synergy—where, for example, communicating what works encourages the new alliance, which then creates more pressure for campaign finance reform, which then allows a fairer debate on what works, which then leads to even more effective communication—and action.

Americans need to pressure our leaders to lead, or we need to get new ones. We know that the budget recommendations made here will not be approved at the federal level during this thirtieth anniversary year of the Kerner Report, but perhaps the necessary political will and leadership can emerge by the fortieth or fiftieth anniversary. To repair the millennium breach and fulfill the legacy of the Kerner Commission, America again needs Franklin Roosevelt's commitment to effective government and Teddy Roosevelt's boldness in establishing the limits of private greed.

Conclusion

America made progress for nearly a decade on the principal fronts that the March 1, 1968, Kerner Report dealt with: race, poverty, and the inner cities. Then that progress stopped, and in some ways we have even regressed.

Among the reasons for the halt and reversal were certain economic shocks and trends: a series of economic recessions; a leveling off of economic growth rates; technological developments and economic globalization, which caused the disappearance of many blue-collar manufacturing jobs and the creation of new jobs requiring high levels of skills and education; the weakening of unions and a decline in unionization. The net result of all of this was that a growing number of working-class families fell into poverty and a lot of already poor Americans became deeply poor.

Government action and inaction also played a part. Particularly during the Reagan and Bush administrations, social programs and social investment suffered badly. The value of income support programs dropped. So did that of the federal minimum wage. Job and training programs and investments in education and infrastructure fell.

As a consequence of these economic shocks and trends and of government action and inaction, there is more poverty in America now than there was thirty years ago. Today, 36.5 million Americans live in poverty, 13.7 percent of our population, compared to 25.4 million poor, 12.8 percent of our people, at the time of the Kerner Report. Child poverty is greater, having grown by a fifth in the 1980s. The income gap between the rich and the rest of Americans—the middle class, the working class, and poor people—has grown wider. The average American family today has less real income than in the 1980s.

Poverty is deeper than it was thirty years ago. Today, 14.4 million

151

Americans live on incomes that amount to less than half of the poverty threshold.

Poverty is more concentrated now. In 1968, only about half of America's poor lived in metropolitan areas; three-fourths of them do today, 42 percent of poor people now live in core inner cities.

As working- and middle-class whites and African Americans have moved out to the suburbs, inner-city poverty has become more concentrated. American housing and schools are resegregating; two-thirds of African American and three-fourths of Hispanic children now attend predominantly minority schools.

Concentrated poverty in the inner cities has produced social disorganization and crime and social isolation for the poor people who live there—largely African American and Hispanic, with some American Indian and Asian American poor, as well. America's inner cities have become the nation's poorhouses, from which many have little hope of escape.

Growing up in poverty, and especially in neighborhoods of concentrated poverty, has a dramatically depressing impact on early childhood development, limiting achievement and cognitive and verbal ability for many children and severely curtailing their chances for a successful life. It is not true that government can do nothing right. What we tried after the Kerner Report largely worked. We just stopped trying it. Or we did not try it hard enough.

We know what works. Head Start and other early childhood development programs work. So do sensible, and working, follow-on programs for older children and youth at risk. Jobs, public school reform, job training and job retention work. Affirmative action and proven desegregation efforts work. We know how to make investments in housing, community development organizations, and public infrastructure work better to generate jobs for the jobs. A livable minimum wage works.

We know what does not work. Trickle-down supply-side economics—incentives for the rich—do not work, not for most Americans. The Job Partnership Training Act has not worked for out-of-school youth. Neither have enterprise zones to subsidize corporate investment in the inner city. Massive prison building and the explosion in incarceration have not worked.

We have the money to do what needs to be done. We must reorder the federal budget and its priorities—moving away from programs and policies that do not work and cutting down on unneeded military expenditures and corporate welfare. We must return to human investment—in programs that do work. We must raise the minimum wage and renew our affirmative-action and desegregation efforts.

To accomplish this, we must, first, help Americans see that things are getting worse again for millions of Americans. Many do not know this. Second, we must communicate what works. Third, we must reduce the growing power of money in American politics, drastically reforming our system of campaign finance—so that our policy and budget priorities can be changed. Fourth, we must all realize our common self-interest in forming political coalitions across racial, ethnic, and class lines that can produce political action.

We must begin to think of our inner cities, and wherever and among whomever else great poverty exists, as internal wastefully underdeveloped areas. It makes economic sense to provide our underskilled, undereducated, underemployed, and underutilized fellow Americans a real chance for success and productivity. It will cost less to do this than what we are doing now. That is fiscal sense. It will save a lot of tragically lost American lives and unrealized human potential. And it will ensure a more stable and secure America for us all.

Notes and Sources

Chapter 1: The Kerner Report Thirty Years Later

1. The section that follows is taken from Fred R. Harris, "The 1967 Riots and the Kerner Commission," in Fred R. Harris and Roger W. Wilkins, eds., *Quiet Riots: Race and Poverty in America* (New York: Pantheon, 1988).

2. *Report of the National Advisory Commission on Civil Disorders* (Washington, D.C.: Government Printing Office, 1968).

3. The discussion of economic trends is based on Kathryn Larin and Elizabeth McNichol, *Pulling Apart: A State-by-State Analysis of Income Trends* (Washington, D.C.: Center on Budget and Policy Priorities, 1997).

4. Jerry Jones, *Federal Revenue Policies That Work: A Blueprint for Job Creation to Support Welfare Reform* (Washington, D.C.: Center for Community Change, 1997).

5. Larin and McNichol, *Pulling Apart*, p. 35.

6. Gary Burtless, "Public Spending for the Poor: Historical Trends and Economic Limits," in Sheldon H. Danziger, Gary D. Sandefur, and Daniel H. Weinberg, eds., *Confronting Poverty: Prescriptions for Change* (Cambridge: Harvard University Press, 1994).

7. Larin and McNichol, *Pulling Apart*, p. vii.

8. Danziger, Sandefur, and Weinberg, *Confronting Poverty*, p. 3.

9. Jeff Faux, "The Economic Case for a Politics of Inclusion," Eisenhower Foundation, Washington, D.C., 1998, p. 4.

10. Robert Reich, "The Missing Options," *American Prospect* (Nov.–Dec. 1997): 8.

11. Faux, "The Economic Case for a Politics of Inclusion," p. 4.

12. Larin and McNichol, *Pulling Apart*, p. 36.

13. The following statistics are from U.S. Census Bureau, *Historical Poverty Tables, 1997* (Washington, D.C.: Government Printing Office, 1997), http://www.census.gov/hhes/poverty/histpov/hstpov8.html; Census Bureau, press release, "Incomes Improve, Poverty Levels Stabilize, Health Insurance Coverage

Slips," Washington, D.C., Sept. 29, 1997, p. 2. See also Steven A. Holmes, "New Reports Say Minorities Benefit in Fiscal Recovery," *New York Times,* Sept. 30, 1997; Editorial, "The Tide Is Not Lifting Everyone," *New York Times,* Sept. 30, 1997.

14. Bob Herbert, "A Loss of Nerve," *New York Times,* Jan. 27, 1997.

15. Isaac Shapiro, *Unequal Shares: Recent Income Trends among the Wealthy,* (Washington, D.C.: Center on Budget and Policy Priorities, 1995), p. 1.

16. Holmes, "New Reports Say Minorities Benefit."

17. Ibid.

18. U.S. Census Bureau, "Income Improves, Poverty Levels Stabilize," p. 2.

19. U.S. Census Bureau, *Historical Poverty Tables, 1997.*

20. U.S. Department of Housing and Urban Development, *The State of the Cities* (Washington, D.C.: Government Printing Office,).

21. Robyn Meredith, "5 Days in 1967 Still Shake Detroit," *New York Times,* July 23, 1997.

22. Martin Carnoy, *Faded Dreams: The Politics and Economics of Race in America* (Cambridge: Cambridge University Press, 1994), pp. 187–94.

23. Ethan Bronner, "Minority Enrollment at U.C. Law, Business Schools Down Sharply," *New York Times,* Jan. 14, 1998.

24. Carnoy, *Faded Dreams,* pp. 191–93.

25. Jones, *Federal Revenue Policies That Work,* p. 4. See also, in regard to hiring discrimination against Hispanics, Marc Bendick Jr., Charles W. Jackson, Victor A. Reinoso, and Laura E. Hodges, "Discrimination against Latino Job Applicants: A Controlled Experiment," *Human Resources Management* 30 (1991): 469–84.

26. *Jobs Fax* (Washington, D.C.: Economics Policy Institute, 1998), http:// stats.bls.gov; Jones, *Federal Revenue Policies That Work,* p. 4.

27. Richard W. Stevenson, "Black-White Economic Gap Narrowing, White House Says," *New York Times,* Feb. 10, 1998.

28. Holmes, "New Reports Say Minorities Benefit."

29. Stevenson, "Black-White Economic Gap Narrowing."

30. Gary Orfield, "Segregated Housing and School Resegregation," in Gary Orfield, Susan E. Eaton, and the Harvard Project on School Desegregation, *Dismantling Desegregation: The Quiet Reversal of Brown v. Board of Education* (New York: New Press, 1996), pp. 318, 319.

31. Gary Orfield, testimony before the President's Advisory Board on Race, Dec. 17, 1997.

32. See Gary Orfield, "The Growth of Segregation: African Americans, Latinos, and Unequal Education," in Gary Orfield, Susan E. Eaton, and the Harvard Project on School Desegregation, *Dismantling Desegregation,* quotations on pp. 53–57.

33. William Julius Wilson, *When Work Disappears: The World of the New Urban Poor* (New York: Vintage, 1996).

34. See Paul A. Jargowsky, "Urban Poverty, Race, and the Central City: The 'Bitter Fruit' of Thirty Years of Neglect," chapter 5.

35. See William Julius Wilson, James M. Quane, and Bruce H. Rankin, "The New Urban Poverty: Consequences of the Economic and Social Decline of Inner-City Neighborhoods," chapter 4.

36. Ibid.

37. Carnoy, *Faded Dreams*, p. 223.

Chapter 2: Urban Poverty, Welfare Reform, and Child Development

The authors would like to thank the National Institute of Child Health and Human Development Research Network on the Child and Family Well-being for supporting the writing of this chapter. Portions of it are drawn from Greg J. Duncan and Jeanne Brooks-Gunn, "Welfare Reform, Poverty, and Child Development," *Issues in Science and Technology*, in press; Jeanne Brooks-Gunn and Greg J. Duncan, "The Effects of Poverty on Children and Youth," *Future of Children* 7 (1997): 55–71.

1. U.S. Bureau of the Census, *Historical Poverty Tables, 1997* (Washington, D.C.: Government Printing Office, 1997) (http://www.census.gov/hhes/poverty/histpov/hstpov8.html).

2. L. Lanison-White, "Poverty in the United States," in U.S. Bureau of the Census, *Current Population Reports,* Series P60-198 (Washington, D.C.: Government Printing Office, 1997).

3. Jeanne Brooks-Gunn, J. Brown, Greg Duncan, and K. A. Moore, "Child Development in the Context of Family and Community Resources: An Agenda for National Data Collection," in National Research Council Institute of Medicine, *Integrating Federal Statistics on Children: Report of a Workshop* (Washington, D.C.: National Academy Press, 1995).

4. See, for example, Greg J. Duncan and Jeanne Brooks-Gunn, *The Consequences of Growing Up Poor* (New York: Russell Sage, 1997); Jeanne Brooks-Gunn and Greg J. Duncan, "The Effects of Poverty on Children and Youth," *Future of Children* 7 (1997): 55–71; Children's Defense Fund, *Wasting America's Future* (Boston: Beacon, 1994).

5. Brooks-Gunn and Duncan, "The Effects of Poverty on Children and Youth," table 1.

6. Duncan and Brooks-Gunn, *The Consequences of Growing Up Poor.*

7. Greg Duncan, Jeanne Brooks-Gunn, J. Yeung, and J. Smith, "How Much Does Childhood Poverty Affect the Life Chances of Children?" *American Sociological Review* 63 (June 1998): pp. 1–18.

8. J. Smith, Jeanne Brooks-Gunn, and P. Klebanov, "The Consequences of

Living in Poverty on Young Children's Cognitive Development," in Duncan and Brooks-Gunn, *The Consequences of Growing Up Poor.*

9. N. Baydar, Jeanne Brooks-Gunn, and F. F. Furstenburg Jr., "Early Warning Signs of Functional Illiteracy: Predictors in Childhood and Adolescence," *Child Development* 64 (1993): 815–29; Jeanne Brooks-Gunn, G. Guo, and F. F. Furstenburg Jr., "Who Drops Out of and Who Continues beyond High School? A 20-Year Follow-up of Black Urban Youth," *Journal of Research on Adolescence* (1993): 271–94.

10. J. Smith, Jeanne Brooks-Gunn, and P. Klebanov, "The Consequences of Living in Poverty on Young Children's Cognitive Development"; and P. K. Klebanov, Jeanne Brooks-Gunn, R. Gordon, and L. Chase-Lansdale, "The Intersection of the Neighborhood and Home Environment and Its Influence on Young Children," in Jeanne Brooks-Gunn, Greg J. Duncan, and J. L. Aber, eds., *Neighborhood Poverty: Context and Consequences for Children* (New York: Russell Sage, 1997).

11. Jeanne Brooks-Gunn, J. Klebanov, and F. Liaw, "The Learning, Physical, and Emotional Environment of the Home in the Context of Poverty: The Infant Health and Development Program," *Children and Youth Services Review* (1995): 251–76.

12. Jeanne Brooks-Gunn, "Strategies for Altering the Outcomes of Poor Children and Their Families," in P. L. Chase-Lansdale and Jeanne Brooks-Gunn, eds., *Escape from Poverty: What Makes a Difference for Children?* (New York: Cambridge University Press, 1995); C. Howes, "Relations between Early Child Care and Schooling," *Development Psychology* 24 (1988): 53–57; S. Hofferth and D. A. Phillips, "Childcare Policy Research," *Journal of Social Issues* 47 (1991): 1–13.

13. I. Lazar and R. B. Darlington, "Lasting Effects of Early Education: A Report from the Consortium for Longitudinal Studies," *Monographs of the Society for Research in Child Development* 47 (1982): 1–151; Infant Health and Development Program, "Enhancing the Outcomes of Low-Birthweight, Premature Babies: A Multisite Randomized Trial," *Journal of the American Medical Association* 263 (1990): 3035–42; Jeanne Brooks-Gunn, C. McCarton, P. Casey, M. McCormick, C. Bauer, J. Bernbaum, J. Tyson, M. Swanson, F. Bennett, D. Scott, J. Tonascia, and C. Meinert, "Early Intervention in Low-Birthweight, Premature Infants: Results through Ages 5 Years from the Infant Health and Development Program," *Journal of the American Medical Association* 272 (1994): 1257–62; M. R. Burchinal, F. A. Campbell, D. M. Bryant, B. H. Wasik, and C. T. Ramey, "Early Intervention and Mediating Processes in Cognitive Performance of Children of Low-Income African-American Families," *Child Development* 68 (1997): 935–54.

14. E. F. Zigler, "Early Childhood Intervention: A Promising Preventative for Juvenile Delinquency," *American Psychologist* 47 (1992): 997–1006; H. Yoshikawa, "Prevention as Cumulative Protection: Effects of Early Family Support

and Education on Chronic Delinquency and Its Risks," *Psychological Bulletin* 115 (1994): 28–54; Brooks-Gunn et al., "Child Development in the Context of Family and Community Resources."

15. A. A. Benasich, Jeanne Brooks-Gunn, and B. C. Clewell, "How Do Mothers Benefit from Early Intervention Programs?" *Journal of Applied Developmental Psychology* 13 (1992): 311–62; P. K. Klebanov, Jeanne Brooks-Gunn, and M. M. McCormick, "Enhancing Maternal Social and Emotional Health via Family-Oriented Early Intervention," *Developmental Psychology,* forthcoming.

16. R. Conger, S. Ge, G. Elder Jr. et al., "Economic Stress, Coercive Family Process, and Developmental Problems of Adolescents," *Child Development* 65 (1994): 541–61.

17. V. McLoyd, "The Impact of Economic Hardship on Black Families and Children: Psychological Distress, Parenting, and Socioeconomic Development," *Child Development* 61 (1990): 311–46.

18. N. Adler, T. Boyce, M. A. Chesney et al., "Socioeconomic Inequalities in Health: No Easy Solution," *Journal of the American Medical Association* 269 (1993): 3140–45.

19. Klebanov, Brooks-Gunn, and McCormick, "Enhancing Maternal Social and Emotional Health."

20. Brooks-Gunn and Duncan, "The Effects of Poverty on Children and Youth."

21. Brooks-Gunn, Guo, and Furstenburg, "Who Drops Out of and Who Continues beyond High School?"

22. R. Sampson, S. Raudenbush, and F. Earls, "Neighborhoods and Violent Crime: A Multilevel Study of Collective Efficacy," *Science* 277 (1997): 918–24.

23. Greg J. Duncan, K. Harris, and J. Boisjoly, "Time Limits and Welfare Reform: New Estimates of the Number and Characteristics of Affected Families," Joint Center for Poverty Research, Northwestern University, 1997.

24. M. Bane and D. Ellwood, *Welfare Realities* (Cambridge: Harvard University Press, 1994).

25. Ibid.; Duncan, Harris, and Boisjoly, "Time Limits and Welfare Reform."

26. T. Fraker, L. Nixon, J. Losby, C. Pringle, and J. Else, *Iowa's Limited Benefit Plan: Summary Report* (Princeton, N.J.: Mathematica Policy Research, 1997).

27. R. Moffitt, "The Effect of the Welfare System on Nonmarital Childbearing," in Department of Health and Human Services, *Report to Congress on Out-of-Wedlock Childbearing* (Washington, D.C.: Government Printing Office, 1996).

28. J. Currie, "Choosing among Alternative Programs for Poor Children," *Future of Children* 7 (1997): 113–31; B. Devancey, M. Ellwood, and J. Love, "Programs That Mitigate the Effects of Poverty on Children," *Future of Children* 7 (1997): 88–112.

29. Benasich, Brooks-Gunn, and Clewell, "How Do Mothers Benefit from Early Intervention Programs?"

30. R. E. Behrman, "Home Visits," *Future of Children* 3 (1993).

Chapter 3: Poverty as a Public Health Issue

Work on this chapter was supported by grants to the Institute for Research on Poverty from the U.S. Department of Health and Human Services and to the Center for Demography and Ecology from the National Institute of Child Health and Human Development.

1. *Report of the National Advisory Commission on Civil Disorders* (Washington, D.C.: Government Printing Office, 1968).

2. Gary D. Sandefur, "Blacks, Hispanics, American Indians, and Poverty—and What Worked," in Fred R. Harris and Roger W. Wilkins, eds., *Quiet Riots: Race and Poverty in the United States* (New York: Pantheon, 1988).

3. Ibid.; Sheldon H. Danziger and Daniel H. Weinberg, "The Historical Record: Trends in Family Income, Inequality, and Poverty," in Sheldon H. Danziger, Gary D. Sandefur, and Daniel H. Weinberg, eds., *Confronting Poverty: Prescriptions of Change* (Cambridge: Harvard University Press, 1994).

4. National Research Council, *Measuring Poverty: A New Approach* (Washington, D.C.: National Academy Press, 1995).

5. To adjust poverty thresholds by family type, the National Research Council committee developed a formula to account for the different consumption needs of adults and children. The committee considered two scale economy factors (0.75 and 0.65) but could not choose between them. Our statistics use the more conservative 0.75-scale economy factor. Using data from the Survey of Income and Program Participation (SIPP) along with that measure, the 1992 poverty rate would have been between 15 and 16 percent, since the SIPP considers more sources of income than does the Current Population Survey (CPS), which is the database currently used in determining official poverty measurements.

6. Danziger and Weinberg, "The Historical Record," p. 18; see also Rebecca M. Blank and Alan Blinder, "Macroeconomics, Income Distribution, and Poverty," in Sheldon H. Danziger and Daniel H. Weinberg, eds., *Fighting Poverty: What Works and What Doesn't* (Cambridge: Harvard University Press, 1986); Timothy M. Smeeding, "Why the U.S. Antipoverty System Doesn't Work Very Well," *Challenge* 35 (1992): 30–35.

7. Eleanor Baugher and Leatha Lamison-White, U.S. Bureau of the Census, *Poverty in the United States: 1995,* Current Population Report P60-194 (Washington, D.C.: Government Printing Office, 1996).

8. The poverty rates for 1959 and 1969 of the Asian population is not available in publications from the U.S. Bureau of the Census. The poverty rates for years between the census years are from data collected in the March Current Population Survey of each year. The report new permits estimates of the poverty rates of Asians and Hispanics as well as of blacks and whites but does not permit estimates of the poverty rate of Native Americans. In addition, one must bear in mind the heterogeneity of each racial and ethnic group, which is most apparent

for Asians and Hispanics, for whom poverty rates vary widely by national origin and nativity.

9. Baugher and Lamison-White.

10. Ibid.

11. The U.S. Bureau of the Census has not published poverty rates for inner-city, metropolitan, and nonmetropolitan areas since 1992. Further, the Current Population Survey public use samples do not provide all information on location necessary for producing these estimates. Consequently, we focus on the 1992 results. Generally, metropolitan areas have a minimum population of 50,000 persons; nonmetropolitan areas have a population less than 50,000 persons, so are not necessarily rural. An inner city is the largest place within a metropolitan area; areas outside the inner city are considered suburbs.

12. Whites include Hispanic whites as well as non-Hispanic whites. Much of the published data we consulted do not allow for this distinction. In some cases, Hispanic whites may be double counted, since the race category and the Hispanic origin category are not mutually exclusive.

13. In the published census data, poverty areas are defined as those with poverty rates of 20 percent or higher.

14. William Julius Wilson, *The Truly Disadvantaged: The Inner City, the Underclass, and Public Policy* (Chicago: University of Chicago Press, 1987); Wilson, *When Work Disappears: The World of the New Urban Poor* (New York: Knopf, 1996).

15. U.S. Bureau of the Census, *Poverty in the United States: 1995.*

16. Wilson, *When Work Disappears.*

17. Danziger, Sandefur, and Weinberg, *Confronting Poverty.*

18. Sheldon Danziger and Peter Gottschalk, eds., *Uneven Tides: Rising Inequality in the 1980s* (New York: Russell Sage, 1993).

19. Ed Gillespie and Bob Schellhas, eds., *Contract with America: The Bold Plan by Rep. Newt Gingrich, Rep. Dick Armey, and the House Republicans to Change the Nation* (New York: Times Books, 1994).

20. Kathryn Edin and Laura Lein, *Making Ends Meet: How Single Mothers Survive Welfare and Low-Wage Work* (New York: Russell Sage, 1997).

21. See Sarah S. Brown and Leon Eisenberg, eds., *The Best Intentions: Unintended Pregnancy and the Well-being of Children and Families* (Washington, D.C.: National Academy Press, 1995), for a discussion of the role of unintended pregnancies in out-of-wedlock childbearing; Ethan A. Nadelmann, "Commonsense Drug Policy," *Foreign Affairs* 77 (1998): 111–26, for a discussion of the implications of treating drugs as a public health issue.

22. Paul A. Jargowsky, *Poverty and Place: Ghettos, Barrios, and the American City* (New York: Russell Sage, 1997), p. 71.

23. Roderick J. Harrison and Claudette E. Bennett, "Racial and Ethnic Diversity," in Reynolds Farley, ed., *Social Trends*, vol. 2 of *State of the Union: America in the 1990s* (New York: Russell Sage, 1995), p. 200.

Chapter 4: The New Urban Poverty

Data used in this chapter were collected for the study "Youth Achievement and the Structure of Inner City Communities," which was funded by the Mac-Arthur Foundation as part of the research program on Successful Adolescent Development in High Risk Areas. Additional funds were made available to the Joblessness and Urban Poverty Research Program at the Malcolm Wiener Center for Social Policy, John F. Kennedy School of Government, Harvard; and by the Ford and Rockefeller Foundations.

1. *Report of the National Advisory Commission on Civil Disorders* (Washington, D.C.: Government Printing Office, 1968).

2. Stephan Thernstrom and Abigail Thernstrom, *America in Black and White: One Nation Indivisible* (New York: Simon and Schuster, 1997).

3. Lawrence Katz, "Wage Subsidies for the Disadvantaged," Working Paper 5679, National Bureau of Economic Research, Cambridge, Mass.; Steven M. Teles, *Whose Welfare? AFDC and Elite Politics* (Lawrence: University Press of Kansas, 1996).

4. Gary Orfield, "Race Tensions and Institutional Support: Social Programs during a Period of Retrenchment," in Margaret Weir, Ann Shola Orloff, and Theda Skocpol, eds., *The Politics of Social Policy in the United States* (Princeton: Princeton University Press, 1988).

5. Michael Katz, *The Undeserving Poor: From the War on Poverty to the War on Welfare* (New York: Pantheon, 1989).

6. Sheldon H. Danziger and Daniel H. Weinberg, "The Historical Record: Trends in Family Income, Inequality, and Poverty," in Sheldon H. Danziger, Gary D. Sandefur, and Daniel H. Weinberg, eds., *Confronting Poverty: Prescriptions for Change* (Cambridge: Harvard University Press, 1994).

7. Michael Katz, *In the Shadow of the Poorhouse: The History of Welfare in America,* rev. ed. (New York: Basic Books, 1996).

8. Danziger and Weinberg, "The Historical Record."

9. Dona Cooper Hamilton and Charles V. Hamilton, *The Dual Agenda: Race and Social Welfare Policies of Civil Rights Organizations* (New York: Pantheon, 1997).

10. Weir, Orloff, and Skocpol, *The Politics of Social Policy.*

11. Katz, *The Undeserving Poor;* James T. Patterson, *America's Struggle against Poverty, 1900–1985,* rev. ed. (Cambridge: Harvard University Press, 1986); Nancy E. Rose, *Workfare or Fair Work: Women, Welfare, and Government Work Programs* (New Brunswick: Rutgers University Press, 1995).

12. See William Julius Wilson, *The Declining Significance of Race: Blacks and Changing American Institutions,* 2d ed. (Chicago: University of Chicago Press, 1980).

13. William Julius Wilson, *When Work Disappears: The World of the New Urban Poor* (New York: Knopf, 1996).

14. David Schwartzman, *Black Unemployment: Part of Unskilled Unemployment* (Westport, Conn.: Greenwood, 1997).

15. Wilson, *When Work Disappears.*

16. Ibid., p. 195.

17. *Report of the National Advisory Commission on Civil Disorders,* p. 401.

18. Katz, *The Undeserving Poor;* Hamilton and Hamilton, *The Dual Agenda.*

19. Michael Hout, "Occupational Mobility of Black Men: 1962–1973," *American Sociological Review* 48 (1984): 308–22; William Julius Wilson, *The Truly Disadvantaged: The Inner City, the Underclass, and Public Policy* (Chicago: University of Chicago Press, 1987); Paul A. Jargowsky, *Poverty and Place: Ghetto, Barrios, and the American City* (New York: Russell Sage, 1997).

20. Wilson, *The Truly Disadvantaged.*

21. Paul A. Jargowsky and Mary Jo Bane, "Ghetto Poverty in the United States, 1970–1980," in Christopher Jencks and Paul E. Peterson, eds., *The Urban Underclass* (Washington, D.C.: Brookings, 1991); John Kasarda, "Jobs, Migration, and Emerging Urban Mismatches," in Laurence E. Lynn Jr. and Michael G. H. McGeary, eds., *Urban Change and Poverty* (Washington, D.C.: National Academy Press, 1993).

22. Jargowsky, *Poverty and Place.*

23. Jargowsky and Bane, "Ghetto Poverty in the United States."

24. Wilson, *When Work Disappears,* p. 14.

25. Ruth R. Kornhauser, *Social Sources of Delinquency* (Chicago: University of Chicago Press, 1978); Robert J. Bursik Jr., "Social Disorganization and Theories of Crime and Delinquency," *Criminology* 26 (1988): 519–15.

26. Robert J. Sampson and W. Byron Groves, "Community Structures and Crime: Testing Social Disorganization Theory," *American Journal of Sociology* 94 (1989): 774–802; Wilson, *When Work Disappears.*

27. Wilson, *The Truly Disadvantaged.*

28. William Julius Wilson, "Studying Inner City Social Dislocations: The Challenge of Public Agenda Research," *American Sociological Review* 56 (1991): 1–14; M. Greene, "Chronic Exposure to Crime and Poverty: Interventions That Work for Youth," *Crime and Delinquency* 39 (1993): 106–24; Kevin Hopkins, "Behavior Routes to Dependency," in Kevin Hopkins, ed., *Welfare Dependency: Behavior, Culture, and Public Policy* (Alexandria, Va.: Hudson Institute, 1987).

29. Wilson, *The Truly Disadvantaged.*

30. Jargowsky, *Poverty and Place.*

31. Wilson, *The Truly Disadvantaged.*

32. Robert J. Bursik Jr. and Harold G. Grasmick, *Neighborhoods and Crime: The Dimensions of Effective Community Control* (New York: Lexington, 1993).

33. Frank Furstenberg, "How Families Manage Risk and Opportunity in Dangerous Neighborhoods," in William Julius Wilson, ed., *Sociology and the Public Agenda* (Newbury Park, Calif.: Sage, 1992).

34. Bursik and Grasmick, *Neighborhoods and Crime.*

35. Wilson, *The Truly Disadvantaged.*

36. Jonathan Crane, "The Epidemic Theory of Ghettos and Neighborhood Effects on Dropping Out and Teenage Childbearing," *American Journal of Sociology* 96 (1991): 1226–59; James M. Quane and Bruce H. Rankin, "Does Living in Poor Neighborhood Reduce Commitment to 'Mainstream' Goals?: The Case of African-American Adolescents and Occupational Expectations," *Journal of Family Issues,* in press.

37. Report of the National Advisory Commission on Civil Disorders, p. 1.

38. Wilson, *When Work Disappears.*

39. Michael Katz, *Improving Poor People: The Welfare State, the 'Underclass,' and Urban Schools as History* (Princeton: Princeton University Press, 1995).

40. Margaret Weir, *The Boundaries of Employment Policy in the United States* (Princeton: Princeton University Press, 1988).

41. Demetrios Caraley, "Washington Abandons the Cities," *Political Science Quarterly* 107 (1992): 1–30; Wilson, *When Work Disappears.*

Chapter 5: Urban Poverty, Race, and the Inner City

1. Sheldon Danziger and Peter Gottschalk, *American Unequal* (New York: Russell Sage, 1995), p. 149.

2. *Report of the National Advisory Commission on Civil Disorders* (Washington, D.C.: Government Printing Office, 1968; New York: Dutton, 1968), p. 244.

3. Douglas S. Massey and Nancy A. Denton, *American Apartheid: Segregation and the Making of the Underclass* (Cambridge: Harvard University Press, 1993); John Yinger, *Closed Doors, Opportunities Lost: The Continuing Costs of Housing Discrimination* (New York: Russell Sage, 1995).

4. *Report of the National Advisory Commission on Civil Disorders,* pp. 244–45.

5. Reynolds Farley and William H. Frey, "Changes in the Segregation of Whites and Blacks during the 1980s: Small Steps toward a More Integrated Society," *American Sociological Review* 59 (1994): 23–45; Douglas S. Massey and Nancy A. Denton, "Trends in the Residential Segregation of Blacks, Hispanics, and Asians: 1970–1980," *American Sociological Review* 52 (1987): 802–25; Massey and Denton, *American Apartheid.*

6. Reynolds Farley, "Residential Segregation of Social and Economic Groups among Blacks, 1970 to 1980," in Christopher Jencks and Paul E. Peterson, eds., *The Urban Underclass* (Washington, D.C.: Brookings, 1991), pp. 274–98.

7. Paul A. Jargowsky, *Poverty and Place: Ghettos, Barrios, and the American City* (New York: Russell Sage, 1997).

8. Paul A. Jargowsky, "Metropolitan Restructuring and Urban Policy," *Stanford Law and Policy Review* 8 (1997): 48.

9. *Report of the National Advisory Commission on Civil Disorders,* p. 12.

10. Ibid., 203–4.

11. Michael Katz, *In the Shadow of the Poorhouse: A Social History of Welfare in America* (New York: Basic Books, 1986).

12. *Report of the National Advisory Commission on Civil Disorders,* quotations on pp. 262, 406.

13. William Julius Wilson, *The Truly Disadvantaged: The Inner City, the Underclass, and Public Policy* (Chicago: University of Chicago Press, 1987).

14. U.S. Congress, Office of Technology Assessment, *The Technological Reshaping of Metropolitan America* (Washington, D.C.: Government Printing Office, 1995).

15. Paul A. Jargowsky and Mary Jo Bane, "Ghetto Poverty in the United States: 1970–1980," in Jencks and Peterson, *The Urban Underclass,* pp. 235–73; Jargowsky, *Poverty and Place.*

16. Jargowsky and Bane, "Ghetto Poverty in the United States."

17. Ingrid Ellen, "The Stability of Racially Mixed Neighborhoods: Revealing New Evidence from 34 Metropolitan Areas," paper presented to the Eighteenth Annual Research Conference of the Association of Public Policy Analysis, 1996; Douglas S. Massey, Andrew B. Gross, and Kumiko Shibuya, "Migration, Segregation, and the Geographic Concentration of Poverty," *American Sociological Review* 59 (1994): 425–45.

18. Jargowsky, *Poverty and Place.*

19. Paul A. Jargowsky, "Take the Money and Run: Economic Segregation in U.S. Metropolitan Areas," *American Sociological Review* 61 (1996): 984–98; Douglas S. Massey and Mitchell L. Eggers, "The Spatial Concentration of Affluence and Poverty during the 1970s," *Urban Affairs Quarterly* 29 (1993): 299–315.

20. William H. Frey, "People in Places: Demographic Trends in Urban America," in Jack Sommer and Donald A. Hicks, eds., *Rediscovering Urban America: Perspectives on the 1980s* (Washington, D.C.: Department of Housing and Urban Development, 1993).

21. Mark Alan Hughes, *Over the Horizon: Jobs in the Suburbs of Major Metropolitan Areas* (Philadelphia: Public/Private Ventures, 1993), 16–17; Wilson, *The Truly Disadvantaged;* William Julius Wilson, *When Work Disappears: The World of the New Urban Poor* (New York: Knopf, 1996).

22. Donald A. Hicks, "Revitalizing Our Cities or Restoring Ties to Them? Redirecting the Debate," *Journal of Law Reform* 27 (1994): 813–75; 815.

23. Peter D. Salins, "Cities, Suburbs, and the Urban Crisis," *Public Interest* 113 (1993): 97.

24. *Report of the National Advisory Commission on Civil Disorders,* p. 235.

25. Ibid., pp. 203–4; emphasis in the original.

26. Ibid., p. 408.

Chapter 6: Race, Violence, and Justice since Kerner

1. Calculated from *Vital Statistics of the United States* (Hyattsville, Md.: National Center for Health Statistics, various years); *Statistical Abstract of the United States* (Washington, D.C.: Government Printing Office, 1997), p. 204.

2. Calculated from World Health Organization, *World Health Statistics, 1994* (Geneva: WHO, 1996); *Health—United States, 1996–97* (Hyattsville, Md.: National Center for Health Statistics, 1997), pp. 156–57.

3. *Health—United States, 1996–97*, pp. 156–57.

4. Donna L. Hoyert and U. Hsing-Chiang Kung, *Asian or Pacific Islander Mortality, Selected States, 1992* (Hyattsville, Md.: National Center for Health Statistics, 1997), p. 3.

5. *Report of Final Mortality Statistics, 1995* (Hyattsville, Md.: National Center for Health Statistics, 1997), pp. 53–55.

6. Ibid.

7. Gopal K. Singh and Stella M. Yu, "Trends and Differentials in Adolescent and Young Adult Mortality in the United States, 1950 through 1993," *American Journal of Public Health* 86 (1996): 564.

8. Calculated from *Report of Final Mortality Statistics, 1995*, p. 19.

9. Romania figure from *Health—United States, 1996–97*, p. 41.

10. *Health—United States, 1996–97*, pp. 156–57.

11. Calculated from *Health—United States, 1995*, pp. 112–13.

12. Rates are approximate. Homicide totals are from Federal Bureau of Investigation, *Uniform Crime Report, 1968*, and *1996 Preliminary Annual Release* (Washington, D.C.: U.S. Department of Justice, 1968, 1997); 1970 census data was used to approximate the 1968 city populations; *Uniform Crime Report* was used to estimate 1996 city populations.

13. H. Range Hutson et al., "Adolescents and Children Injured in Drive-by Shootings in Los Angeles," *New England Journal of Medicine* 330 (1994): 325.

14. Craig A. Perkins, *Age Patterns of Victims of Serious Violent Crime* (Washington, D.C.: U.S. Bureau of Justice Statistics, 1997), pp. 5–6. In this calculation, the author includes homicide among violent crimes, though homicide is not counted in victim surveys.

15. Michael R. Rand, *Violence-Related Injuries Treated by Hospital Emergency Departments* (Washington, D.C.: U.S. Bureau of Justice Statistics, 1997), pp. 2–8.

16. Donald F. Schwartz et al., "A Longitudinal Study of Injury Morbidity in an African-American Population," *Journal of the American Medical Association* 27 (1994): 755–60.

17. These figures, and most that follow, are from *Prisoners in 1996* (Washington, D.C.: U.S. Bureau of Justice Statistics, 1997); and *Correctional Populations in the United States, 1995* (Washington, D.C.: U.S. Bureau of Justice Statistics, 1997).

18. *Census of State and Federal Correctional Facilities, 1995* (Washington, D.C.: U.S. Bureau of Justice Statistics, 1997), p. 3.

19. Hispanic prison figures from Patrick A. Langan, *Race of Prisoners Admitted to State and Federal Institutions, 1926–86* (Washington, D.C.: U.S. Bureau of Justice Statistics, 1991), p. 8. Jail figures from Margaret W. Cahalan, *Historical Corrections Statistics in the United States, 1850–1984* (Washington, D.C.: U.S. Bureau of Justice Statistics, 1986), p. 91.

20. Thomas P. Bonczar and Allen J. Beck, *Lifetime Likelihood of Going to State or Federal Prison* (Washington, D.C.: U.S. Bureau of Justice Statistics, 1997), p. 1. Note that this calculation does not include the chance of going to a local jail or a juvenile institution.

21. *Correctional Populations in the United States, 1995,* p. 7.

22. National figure from Marc Mauer and Tracy Huling, *Young Black Americans and the Criminal Justice System, Five Years Later* (Washington, D.C.: Sentencing Project, 1995); California figure from Vincent Schiraldi, Sue Kuyper, and Sharen Hewitt, *Young African Americans and the Criminal Justice System in California: Five Years Later* (San Francisco: Center on Juvenile and Criminal Justice, 1996); Baltimore figure from Jerome Miller, *Hobbling a Generation* (Alexandria, Va.: National Center on Institutions and Alternatives, 1992). These figures may double count some offenders who show up in more than one of these correctional populations—but not many. On this point, see Michael Tonry, *Malign Neglect: Race, Crime, and Punishment in America* (New York: Oxford University Press, 1995), pp. 30–31.

23. *Correctional Populations in the United States, 1995,* p. 7.

24. State incarceration figures from *Correctional Populations in the United States, 1995,* various pages; state population figures from *Statistical Abstract of the United States, 1997,* p. 34.

25. *Prisoners in 1996,* p. 10. In Massachusetts, blacks and Hispanics make up 9 percent of the general population, but 83 percent of state prison inmates sentenced under mandatory terms for drug offenses. Cary Goldberg, "Study Casts Doubt on Wisdom of Mandatory Terms for Drugs," *New York Times* (November 25, 1997).

26. Kathleen Connolly, Lea McDermid, Vincent Schiraldi, and Dan Macallair, *From Classrooms to Cellblocks* (San Francisco: Center on Juvenile and Criminal Justice, 1996), p. 2.

27. See generally Cassia C. Spohn, "Courts, Sentences, and Prisons," *Daedalus* 124 (1995): 119–43.

28. Tonry, *Malign Neglect,* pp. 30–31.

29. Alfred Blumstein, "On the Racial Disproportionality of United States Prison Populations," *Journal of Criminal Law and Criminology* 73, 1259–81.

30. Patrick A. Langan, "Racism on Trial: New Evidence to Explain the Racial Composition of Prisons in the United States," *Journal of Criminal Law and Criminology* 76, 666–83.

31. Robert D. Crutchfield, George S. Bridges, and Susan R. Pitchford, "Analytical and Aggregation Biases in Analyses of Imprisonment: Reconciling Dis-

crepancies in Studies of Racial Disparity," *Journal of Research in Crime and Delinquency* 31 (1994): 177–79.

32. Ibid.

33. James F. Nelson, *Disparities in Processing Felony Arrests in New York State, 1990–92* (Albany: New York State Division of Criminal Justice Services, 1995).

34. See Donna M. Bishop and Charles E. Frazier, "Race Effects in Juvenile Justice Decision-Making: Findings of a Statewide Analysis," *Journal of Criminal Law and Criminology* 86 (1996): pp. 404–9. Note that the disadvantage seemed to work in the other direction for "status" offenses.

35. Ibid.

36. Madeline Wordes, Timothy S. Bynum, and Charles J. Corley, "Locking Up Youth: The Impact of Race on Detention Decisions," *Journal of Research in Crime and Delinquency* 31 (1994): 149–65.

37. See Robert J. Sampson and John H. Laub, "Structural Variations in Juvenile Court Processing," *Law and Society Review* 27 (1993): 306.

38. Ibid., p. 306.

39. Darlene J. Conley, "Adding Color to a Black and White Picture: Using Qualitative Data to Explain Racial Disproportionality in the Juvenile Justice System," *Journal of Research in Crime and Delinquency* 31 (1994): 135–48.

40. J. D. Unnever, "Direct and Organizational Discrimination in the Sentencing of Drug Offenders," *Social Problems* 30 (1982): 212–25.

41. Marjorie S. Zatz, "Race, Ethnicity, and Determinate Sentencing," *Criminology* 22 (1984): 147–71.

42. Gary D. LaFree, "Official Reactions to Hispanic Defendants in the Southwest," *Journal of Research in Crime and Delinquency* 22 (1985): 213–37.

43. Cf. Harold Watts and Demetra Smith Nightingale, "Adding It Up: The Economic Impact of Incarceration on Individuals," in *The Unintended Consequences of Incarceration* (New York: Vera Institute of Justice, 1996).

44. See John Hagan, "The Next Generation: Children of Prisoners," in *Unintended Consequences of Incarceration*.

45. Connolly et al., *From Classrooms to Cellblocks*, pp. 1–15.

Chapter 7: Racism and the Poor

1. *Report of the National Advisory Commission on Civil Disorders* (Washington, D.C.: Government Printing Office, 1968).

2. *Brown v. Board of Education*, 347 U.S. 483 (1954); Civil Rights Act of 1964, Pub. L. No. 88-352, 78 Stat. 241 (codified as amended at 28 U.S.C. § 1447, 42 U.S.C. §§ 1971, 1975, 2000 [1988]). The Head Start program was created under the Economic Opportunity Act of 1964, Pub. L. No. 88-452, 78 Stat. 508. It was reauthorized under the Head Start Act of 1981, Pub. L. No. 97-35, 96 Stat. 499, and was amended by the Human Services Amendments of

1994, Pub. L. No. 103-252, 108 Stat. 623 (codified as amended in scattered sections of 20 and 42 U.S.C.). Elementary and Secondary Education Act of 1965, Pub. L. No. 89-10, 79 Stat. 27 (codified as amended in scattered sections of 20 U.S.C.). The act was reauthorized by the Augustus F. Hawkins—Robert T. Stafford Elementary and Secondary School Improvement Amendments of 1988, Pub. L. No. 100-297, 102 Stat. 230, and by the Improving America's Schools Act of 1994, Pub. L. No. 103-382, 108 Stat. 3518.

3. Civil Rights Act of 1968, Tit. VIII, § 812, Pub. L. No. 90-284, 82 Stat. 73, 88 (codified as amended at 42 U.S.C. § 3612).

4. *Keyes v. School District No. 1,* 413 U.S. 189, 207 (1973) (holding that intentionally segregative conduct by a school board in a "meaningful portion" of a school system would require a systemwide remedy); *Swann v. Charlotte-Mecklenburg Board of Education,* 402 U.S. 1, 28-29 (1971) (holding that a district court has broad discretion to administer remedies, including systemwide desegregation through the use of busing); *Green v. County School Board of New Kent County,* 391 U.S. 430, 438 (1968) (holding that a school board has an affirmative duty to eliminate a dual system "root and branch").

5. *Griggs v. Duke Power Co.,* 401 U.S. 424, 429-33 (1971).

6. See, for example, Title IX of the Education Amendments of 1972, 20 U.S.C. §§ 1681-88 (preventing discrimination on the basis of gender in educational programs receiving federal assistance); Americans with Disabilities Act of 1990, Pub. L. No. 101-36, 104 Stat. 327 (codified as amended in scattered sections of 42 and 47 U.S.C. and 29 U.S.C. § 706 [1988]) (providing equal access to persons with disabilities in the areas of employment, public accommodations, and transportation); *Franklin v. Gwinnett County Public Schools,* 112 S.Ct. 1028, 1087 (1992) (holding that Title IX remedies include monetary damages); *Lau v. Nichols,* 414 U.S. 563, 564 (1974) (holding that non-English-speaking students are entitled to equal educational opportunity under 42 U.SC. § 2000d [1988]).

7. See Voting Rights Act Amendments of 1982, Pub. L. No. 97-205, 96 Stat. 131 (codified as amended at 42 U.S.C. § 1973 [1988]) (reversing *City of Mobile v. Bolden,* 446 U.S. 55 [1980]); Civil Rights Act of 1991, Pub. L. No. 102-166, 105 Stat. 1071 (codified as amended in scattered sections of 2, 16, 29, and 42 U.S.C.A. [West Supp. 1991]) (reversing *Wards Cove Packing Co., Inc. v. Atonio,* 490 U.S. 642, 655-58 [1989] and other Supreme Court decisions in 1989); Civil Rights Restoration Act of 1988, Pub. L. No. 100-259, 102 Stat. 28 (codified as amended at 20 U.S.C.A. §§ 1681, 1687, 1688; 29 U.S.C.A. §§ 4, 706; 42 U.S.C.A. §§ 2000—4, 6107 [West Supp. 1991]) (reversing *Grove City College v. Bell,* 465 U.S. 555, 570–75 [1984]).

8. See Bill McAllister, "Call for a Panel on L.A. Unrest Echoes Historical Response," *Washington Post,* May 4, 1992; Carla Rivera, "Riots' Causes Same as in '60s, State Panel Says," *Los Angeles Times,* Oct. 2, 1992.

9. See, for example, John F. Kain, "Housing Segregation, Negro Employ-

ment, and Metropolitan Decentralization," *Quarterly Journal of Economics* 82 (1968): 175 (addressing the link between discrimination and segregation in metropolitan housing markets and the distribution and level of minority employment); John F. Kain, "The Spatial Mismatch Hypothesis: Three Decades Later," *Housing Policy Debate* 3 (1992): 371 (reviewing research regarding the impact of housing discrimination on black employment); John D. Kasarda, "Urban Industrial Transition and the Underclass," *Annals of the American Academy of Political and Social Science* 501 (1989): 26 (noting the transformation of cities from "centers of production and distribution of goods to centers of administration, finance and information exchange," and a resulting loss in available blue-collar employment).

10. See, for example, *Abbott v. Burke*, 199 N.J. 287, 355–57, 575 A.2d 359, 393–94 (1990) (discussing the relationship between "municipal overburden" and substandard education in urban areas).

11. Douglas S. Massey and Nancy A. Denton, *American Apartheid: Segregation and the Making of the Underclass* (Cambridge: Harvard University Press, 1993), pp. 129–30. Massey and Denton construct an index of concentrated poverty based on the percentage of poor families in the neighborhood of the average poor family. They then compare the percentage poor in the neighborhood of the average poor black family with a like percentage for the average white family.

12. *Brown v. Board of Education.*

13. *Strauder v. West Virginia*, 100 U.S. 303, 307–308 (1880).

14. James S. Coleman, Ernest Q. Campbell, Carol J. Hobson, James McPartland, Alexander M. Mood, Frederic D. Weinfeld, and Robert L. York, *Equality of Educational Opportunity* (Washington, D.C.: Government Printing Office, 1966) (the Coleman Report). *See also* U.S. Commission on Civil Rights, *Racial Isolation in the Public Schools* (Washington, D.C.: Government Printing Office, 1967).

15. Abt Associates, *Prospects: The Congressionally Mandated Study of Educational Growth and Opportunity* (Washington, D.C.: Department of Education, 1993).

16. In high-poverty schools, 30 percent of poor children scored in the lowest tenth percentile, three times the percentage of those in low-poverty schools. In contrast, 30 percent of poor children in low-poverty schools scored in the top half, compared with only 16 percent of those in high-poverty schools.

17. National Assessment of Educational Progress, *Three Assessments of Progress in Reading Performance, 1970–1980* (Denver: Education Commission of the States, 1981).

18. Marshall Smith and Jennifer O'Day, "Educational Equality: 1966 and Now," in Deborah A. Verstegen and James G. Ward, eds., *Spheres of Justice in Education: The 1990 American Education Finance Association Yearbook* (New York: Harper Business, 1991), p. 75.

19. David W. Grissmer, Sheila Natarj Kirby, Mark Berends, and Stephanie

Williamson, *Student Achievement and the Changing American Family: An Executive Summary* (Santa Monica, Calif.: Rand, 1994), p. 22.

20. Other factors may have been the increased investments in public education in the South, after enactment of Title I of the Elementary and Secondary Education Act and the availability of more early childhood education opportunities for poor children after passage of Head Start.

21. Robert L. Crain and Rita E. Marhard, "Minority Achievement: Policy Implications of Research," in Willis D. Hawley, ed., *Effective School Desegregation: Equity, Quality, and Feasibility* (Beverly Hills, Calif.: Sage, 1981).

22. James McPartland and JoMills Braddock, "Going to College and Getting a Good Job: The Impact of Desegregation," in Hawley, *Effective School Desegregation*, n. 24. In addition, low-income black students who receive a desegregated education have a good chance of avoiding situations and behavior (such as teenage pregnancy and hostile encounters with police) that blight the prospects of many of their peers. These findings emerge from a long-term study of some seven hundred low-income students in Hartford, Connecticut, one group of which began desegregation in the 1960s while the other remained in segregated schools. See "Study Finds Desegregation Is an Effective Social Tool," *New York Times*, Sept. 17, 1985. See also Robert L. Crain and Jack Strauss, *School Desegregation and Black Occupational Attainments: Results from a Long-Term Experiment* (Baltimore: John Hopkins University, Center for Social Organization of Schools, 1985) (analyzing the impact of the Hartford desegregation program on occupational outcomes).

23. Amy Stuart Wells and Robert L. Crain, *Stepping over the Color Line: African-American Students in White Suburban Schools* (New Haven: Yale University Press, 1997), pp. 197–99.

24. Dennis W. Brogan, *The American Character* (New York: Time, 1956), pp. 170, 174–75.

25. Gary Orfield and Sean Reardon, "Working Papers: Race, Poverty, and Inequality," in Susan M. Liss and William L. Taylor, eds., *New Opportunities: Civil Rights at a Crossroads* (Washington, D.C.: Citizens' Commission on Civil Rights, 1992).

26. *Education Watch: The 1996 Education Trust State and National Data Book* (Washington, D.C.: Education Trust, 1996), p. 5.

27. White House Press Release, "Remarks by the President in Ceremony Commemorating the 40th Anniversary of the Desegregation of Central High School" (White House: Office of the Press Secretary, Sept. 25, 1997).

28. See *ICCM Employ. Prac. Guide* (1973), p. 1860; U.S. Commission on Civil Rights, *Federal Civil Rights Enforcement Effort—1974* (Washington, D.C.: Government Printing Office, 1975), pp. 552–53.

29. One critic of this point argues that the initiatives I cite are dated, going back to the 1970s and 1980s. But Richard D. Kahlenberg, *The Remedy: Class, Race, and Affirmative Action* (New York: Basic Books, 1996), fails to note that the

continued presence of minorities in these fields into the 1990s indicates that affirmation action is continuing to provide opportunity and mobility. Nor does he deal with the precipitous drop in minority enrollments at higher education institutions that have been forced by court orders to eliminate their affirmative action policies, an omen of what may happen both in higher education and employment if affirmative action is ended.

30. See Marcus Alexis, "The Effect of Admission Procedures on Minority Enrollment in Graduate and Professional Schools," in *Working Papers: Bakke, Weber and Affirmative Action* (New York: Rockefeller Foundation, 1979), pp. 52–71.

31. Grissmer et al., *Student Achievement and the Changing American Family,* n. 22.

32. See especially Richard J. Herrnstein, *The Bell Curve: Intelligence and Class Structure in American Life* (New York: Free Press, 1994).

33. Title I of the Improving America's Schools Act, Pub. L. 103-382, 108 Stat. 3518 (codified at 20 U.S.C. §§ 6301–6514) (1994).

34. There is also room for enlightened judicial action at the state level. In *Sheff v. O'Neill,* 238 Conn. 1, 678 A.2d 1267 (1996), the Connecticut Supreme Court found that the equal protection provisions of the state constitution required a remedy for poor children of color in isolated schools of the inner city.

35. Franklin Delano Roosevelt, Second Inaugural Address, January 20, 1937, in Davis Newton Lott, ed., *The Inaugural Addresses of the American Presidents from Washington to Kennedy* (New York: Holt, Rinehart, and Winston, 1961), pp. 239–40.

Chapter 8: Policy for the New Millennium

1. This chapter is a summary of the Milton S. Eisenhower Foundation's thirty-year update of the Report of the National Advisory Commission on Civil Disorders, *The Millennium Breach: Richer, Poorer and Racially Apart* (Washington, D.C.: Milton S. Eisenhower Foundation, 1998). Written by Lynn A. Curtis and Fred R. Harris, with inputs from other Eisenhower Trustees, the update is available from the Milton S. Eisenhower Foundation.

2. See chapter 1.

3. Center for Community Change, *Newsletter* (Issue 19, Fall 1997); Alan Okagaki, *Developing a Public Policy Agenda on Jobs* (Washington, D.C.: Center for Community Change, 1997).

4. Jerry Jones, *Federal Revenue Policies That Work: A Blueprint for Job Creation to Support Welfare Reform* (Washington, D.C.: Center for Community Change, 1997).

5. See chapter 4. Also see William Julius Wilson, *When Work Disappears: The World of the New Urban Poor* (New York: Knopf, 1996).

6. Data are from the Congressional Budget Office. See Jason DeParle, "Richer Rich, Poorer Poor, and a Fatter Green Book," *New York Times,* May 26, 1991; and Lynn A. Curtis, *Family, Employment and Reconstruction* (Milwaukee: Family Service America, 1995).

7. Kevin Phillips, *The Politics of Rich and Poor* (New York: Random House, 1990).

8. U.S. Census, *Historical Poverty Tables* (Washington, D.C.: U.S. Census, 1997); Children's Defense Fund, *The State of America's Children* (Washington, D.C.: Children's Defense Fund, 1994); Felicity Baringer, "Rich-Poor Gulf Widens among Blacks, *New York Times,* Sept. 25, 1992; Keith Bradsher, "Gap in Wealth in U.S. Called Widest in West," *New York Times,* Apr. 17, 1995; and Editorial "The Tide Is Not Lifting Everyone," *New York Times,* Sept. 30, 1997.

9. Glenn C. Loury, "Unequalized," *New Republic,* Apr. 6, 1998.

10. Ibid.

11. Bradsher, "Gap in Wealth in U.S. Called Widest in West."

12. American Federation of State, County, and Municipal Workers, *Why Isn't the Economy Working for Workers?* (Washington, D.C.: American Federation of State, County, and Municipal Workers, 1997).

13. Gary Orfield, "Segregated Housing and School Desegregation," in Gary Orfield, Susan E. Eaton, and the Harvard Project on School Desegregation, *Dismantling Desegregation: The Quiet Reversal of Brown vs. Board of Education* (New York: New Press, 1996).

14. "Quality Counts 1998: The Urban Challenge," *Education Week,* Jan. 6, 1998.

15. John Atlas and Peter Drier, *A National Housing Agenda for the 1990s,* (Washington, D.C.: National Housing Institute, 1992); Lynn A. Curtis, *Family, Employment and Reconstruction;* and Sentencing Project, *Crime Rates and Incarceration: Are We Any Safer?* (Washington, D.C.: Sentencing Project, 1992).

16. Roberto Suro, "More Is Spent on New Prisons Than Colleges," *Washington Post,* Feb. 24, 1997; and Beatrix Hamburg, "President's Report," *Annual Report, 1996* (New York: William T. Grant Foundation, 1997).

17. Mark Mauer, *Young Black Men and the Criminal Justice System* (Washington, D.C.: Sentencing Project, 1990); and Mark Mauer, *Intended and Unintended Consequences: State Racial Disparities in Imprisonment* (Washington, D.C.: Sentencing Project, 1997).

18. Milton Freidman, "There's No Justice in the War on Drugs," *New York Times,* Jan. 11, 1998.

19. Elliott Currie, *Crime and Punishment in America* (New York: Metropolitan Books, 1998); and Editorial, "Crack Sentences Revisited," *Washington Post,* May 5, 1997.

20. James Brooke, "Prisons: Growth Industry for Some," *New York Times* Nov. 2, 1997. Also see Steven R. Donziger, *The Real War on Crime: Report of the National Criminal Justice Commission* (New York: Harper Collins, 1996).

21. Jeffrey A. Roth, "Understanding and Preventing Violence," in *Research in Brief* (Washington, D.C.: National Institute of Justice, 1994); and Richard A. Mendel, *Prevention or Pork? A Hard Look at Youth-Oriented Anti-Crime Programs* (Washington, D.C.: American Youth Policy Forum, 1995).

22. Much of the same breach applies to those living in pockets of rural poverty. The original Kerner Report focused on urban poverty. Accordingly, our priority in the Eisenhower Foundation's thirty-year update upon which this chapter is based also is on urban poverty.

23. Urban Institute, *Confronting the Nation's Urban Crisis: From Watts (1965) to South Central Los Angeles (1992)* (Washington, D.C.: Urban Institute, 1992); William J. Cunningham, "Enterprise Zones," Testimony before the Committee on Select Revenue Measures, Committee on Ways and Means, United States House of Representatives, July 11, 1991; and Tom Furlong, "Enterprise Zone in L.A. Fraught with Problems," *Los Angeles Times,* May 19, 1992.

24. "Reinventing America," *Business Week,* Jan. 19, 1993; and "Not So EZ," *Economist,* Jan. 28, 1989.

25. "Job Training Partnership Act: Youth Pilot Projects," *Federal Register,* April 13, 1994.

26. Doris L. MacKenzie and Claire Souryal, *Multiple Evaluation of Shock Incarceration* (Washington, D.C.: National Institute of Justice, 1994).

27. Lynn A. Curtis, *Youth Investment and Police Mentoring: Final Report* (Washington, D.C.: Milton S. Eisenhower Foundation, 1998).

28. See Lynn A. Curtis and Fred R. Harris, *The Millennium Breach: Richer, Poorer and Racially Apart* (Washington, D.C.: Milton S. Eisenhower Foundation, 1998), chapter 4.

29. Lisbeth B. Schorr, "Helping Kids When It Counts," *Washington Post,* Apr. 30, 1997; and Committee for Economic Development, *Children in Need: Investment Strategies for the Educationally Disadvantaged* (New York: Committee for Economic Development, 1987).

30. See Curtis, *Youth Investment and Police Mentoring.*

31. Andrew Hahn, *Quantum Opportunities Program: A Brief on the QOP Pilot Program* (Waltham, Mass.: Center for Human Resources, Heller Graduate School, Brandeis University, 1995).

32. James P. Comer, *Waiting for a Miracle* (New York: Dutton, 1997).

33. Robert D. Felner et al., "The Impact of School Reform for the Middle Years," *Phi Delta Kappa,* Mar., 1997, 528–50.

34. Joy G. Dryfoos, *Safe Passage: Making It through Adolescence in a Risky Society* (New York: Oxford University Press, 1998).

35. Ibid.

36. Ibid.

37. Ibid.

38. Jonathan Kozol, "Saving Public Education," *Nation,* Feb. 17, 1997.

39. Curtis and Harris, *The Millennium Breach.*

40. Ibid.

41. Alan Okagaki, *Developing a Public Policy Agenda on Jobs.*

42. Curtis, *Family, Employment and Reconstruction;* and David Rusk, *Cities without Suburbs* (Washington, D.C.: Woodrow Wilson Center Press, 1993).

43. Ibid.

44. Michael Quint, "This Bank Can Turn a Profit and Follow a Social Agenda," *New York Times,* May 24, 1992.

45. Okagaki, *Developing a Public Policy Agenda on Jobs.*

46. Curtis, *Family, Employment and Reconstruction.*

47. Ibid.

48. Ann Mariano, "Paradise at Parkside Reclaims Its Legacy," *Washington Post,* June 29, 1991; and Bill Gifford, "Paradise Found," *Washington City Paper,* Jan. 29, 1993.

49. Jeff Faux, "The Economic Case for a Politics of Inclusion," paper prepared for the Eisenhower Foundation's 30th Anniversary Update of the Kerner Riot Commission (Washington, D.C.: Economic Policy Institute, 1998); Jeff Faux, "You Are Not Alone," in Stanley B. Greenberg and Theda Skocpol, eds., *The New Majority: Toward a Popular Progressive Politics* (New Haven and London: Yale University Press, 1997).

50. Ibid.

51. Ibid.

52. The details for this section are found in Curtis and Harris, *The Millennium Breach,* chapter 6.

53. Ibid.

54. Ibid.

55. Details for how the line items in table 8.1 were calculated are found in Curtis and Harris, *The Millennium Breach.* The $7 billion per year for Head Start is the estimated cost for expanding the existing Head Start program to all eligible poor children. The $15 billion per year for replication of successful public inner-city school reform initiatives is based on estimates by Joy Dryfoos that roughly 15,000 schools in the United States serve disadvantaged urban youth, children, and teenagers; that the average number of students per school is about 1,000; and that the average cost per student to implement reforms that work is about $1,000. The $1 billion per year for the Corporation for Youth Investment is a conservative estimate for funding, technically assisting and evaluating safe haven-type and Quantum Opportunities-type replications for a fraction of the children, youth, and teenagers who could benefit from them. The $4.5 billion per year for job training reform modeled after the Argus Community would allow training each year for a fraction of the 2,000,000-plus inner-city unemployed who need it. The $1 billion per year for the National Community Development Bank is expected to generate a fraction of the 1,000,000 new private jobs that is our goal for the inner city. The $5 billion per year for 250,000 public sector construction and urban repair jobs each year is based on estimates in United

States Conference of Mayors, *Ready to Go: New Lists of Transportation and Community Development Projects* (Washington, D.C.: United States Conference of Mayors, 1993). The $20 billion per year for 1,000,000 public service jobs is based on a minimum wage that averages to $20,000 per year, with benefits and administrative expenses. This is somewhat higher than the average assumed in Richard McGahey, *Estimating the Economic Impact of a Public Jobs Program* (Washington, D.C.: Center for Community Change, 1997). The $100 million per year for replication of race-specific solutions is a conservative estimate of the cost of significantly expanding proven successes, like the Gatreaux program for housing integration, along with the costs of a new on-line system to share facts on race and models of successful racial dialogue. The $2.4 billion per year is based primarily on estimates for expanding proven drug treatment for a fraction of those who need it, as calculated in Joseph A. Califano Jr., "Crime and Punishment—And Treatment, Too," *Washington Post,* Feb.8, 1998.

56. Robert B. Reich, *Locked in the Cabinet* (New York: Knopf, 1997).

57. McGahey, *Estimating the Economic Impact of a Public Jobs Program.*

58. Editorial, "150B a Year: Where to Find It," *New York Times,* Mar. 8, 1990; Editorial, "Star Wars in the Twilight Zone," *New York Times,* June 14, 1992; Editorial, "Who Needs Four Air Forces?" *New York Times,* Nov. 30, 1992; Jeffrey R. Smith, "Two Missiles Unnecessary, Ex Chiefs Say," *Washington Post,* Feb. 3, 1990; and Patrick E. Tyler, "Halving Defense Budget in a Decade Suggested," *Washington Post,* Nov. 21, 1989).

59. Ibid.

60. Jill Abramson, "Money Buys a Lot More Than Access," *New York Times,* Nov. 9, 1997; Kent Cooper, *Comments for the 30 Year Eisenhower Foundation Update of the Kerner Commission* (Washington, D.C.: Center for Responsive Politics, 1998); Ruth Marcus, "Business Donations Show Money Follows the Leaders," *Washington Post,* Nov. 25, 1997; Jamin B. Raskin, "Dollar Democracy," *Nation,* May 5, 1997; E. Joshua Rosenkranz, "Campaign Reform: The Hidden Killers," *Nation,* May 5, 1997; and Fred Wertheimer, "Unless We Ban Soft Money," *Washington Post,* Aug. 10, 1997.

61. Ibid.

62. James Ridgeway, "Heritage on the Hill," *Nation,* Dec. 22, 1997.

63. George Gerbner, "Reclaiming Our Cultural Mythology," *In Context,* (1994): 40–42.

64. For details on the Dorchester Youth Collaborative, see Curtis, *Youth Investment and Police Mentoring,* chapter 7.

65. For examples of how new stories were "framed" by the print media, see Michael A. Fletcher, "Kerner Prophecy on Race Relations Came True, Report Says," *Washington Post,* Mar. 1, 1998; Alissa J. Rubin, "Racial Divide Widens, Study Says," *Los Angeles Times,* Mar. 1, 1998; "Kerner Commission's Separate and Unequal Societies Exist Today: Report," *Jet,* Mar. 23, 1998; and Domenica Marchetti, "Charities Must Work to Build on Successes in Fight against Poverty, Report Says," *Chronicle of Philanthropy,* Mar. 12, 1998.

66. For examples of how we dismissed naysayers, see Elliott Currie, "Inequality and Violence in Our Cities," *Wall Street Journal*, Mar. 23, 1998; Lynn A. Curtis, "Kerner Update Used Scientific Evidence," *Chronicle of Philanthropy*, Apr. 9, 1998; Lynn A. Curtis, "A Long Way to Go," *Chicago Sun-Times*, Apr. 26, 1998; and Lynn A. Curtis, "Supply-Side Policies of the 1980s Opened Up a Class Breach," *Washington Times*, Apr. 27, 1998.

67. For examples of supportive opinion, see Editorial, "New War on Poverty," *Philadelphia Inquirer*, Mar. 8, 1998; Editorial, "Progress and Need," *Christian Science Monitor*, Mar. 5, 1998; Editorial, "Kerner at 30," *Minneapolis St. Paul Star Tribune*, Mar. 4, 1998; Editorial, "Racial Equity Continues to Elude Nation," *Milwaukee Journal Sentinel* Mar. 7, 1998; Editorial, "The Kerner Report, 30 Years Later," *Boston Globe*, Mar. 1, 1998; Barbara Reynolds, "Racial Divides Still Deserves Our Attention," *Detroit News and Free Press*, Mar. 8, 1998; Gregory Stanford, "Still the Chasm: Racial Gap Remains Unbridged," *Milwaukee Journal Sentinel*, Mar. 8, 1998; Brenda Payton, "Heed the Warnings," *Oakland Tribune* Mar. 5, 1998; Linda Wright Moore, "Deep Resolve Needed to Bridge the Race Abyss," *Philadelphia Daily News*, Mar. 5, 1998; Dwight Lewis, "Nation's Strides towards Equality Have Been Great, But Far More Is Needed on the Economic Front," *Tennessean*, Mar. 1, 1998; Gracie Bonds Staples, "Still Separate But Unequal Societies—And School Districts," *Fort Worth Star Telegram*, Mar. 1, 1998; Charlie James, "Millennium Report Shows It's Time to Close Black-White Economic Gap," *Seattle Post Intelligencer*, Mar. 6, 1998; Jesse Jackson, "Inequality Is Deeply Rooted," *Syracuse Herald Journal*, Mar. 9, 1998; Elizabeth Bennett, "Read Any Good Reports Lately?" *Mishawaka Enterprise*, Mar. 5, 1998; and Editorial, "Kerner Panel Decries Racism, While Industry Seeks Workers," *Waterloo Courier*, Mar. 4, 1998.

68. William Julius Wilson, "The New Social Inequality and Affirmative Opportunity," in Stanley B. Greenburg and Theda Skocpol, eds., *The New Majority: Toward a Popular Progressive Politics*.

69. Peter Applebone, "From Riots of the '60s, A Report for a Nation with Will and Way for Healing," *New York Times*, May 8, 1992; and Robin Toner, "Los Angeles Riots Are a Warning, Americans Fear," *New York Times*, June 14, 1992.

70. Children's Partnership, *Next Generation Reports*, Apr. 1997.

71. Susan Page and W. Welch, "Poll: Don't Use Surplus to Cut Taxes," *USA Today*, Jan. 9–11, 1998.

72. Faux, "The Economic Case for a Politics of Inclusion"; and Faux, "You Are Not Alone." Also see John Jeter, "Cities, Oldest Suburbs Becoming Allies," *Washington Post*, Feb. 22, 1998.

73. Most of the message is based in Faux, "The Economic Case for a Politics of Inclusion," and Faux, "You Are Not Alone," with some additions by the author.

74. Sidney Verba, Kaye Lehman, and H. Bradey, "The Big Tilt: Participatory Inequality in America," *American Prospect*, May/June 1997.

Index

Academy for Peace and Justice (Brooklyn), 135
adolescents, low income and, 25
affirmative action, 140; attacks on, 16–17; beneficial effects of, 16; as mobility strategy, 119, 123–25, 126–27, 171n29; for rich, 143
Aid to Families with Dependent Children (AFDC), 22, 27, 52, 53, 58, 77
Alabama, African Americans incarcerated in, 105–6, 110
American Indians: affirmative action and, 16; incarceration of, 103–4; in inner cities, 18; poverty and, 37–48, 49, 50, 55–56; violence and, 97
Americans with Disabilities Act of 1990, 169n6
Argus Community (South Bronx), 136–37, 139, 175n55
Asians: incarceration of, 103–4; in inner cities, 18; poverty and, 34–35, 38, 39, 40, 41, 42, 43, 44, 46, 47, 48, 49, 50, 55–56, 160n8; violence and, 97–98, 99
Atlanta: inner-city poverty in, 90; riots in (1967), 10
AT&T, 123

Baltimore: homicide in, 101; inner-city poverty in, 90
Bensonhurst, New York, riots in, 118
Birmingham: demonstration in (1963), 58; homicide in, 101; inner-city poverty in, 90
Black Power movement, Kerner Commission Report and, 92
boot camps, failure of, 132
Boston, inner-city poverty in, 90
Brennan, William, 126
Brown v. Board of Education, 117, 119–20, 168n2
Buffalo: inner-city poverty in, 89, 90; riots in (1967), 10
Burtless, Gary, 13
Bush, George, 76; affirmative action and, 16; recession and, 12

California: affirmative action in, 16, 125; African Americans incarcerated in, 105, 107, 114–15
Cambridge (Maryland), riots in (1967), 10
Camden, New Jersey, homicide in, 101
Carnoy, Martin, 19
caseloads, welfare reform and decrease in, 27–29
Center for Community Change, 12, 143
Center for Defense Information, 143
Centro Sister Isolina Ferré (San Juan, Puerto Rico), 134
Chicago: economic and social transformation of neighborhoods of, 64–74, 76; inner-city poverty in,

90; neighborhoods in, 26–27; peer group orientation in, 72–74, 75; riots in (1966), 8; social disorganization in, 65–69, 70; social isolation in, 72–73; unemployment in, 64–65; violence and crime in, 69–71; welfare assistance in, 65, 67

children, in poverty, 14, 15, 38, 39, 44, 46, 48, 52, 53, 130; development and, 15, 21–32

Child Support Enforcement program, 27

Cincinnati, riots in (1967), 10

cities, African American migration to, 7. *See also* inner cities; *specific cities*

Civil Rights Act of 1964, 117, 120

Civil Rights Act of 1968, 117, 169n3

Civil Rights Act of 1991, 169n7

Civil Rights Restoration Act of 1988, 169n7

Cleveland: inner-city poverty in, 90; riots in (1966), 8

Clinton, Bill, 13; affirmative action and, 126; desegregation and, 122, 126; welfare reform and, 22, 52–53, 54, 55, 57

cognitive development, child poverty and, 24–25, 31

Coleman Report, 120

collective efficacy, neighborhoods and, 26–27

Comer, James, 135

Community Reinvestment Act of 1977, 138

concentration effects, in inner cities, 62

Contract with America, 52–53

Conyers, John, 16

corporate welfare, elimination of, 133, 140–43

Corporation for Youth Investment, creation of, 134–35, 141, 175n55

corporations: elimination of welfare for, 133, 140–43; hiring practices of, 140

crime/violence: in Chicago, 69–71; in inner cities, 62, 63, 69–71, 95–103; in Newark, 8

criminal justice system: discrimination in, 107–15; juvenile, 110–12; proposed investments in, 139–40, 141; *See also* incarceration of minorities

Crown Heights, New York, riots in, 118

Dallas, inner-city poverty in, 90

defense budget, inner-city policy funded with reduction in, 143

desegregation, as antipoverty strategy, 117–18, 119–23, 125–26, 168n2, 169nn3–7, 171n22

Detroit: African American migration to, 7; homicide in, 101; inner-city poverty in, 90; in 1967, 8; poverty in, 15–16; riots in, 8, 9–10

discrimination: in criminal justice system, 107–15; in education, 17–18; in employment, 17, 117–18, 169n5; in housing, 17, 82–83, 117, 169n3; by income, 91; in North, 7

Dorchester Youth Collaborative (Boston), 134, 146

drug war: minority incarceration and, 105, 106–7, 109; sentencing and, 131, 140; treatment and, 175n55

Dryfoos, Joy, 135, 136, 175n55

economy: poverty and, 12, 34, 51, 54, 59–60, 76; unemployment and, 59–60

education. *See* schools

Education Amendments of 1972, 169n6

Eisenhower, Milton S., 1

Eisenhower, Milton S., Foundation, 1–2, 146–47

Eisenhower Commission, 1, 95

elderly, poverty among, 38, 39, 40

Elementary and Secondary Education Act of 1965, 117, 120, 168n2

employment: affirmative action and, 123–24; discrimination in, 17, 117–18, 169n5; 1970s and, 12; poverty and, 44–50; private sector inner-city jobs generated for, 137–

38, 141; public sector inner-city jobs generated for, 138–39, 141, 175n55; in suburbs, 15, 45; welfare policy and, 58–60. *See also* job training; jobs; unemployment

Employment Program of the Portland (Oregon) Development Commission, 137

empowerment, inadequacy of, 132

enterprise zones, failure of, 132, 138

Europe, child welfare in, 30

Fair Housing Act of 1968, 83

Family Support Act of 1988, 51

Faux, Jeff, 13

female-headed families, poverty in, 8, 38, 39, 40, 44, 45, 46, 47, 48, 50

food stamp program, 27, 33, 35, 51

foreign born, poverty and, 44–49

Forsythe County, Georgia, riots in, 118

Fourteenth Amendment, 119

Franklin v. Gwinnett County Public Schools, 169n6

Friedman, Milton, 131

Gary, Indiana, homicide in, 101

Gerbner, George, 145

ghetto. *See* inner cities

government: action and inaction in 1970s and, 12–14; inner city and, 91–92. *See also* inner-city polity, proposal for; integration and, 17, 117–18, 119–23, 125–26, 168n2, 169nn3–7, 171n22, 172n34; poverty policy and, 33, 34, 50–53. *See also* affirmative action; municipal governments; state government

Grand Rapids, riots in (1967), 10

Green v. County School Board of New Kent County, 117, 169n3

Griggs v. Duke Power Co., 117–18, 169n5

Grove City College v. Bell, 169n7

Harlem, riot in (1964), 58

Head Start, 51, 117, 168n2; full funding needed for, 133–34, 141, 175n55

Hispanics: affirmative action and, 16; employment discrimination and, 17; housing and, 17; incarceration of, 103, 104, 105, 111, 112, 113; in inner cities, 18; median family income for, 17; poverty and, 17, 18, 34–50, 55–56, 87, 160n8; schools and, 17–18; unemployment and, 17; violence and, 97, 98, 99, 101

home environment, cognitive development and, 25

homicide: minorities and, 96–101; whites and, 97, 98, 99

housing, 7, 152; in Detroit, 8; discrimination in, 17, 82–83, 117, 169n3; in Newark, 8; prisons built instead of, 131

Houston, inner-city poverty in, 90

Howard Beach, New York, riots in, 118

incarceration of minorities, 103–15, 131; prisons and, 131, 133. *See also* criminal justice system

income: of African Americans, 17, 80–81; child development and, 23–27; in Detroit, 15–16; of Hispanics, 17; inequality in, 14–15, 16–17, 80–81, 130; minimum wage and, 14; in 1970s, 12; in 1996, 14; segregation by, 91

Indiana, African Americans incarcerated in, 110

infrastructure, decrease in government spending on, 13–14

Inglewood, California, homicide in, 101

inner cities, 57–78; alliance with middle and working classes for inner-city policy, 148–50; concentration effects in, 62; economic shocks and trends of 1970s and, 12; expansion of, 62–63, 79–80; female-headed families in, 64–65; government policy toward, 91–92; isolation and, 63, 72–73, 77; Kerner Commission Report and, 83, 84–85, 88; migration to, 17; outmigration and, 60–64, 76, 91, 115, 118; peer group orientation in, 72–74, 75, 77; poverty in, 15–19, 21, 22, 34, 40–47, 49, 50, 55, 60, 88–92, 161n11; rejection of American institutions and, 94; social disorganization in, 62, 63, 65–69, 70, 76–77; spatial organization of poverty in, 83–88, 92–94; unemployment in, 58–60, 63, 64, 65, 76, 77; violence and crime in, 62, 63, 69–71, 95–103; welfare assistance in, 65, 67, 77

inner-city policy, proposal for, 129–50; corporate welfare elimination, 133, 140–53; Corporation for Youth Investment, 134–35, 141, 175n55; cost of, 140; defense budget reduction for, 143; facts as bases for, 129–32; financing, 140–43, 175n55; fully funded Head Start, 133–34, 141, 175n55; ineffective urban policy and, 132–33; investments in criminal justice, 139–40, 141; job training, 136–37, 141; leadership for, 150; National Community Development Bank, 137–38, 175n55; obstacles to, 144–46; political alliance needed for, 148–50; private sector inner-city jobs, 137–38, 141; public opinion on, 146–48; public sector inner-city jobs, 138–39, 141, 175n55; school reform, 135–36, 140, 141, 175n55

integration, as antipoverty strategy, 117–18, 119–23, 125–26, 168n2, 169nn3–7, 171n22

Iowa: African Americans incarcerated in, 106; welfare recipients in, 29

isolation, inner cities and, 63, 72–73

Jackson, Mississippi, homicide in, 101

Jargowsky, Paul A., 18

Job Corps Act of 1964, 59

jobs: creation of for full employment, 137–39, 141, 175n55; in suburbs, 15, 45. *See also* employment; job training

job training, 51, 59; decreased government spending on, 13; failure of, 132; reform of, 136–37, 141

Job Training Partnership Act (JTPA), 132, 136, 137, 152

Johnson, Lyndon B., 126; affirmative action and, 123; Kerner Commission Report and, 1, 10, 11, 78; War on Poverty and, 51

Jones, Jerry, 12

juvenile justice system, discrimination in, 110–12

Kansas City, inner-city poverty in, 90

Katzenbach crime commission, 95

Kaufman, William W., 143

Kennedy, John F., 75; affirmative action and, 123

Kennedy, Robert F., 1

Kerner Commission Report, 7, 21, 115, 150, 151; on America as two separate and unequal societies, 74–75, 94, 117, 127, 131; Black Power movement and, 92; contents of, 10–11; criminal justice system and, 114; Eisenhower Foundation updating, 146–47; ghetto and, 83, 84–85, 88; ghetto enrichment and, 61; inner-city youth and, 77; recommendations of, 11, 140; segregation and, 82, 83; situation thirty years after, 11–20, 26, 30–56, 78, 125; urban riots and, 7–11, 34, 57–58, 95, 118; white racism and, 92–93

Keyes v. School District No. 1, 117, 169n3

King, Martin Luther, Jr., 1, 117, 126

King, Rodney, 118

Koban, Inc. (Columbia, South Carolina), 134

Kozol, Jonathan, 136

labor force participation. *See* employment
Lau v. Nichols, 169n6
Learninggames curriculum, 31
Lewis, Isabelle, 31
Linder, Father William, 138
Los Angeles: homicide in, 101; inner-city poverty in, 90; riots in (1992), 118, 138
Loury, Glenn, 130

McGahey, Richard, 143
Manpower Demonstration and Training Act of 1962, 59
Marshall, Ray, 129
Marshall, Thurgood, 16, 126
Martin, Molly, 18
Massachusetts, African Americans incarcerated in, 110
Medicaid, 33, 35, 51
Medicare, 51
Memphis: homicide in, 101; inner-city poverty in, 90
metropolitan areas: decentralization in, 91–92; poverty in, 40–47, 49, 50, 55, 161n11
Miami, riots in, 118
Michigan, school finance in, 137
middle class, 148; African Americans in, 124–25; alliance with poor and working class for inner-city policy, 148–50
migration, from inner cities, 60–64, 76, 91, 115, 118
Millennium Breach, The (Eisenhower Foundation), 2
Milwaukee: homicide in, 101; riots in (1967), 10
Minneapolis: area-wide tax base of, 137; homicide in, 101; riots in (1967), 10
Minnesota, African Americans incarcerated in, 106
Mississippi, African Americans incarcerated in, 110
Missouri, African Americans incarcerated in, 110

Mobile, inner-city poverty in, 90
Mobile v. Bolden, 169n7
mobility strategies: affirmation action as, 119, 123–25, 126–27, 171n29; integration as, 117–18, 119–23, 125–26, 168n2, 169nn3–7, 171n22, 172n34
Moyers, Bill, 146
municipal governments, African American representation in, 8
Myrdal, Gunnar, 108

National Advisory Commission on Civil Disorders. *See* Kerner Commission Report
National Assessment of Education Progress (NAEP), 120–21
National Association for the Advancement of Colored People (NAACP), 58
National Commission on the Causes and Prevention of Violence. *See* Eisenhower Commission
National Community Development Bank, 137–38, 175n55
National Criminal Victimization Survey (NCVS), 102
National Research Council (NRC), 35–37, 160n5
National Welfare Rights Organization, 58
Native Americans. *See* American Indians
neighborhoods: child development and, 26–27; resegregation of, 130–31
Newark: African American migration to, 7; inner-city poverty in, 89, 90; in 1967, 8; riots in (1967), 8–9, 138
New Community Corporation, 138
New England, African Americans incarcerated in, 105, 106, 110
New Hampshire, African Americans incarcerated in, 106, 110
New Orleans: homicide in, 101; inner-city poverty in, 90
New York: African Americans incar-

cerated in, 105, 110; inner-city
  poverty in, 89, 90
Nixon, Richard, 123
nonmetropolitan areas, poverty in,
  40–47, 49, 50, 55, 161n11

Office of Economic Opportunity, 58
Orfield, Gary, 17–18
outmigration, from inner cities, 60–
  64, 76, 91, 115, 118

parental health, income and, 26
peer group orientation: in Chicago,
  72–74, 75; in inner cities, 72–74,
  75, 77
Personal Responsibility and Work
  Opportunity Reconciliation Act
  (PRWORA) of 1996, 22–23, 27–
  29, 52–53, 77
Philadelphia: affirmative action in,
  124; homicide in, 101,; inner-city
  poverty in, 89, 90
Phillips, Kevin, 130
Pittsburgh, inner-city poverty in, 89,
  90
Plainfield (New Jersey), riots in
  (1967), 10
police, in Newark, 8–9
political alliance, for proposed inner-
  city policy, 148–49
poverty: African Americans and, 34,
  36–47, 49, 50, 55–56, 60, 130,
  160n8; American Indians and, 37–
  47, 49, 50, 55–56; Asians and, 38–
  50, 55–56, 160n8; characteristics of
  those in, 43–47, 48; child development and, 15, 21–32; children in,
  14, 15, 21–32, 38, 39, 44, 46, 48,
  52, 53, 130; current worsening of,
  14–15; definition of, 35–37,
  160n5; economy and, 12, 34, 51,
  54, 59–60, 76; education and,
  44–50; elderly and, 38, 39, 40; employment and, 44–50; expansion of
  in inner cities, 88–92; female-
  headed households and, 38, 39, 40,
  44, 45, 46, 47, 48, 50; foreign born

and, 44, 45, 46, 47, 49; by geographical area, 40–43; government
  policy and, 33, 34, 50–53; by
  group, 47, 49–50; Hispanics and,
  34, 36–50, 55–56, 87, 160n8; inner
  cities and, 15–19, 21, 22, 34, 40–
  47, 49, 50, 55, 60, 161n11; in metropolitan areas, 40–47, 49, 50, 55,
  161n11; in nonmetropolitan areas,
  40–47, 49, 50, 55, 161n11; personal responsibility for, 53–54;
  prevalence of, 33, 34; as public
  health issue, 33–56; since 1960s,
  37–50; since 1968, 50–53; spatial
  organization of, 83–88, 92–94; unemployment and, 54–55; whites
  and, 37, 39, 40, 41, 42, 43, 44, 46,
  47, 49, 50, 55–56, 87, 160n8
President's Initiative on Race, 17
prisons. See incarceration of minorities
Public Campaign, 144
public health issue, poverty as, 33–56
public opinion, on proposed inner-
  city polity, 146–48

Quane, James, 18–19
Quantum Opportunities (Ford Foundation), 134, 175n55

Rankin, Bruce, 18–19
Reagan, Ronald, 12–13, 76; affirmative action and, 16; recession and,
  12
recessions, of 1970s, 12
Rehnquist, William, 16, 126
Reich, Robert, 13, 140
resegregation, 17–18, 129–30
Richmond, Virginia, homicide in,
  101
riots, See urban riots
Roosevelt, Franklin D., 127, 150
Roosevelt, Theodore, 150

Safe Passage Commission, 136
Safe Passages (Dryfoos), 135
St. Louis: inner-city poverty in, 90;

school desegregation and, 121, 122, 126

Salome Arena Middle Academy (New York), 135

Sandefur, Gary, 18

San Francisco: inner-city poverty in, 90; riots in (1966), 8

School Development Plan, 135

schools: affirmative action and, 16, 124–25, 127; child poverty and, 24–25, 31; decrease in government spending on, 13; desegregation and, 117, 119–23, 125–26, 168n2, 169n4, 5–6, 170n16, 161n22, 172n34; in Detroit, 8; inadequacy of, 131; in inner cities, 73–74, 77; in Newark, 8; poverty and, 44–50; reform of, 135–36, 140, 141; resegregation of, 130–31; segregation in, 17–18

segregation. *See* discrimination

self-sufficiency, inadequacy of, 132

Sentencing Project, 105

single-parent families, in Newark, 8. *See also* female-headed families, poverty in

social disorganization: in Chicago, 65–69, 70, 76–77; inner cities and, 62, 63, 65–69, 70, 76–77

social isolation, in Chicago, 72–73, 77

Social Security amendments (1962), 58

South Shore Bank (Chicago), 137

Sparling, Joe, 31

state governments: affirmative action and, 16; inner cities and, 92; school desegregation and, 172n34

steel industry, affirmative action and, 123

Stoneman, Dorothy, 138

suburbs: employment in, 15, 45; migration to, 15, 91, 118

Supplemental Security Income, 27

Supreme Court: affirmative action and, 16, 126; desegregation and, 5–7, 117–18, 119–20, 122, 169n3

Survey of Injured Victims of Violence (SIVV), 102–3

Swann v. Charlotte-Mecklenburg Board of Education, 117, 169n3

Tampa, riots in (1967), 10

TANF. *See* Temporary Assistance for Needy Families

Target Industries, 137

tax breaks for rich, inner-city policy financing versus, 133, 140–43

Tax Reform Act of 1986, 51

teenage pregnancy, legislation discouraging, 53

Telesis Corporation, 138

Temporary Assistance for Needy Families (TANF), 22–23, 29, 53

Texas, affirmative action in, 125

Thomas, Clarence, 16

Tocqueville, Alexis de, 8

trickle-down supply-side economics, failure of, 132

Turning Points plan (Carnegie Council on Adolescent Development), 135

unemployment, 129–30; for African Americans, 17; in Chicago, 64–65; in inner cities, 58–60, 63, 64, 65, 76, 77; in Newark, 8; poverty and, 54–55. *See also* employment

unionization: decline in, 151; 1970s and, 12

University of California, affirmative action and, 16

urban riots, 1, 7–10; causes of, 7–8; in Chicago, 8; in Cleveland, 8; in Detroit (1967), 9–10; in Harlem (1964), 58; Kerner Commission Report and, 7–11, 34, 57–58, 95, 118; in Los Angeles (1992), 118, 138; in Newark (1967), 8–9, 138; in 1992, 34–35; in 1990s, 118; in San Francisco, 8; in Watts (1965), 8, 58

violence. *See* crime/violence

volunteerism, inadequacy of, 132

Voting Rights Act Amendments of 1982, 169n7

wages. *See* income

War on Poverty, 33, 51, 52, 117; child development studies and, 21–22

Wards Cove Packing Co., Inc. v. Atonio, 169n7

Warren, Earl, 120, 126

Washington, D.C.: homicide in, 101; inner-city poverty in, 90

Washington State, African Americans incarcerated in, 110

Watts, riot in (1965), 8, 58

welfare assistance: in Chicago, 65, 67; decrease in, 13; employment opportunities and, 58–60; in inner cities, 77

welfare reform: child poverty and, 22–23, 24, 27–29, 30–32; Clinton and, 22, 52–53, 54, 55, 77

Wells, Thomas, 18

white racism, Kerner Commission Report and, 92–93

whites: homicide and, 97, 98, 99; incarceration of, 104, 105, 106; poverty and, 37, 39, 40, 41, 42, 43, 44, 46, 47, 49, 50, 55–56, 87, 160n8

Wilson, William Julius, 18–19

Wisconsin: African Americans incarcerated in, 106, 110; caseload decrease in, 27, 28

women, incarceration of, 105. *See also* female-headed families, poverty in

Work Incentive Program of 1967, 59

working class, 148; alliance with middle class and poor for inner-city policy, 148–50

years of potential life lost (YPLL), violence and, 100

Youth Build USA, 138

About the Contributors

Jeanne Brooks-Gunn is a member of the faculty of Columbia University. She has written extensively on poverty and its effects on children, including, with Greg J. Duncan, *Consequences of Growing Up Poor,* published in 1997.

Elliott Currie is a professor in the Legal Studies Program at the University of California—Berkeley and is affiliated with its Center for the Study of Law and Society. He is the author of a number of books, including *Crime and Punishment in America,* published in 1998.

Lynn A. Curtis is president of the Milton S. Eisenhower Foundation. He served as an urban policy adviser to the U.S. Secretary of Housing and Urban Development, was director of President Carter's Urban and Regional Policy Group, and is the author or editor of nine books.

Greg J. Duncan is professor of education and social policy at Northwestern University and director of the Northwestern University/University of Chicago Center for Poverty Research. He is the author of *Years of Poverty, Years of Plenty,* published in 1984, and more recently, numerous articles on poor families, poor neighborhoods, and child development.

Fred R. Harris is a former U.S. senator from Oklahoma. He served on the Kerner Commission. He is professor of political science at the University of New Mexico, author or editor of fifteen books, including, as co-editor, *Quiet Riots: Race and Poverty in the United States,* published in 1988. He is co-chair of the board of trustees of the Milton S. Eisenhower Foundation.

Paul A. Jargowsky is visiting associate professor at Harvard University's John F. Kennedy School of Government and associate professor at

187

the University of Texas—Dallas. He is the author of *Poverty and Place: Ghettos, Barrios, and the American City,* published in 1996.

Molly Martin is a graduate student in sociology and a trainee in demography at the Center for Demography and Ecology at the University of Wisconsin. Her research focuses on the effects of welfare reform on out-of-wedlock childbearing.

James M. Quane is associate director of the Joblessness and Urban Poverty Research Program at Harvard University's John F. Kennedy School of Government. His research focuses on the effects of concentrated unemployment and disadvantaged neighborhoods on low-income youth. He is also involved in a multicity study of the impact of welfare reform on families and children.

Bruce H. Rankin is a research associate in the Joblessness and Urban Poverty Research Program at Harvard University's John F. Kennedy School of Government. His research focuses on the relationship between neighborhood characteristics, social isolation, and the life chances of inner-city residents.

Gary Sandefur is professor of sociology at the University of Wisconsin—Madison and is affiliated with its Institute for Research on Poverty. He is the author or editor of a number of books, including, as co-editor, *Confronting Poverty: Prescriptions for Change,* published in 1994.

William L. Taylor practices law in Washington, D.C., and teaches education law at Georgetown Law School. An advocate for low-income and minority students, he is a former member of the legal staff of the NAACP Legal Defense and Education Fund and former staff director of the U.S. Commission on Civil Rights.

Thomas Wells is a doctoral candidate in sociology at the University of Wisconsin—Madison. His areas of interest include stratification, occupational mobility, and racial inequality.

William Julius Wilson is Malcolm Wiener Professor of social policy at Harvard University's John F. Kennedy School of Government and professor of African American studies at Harvard University. A past president of the American Sociological Association and a past MacArthur Prize fellow, he is the author of numerous works, including *When Work Disappears: The World of the New Urban Poor,* published in 1996.